D1607521

Reading, Writing, and Segregation

WOMEN IN AMERICAN HISTORY

Editorial Advisors
Anne Firor Scott
Susan Armitage
Susan K. Cahn
Deborah Gray White

A list of books in the series appears
at the end of this book.

Reading, Writing, and Segregation

A CENTURY OF BLACK WOMEN TEACHERS IN NASHVILLE

Sonya Ramsey

University of Illinois Press
Urbana and Chicago

Portions of chapter 3 appeared in the *Journal of African American History* 90 (Winter–Spring 2005): 29–52, and are reprinted here with permission from that journal.

Library of Congress Cataloging-in-Publication Data
Ramsey, Sonya Yvette.
Reading, writing, and segregation : a century of Black women
teachers in Nashville / Sonya Ramsey.
p.   cm. — (Women in American history)
Includes bibliographical references and index.
ISBN 978-0-252-03229-5 (cloth : alk. paper)
1. African American women teachers—Tennessee—Nashville—History.
2. Segregation in education—Tennessee—Nashville—History.
3. Discrimination in education—Tennessee—Nashville—History.
I. Title.
LC2731.R36   2008
371.10092'2—dc22 [B]   2007018916

This book is dedicated to my mother,
Betty J. Cunningham, with love

Contents

Illustrations follow page 80.

Acknowledgments

As a graduate student at the University of North Carolina at Chapel Hill, I was fortunate to work as an interviewer in the Ford Foundation–sponsored Behind the Veil Project. In one summer I had the opportunity to interview people from all walks of life, but the stories of African American teachers had the most impact on me and led me to study the experiences of black women teachers in my hometown, Nashville, Tennessee.

Now, after many years, there are many people and organizations I thank for helping with my academic and professional journeys. My mother, Betty Cunningham, tirelessly read repeated revisions of my work and provided constant support; my father, Charles Ramsey II, offered much-needed advice on how to navigate academia; and my brothers, Edward Audain and Charles Ramsey III, as well as the rest of my family also provided encouragement. I also thank several colleagues: Jacquelyn Dowd Hall, my Ph.D. advisor, who still offers advice; Peter Filene, Reginald Hildebrand, Jerma Jackson, James Leloudis, and George Noblitt; and my wonderful manuscript readers Glenda Gilmore and Anne Firor Scott. I also thank the friends and colleagues who graciously reviewed chapters of this manuscript: Stefan Bradley, Prudence Cumberbatch, Bobby Lovett, Kathy Nasstrom, Kathryn Walbert, Adam Fairclough, and Houston Roberson.

I am also indebted to my former colleagues at the University of Texas at Arlington for encouragement and guidance and my new ones at the University of North Carolina at Charlotte. Among the many friends who kept their telephone lines open to hear my frequent and frantic discussions of this project are Oscar Crawford Jr., Dwight Ferguson, Yeae Hagler, Denise Johnson, Andrea Harper, Thelma Moultrie, Ana Ramos-Zayas, Marva Roberts, Harry Robinson Jr., Judy Cain Steele, Sandra Rodriguez, Maria Archibald, Kelly Thompson, and Rolanda Warner.

This endeavor would have been much more difficult without financial support, and I am very grateful for fellowships from the Spencer Foundation and the Faculty/Independent Scholar Fellowship Program offered by Tulane University and the use of resources from the Southern Oral History Program, a part of the UNC Center for the Study of the American South at Chapel Hill. I also appreciate the librarians and archivists at the Pearl Senior High Alumni Museum, the Tennessee State Library Archives, the Metropolitan Archives of Nashville, Davidson County, the Nashville Room of the Metropolitan Nashville Public Library, the Amistad Research Center at Tulane University, and the libraries of the University of Texas at Austin, Southern Methodist University, and the University of Texas at Arlington as well as those in the special collections of Tennessee State, Fisk, and Vanderbilt universities and Melissa Bryant of the Metropolitan Nashville Board of Education.

Of course, this project could not have been completed without the many teachers and others who served as interview subjects and recommended educators such as LaMona McCarter, Ossie Trammel, William McMakin, Gwendolyn Vincent, and Anne and Theodore Lenox. I especially thank Lillian Dunn Thomas for direction and help. Unfortunately, I was unable to cite information from all the wonderful teachers who served as subjects for this book, but each interview helped contribute to my larger goals. The following were interview subjects: Dorothy Baines, Thelma Baker Baxter, Novella Bass, Lillie D. Bowman, Mary Carver-Patrick, Ivanetta H. Davis, Novella Davis, Myra Dixon, Bonnie S. Dobbins, Eva Dorsey, Edith Dowdy, Mary Driscoll, Lillian Dunn Thomas, Mary Alice Goldman, Jeannie G. Gore, Mary R. Hardy, Rose Marie Howell, Ola Hudson, Ada J. Jackson, Elene Jackson, Roberta S. Jackson, Helen L. James, Donzell Johnson, Minerva H. Johnson Hawkins, Sadie G. Johnson, Laurie Lane, Sadie Madry, Ida K. Martin, Helen Anne Mayes, Peggy Mazur, Tennie Mai McGill, Edna Minaya, Frances Reeds, Charleene Spencer, Albert Shaw, Foster Shockley, Leathra S. Shockley, Margaret Sims, Oliver Smith, Omega Stratton, Thelma Tears, Ethel Thomas, Ella H. Thompson, Lynda Thompson, Elizabeth Tune, Virginia G. Westbrook, Margaret C. Whitfield, Fannie B. Williams, Martha E. Woods, Helen M. Young, and Ruth T. Young.

Introduction

Reading, Writing, and Segregation: A Century of Black Women Teachers in Nashville begins in 1867 with the inception of the city's segregated black schools and ends in 1983, more than ten years after federal court–ordered public school desegregation. A consideration of these teachers over such a long expanse of time reveals various changes in how black women defined themselves as middle-class professionals and influenced and responded to social forces, from racial uplift to the civil rights and women's movements.

Reading, Writing, and Segregation also explores how critical moments and episodes, including the rise of Jim Crow, World War I, the Great Depression, World War II, and the *Brown v. Board of Education* decision, influenced the working and personal lives of black urban teachers. The black female teachers of Nashville belie the image of undertrained rural educators. Instead, this book, along with several other excellent studies of black teachers during the Jim Crow era, chronicles the experiences of sophisticated, highly educated, urban women who valued having a middle-class status and position and provides information on African American educational experiences in the urban South.[1]

In the first chapter, a wide-reaching examination of African American education in Nashville from the end of the Civil War to the beginning of the Great Depression, I describe and discuss the development of African American segregated public schools in Nashville and the black community's simultaneous effort to secure black teachers for its children. In an almost twenty-year struggle, leaders and parents petitioned the school board to hire blacks instead of southern whites. Most African Americans of the era maintained that black teachers cared about their children and believed in their abilities; the teachers were also connected to the community's progress.

This quest by black Nashvillians was a way of countering the deplorable physical and financial conditions of segregated schools. During the first decades of the twentieth century the city's black leaders also successfully petitioned the state to open a normal (teacher-training) school in Nashville. Such efforts represented not only the community's struggle against racial injustice but also its quest to strengthen the professional class. Black America debated the nature and scope of how millions of southern blacks would learn at the turn of the century. Being the location of Fisk University, a liberal arts institution, as well as Tennessee Agricultural and Industrial State, an industrial education–based normal school, Nashville epitomized both sides of the issue. In addition, Booker T. Washington and W. E. B. Du Bois each had ties to the city. Teachers responsible for conveying these philosophies remain at the center of the discussion, and those in Nashville exercised both options for learning.

The institutions of higher learning promoted different educational objectives, but both Fisk and Tennessee A&I helped students create a model of the professional urban teacher, one who serves by precept and example in the classroom and as a leader in the community. In an effort to reinforce their status as middle-class professionals, teachers sometimes separated themselves from being "uplifters of the race" and participated in exclusive organizations. Chapter 1 explores how Nashville's black women teachers influenced the parameters and characteristics of middle-class life from the post-Reconstruction era to the Great Depression.

The second chapter traces the actions and activities of the teachers throughout the 1940s and early 1950s. Along with parents and religious leaders, they were role models for students yet still struggled for parity and respect from white colleagues. Ironically, although African American teachers considered themselves to be distinguished and capable professionals, they consistently encountered claims from the larger educational profession that blacks were incompetent and inferior. Black women teachers in Nashville and many other urban southern cities had more college degrees than their white counterparts yet still received lower salaries. During the late 1930s and early 1940s the National Association for the Advancement of Colored People (NAACP) began the attack on segregation in education by fighting for the equalization of teachers' salaries. In Nashville, African American teachers won that battle in 1942 with the *Thomas v. Hibbits* case against the city's all-white board of education. Such efforts eventually resulted in a single pay schedule for all teachers from elementary to high school, thus benefiting all Nashville teachers. Most black women teachers supported the case, but some feared negative reprisals. For those who based their self-identities upon their positions, job loss and a possible expulsion from middle-class society could be devastating.

During World War II, African American teachers supported patriotism while inculcating a thirst for tolerance, equality, and freedom in their students. They restyled the meaning of American democracy to suggest that the students merited equality. The last part of chapter 2 discusses how teachers responded to the NAACP's early legal strategies to end segregation and how the push for complete desegregation affected their impact.

When the Supreme Court declared through the *Brown v. Board of Education* decision that educational segregation violated the Constitution, Nashville's black women teachers reacted with a wide range of emotions. Chapter 3 describes the struggle to desegregate that concluded with federal intervention. In an effort to hinder integration, the Nashville City Board of Education allocated more funding for African American schools, which led to new construction and increased access to materials. African American parents, students, and teachers celebrated the positive changes, although massive funding inequities remained between black schools and white. At the same time, the board was continually being challenged to remedy problems. By sponsoring cultural events or career days, Nashville's African American faculties attempted to create a rich culture for students and the surrounding community.

Teachers supported the civil rights movement in a plethora of ways that included being drivers or organizers and offering financial support. The women teachers watched from the sidelines, their emotions ranging from anxious disdain to delighted pride as students took to the streets and developed new strategies for freedom. African American schools remained segregated, but students refused to accept the status quo. They internalized their teachers' cold war promotion of democracy and simultaneously discarded the instructors' belief in the merits of educational attainment as the primary vehicle for social equality.

The fourth and final chapter examines the experiences of those who desegregated formerly all-white public schools and those who remained at previously all-black ones. After repeated local NAACP court challenges, federal courts mandated that public schools adhere to a comprehensive desegregation plan that involved teacher transfers, quotas, school closings, and busing to achieve racial balance. The summers of 1970 and 1971 were marked by apprehension as thousands of Nashville's African American teachers received notices to report to predominately white schools. Those who remained in traditionally black schools saw younger, white instructors occupy former colleagues' classrooms. Some black women teachers celebrated the opportunity to work in modern surroundings that had ample supplies; others, however, still lament the dismantling of their comfortable, culturally familiar worlds and the loss of support systems. They encountered colleagues, parents, and students who sometimes resented their presence. As a result, the African American female instructors attempted to forge biracial coalitions and construct new identities as teachers and professionals.

When Nashville's African American community protested closing the venerated Pearl Senior High School and other black schools as a part of the board's desegregation plan they did not realize that the institutions had already changed. By the mid-1970s the majority of students at Nashville's oldest African American secondary school were black, but most of its faculty were white. Schools could never return to what they had been during the 1950s and early 1960s without the presence of the African American teachers who had helped create places where teaching was encouraged and students were expected to succeed. My exploration of how desegregation transformed their roles as professionals in the classroom and in the black community illuminates the complicated and often controversial consequences of desegregation.

Reading, Writing, and Segregation

ONE

"By Precept and Example": Schools, Community, and Professional Teachers from 1867 through the 1930s

In 1878 the prominent black attorney and businessman James Carroll Napier won a seat on the Nashville city council by pledging to have African American teachers hired in the city's black schools. He claimed that they offered an "incentive to colored pupils" and that southern white teachers cared more for their salaries than for helping black children.[1] Napier's campaign promise to voters in his predominately black Fourth Ward was part of the local community's ongoing drive to obtain African American teachers for their children. The struggle had begun in 1868 when black residents first petitioned the Nashville City Board of Education, and continued until 1887, when the board employed a new African American teaching staff at the last remaining black school with an all-white faculty. When the Tennessee General Assembly passed several segregation acts in 1901, including one barring teachers from instructing students of another race, Nashville's African American community did not object because the law reinforced their desire for black teachers in black schools.

The black residents of Nashville continued to ask an indifferent board of education to remedy glaring inequities in funding and resources. The battle to end segregation was in the future. Set in the context of the appalling state of Nashville's institutions and the city's tense racial climate during the late nineteenth and early twentieth centuries, the quest for improved black schools and a black faculty was a profound response to society's broken promises of freedom and equality. The struggle bore upon the entire black community and would continue throughout the twentieth century.[2]

Answering the community's call, African American teachers embarked on a journey that required them to combat the impact of segregation and oppression at a variety of levels. They assumed leadership roles in service organizations and even provided lunches and clothing for needy students. Some were armed with little more than confidence and self-respect, but they struggled to keep students from internalizing the larger society's views of black inferiority. Working against overwhelming circumstances, black women teachers sometimes fell short of the mandate to uplift the race through education, but their efforts offered the black community the comfort of knowing that its children had caring and accountable instructors.

Improved schooling was entwined with the black community's desire to expand its middle class. In addition to securing more teachers for their children's benefit, the establishment of Tennessee Agricultural and Industrial State Normal School (A&I) in 1912 allowed greater numbers of blacks to become professionals. A&I's motto charged students to "Think, Work, and Serve," and the education they and their Fisk University counterparts received prepared them to adapt to the complicated issue of being role models for the race. As national leaders, especially Booker T. Washington and W. E. B. Du Bois, debated the best strategies for educational progress, black institutions of higher learning in Nashville employed a variety of ideas that helped black women develop as professional teachers. They were encouraged to overcome inferior surroundings, become leaders and activists in racial uplift, and maintain social standing by participating in professional associations and exclusive clubs and organizations.

The experiences of black teachers in Nashville from the 1880s, when they first began working in sizable numbers in schools, to the 1930s, when they became the majority of black professional women in the city, demonstrate their belief that becoming educated, middle-class community leaders would help them adapt to—and sometimes overcome—the economic and social obstacles of a racially inequitable system. Their efforts to "serve by precept and example" outside their classrooms also reveal the educators' drive to embody and shape the city's female black middle class.

The majority of teachers who worked among blacks in Nashville during the 1860s and 1870s were white, most of them former missionaries who had traveled south during and after the Civil War to teach in schools for freed people.[3] Along with teaching basic literacy, these northerners felt obligated to promote the moral development of former slaves and help mold them into acceptable citizens.[4] Some of these men and women mixed paternalistic and racist attitudes with missionary zeal. They most likely agreed with Fisk teacher Ester W. Douglass, who observed, "Perhaps, I shouldn't say this. But, I think the scholars (students) here are trying to do more than they, with little previous culture, are capable of doing well."[5] Despite the subtle prejudice of teachers like Douglass, black Nashvillians appreciated and respected the efforts of the men and women who sacrificed possible economic comforts and social acceptance to help instruct their children.[6]

As the former missionaries labored in black public schools, however, some city leaders considered them a threat to white supremacy.[7] In an effort to discourage the teachers from the North, the Nashville city council passed a residency requirement in 1869 that forbade teachers from leaving for summer vacation. To the dismay of the council, however, most of the northern teachers, including five of the seven faculty at Belle View, the city's first black public school, remained and reported back to work in the fall.[8]

Although local residents valued the services of the northern white teachers, in July 1868 black leaders asked the board to appoint qualified African American teachers in one department of the colored schools. A month later the board decided to open a separate section staffed with black teachers in a building adjacent to Gun Factory Elementary School at 305 North Summer Street. The new facility, known as the Broad Street School, was located near the railroad crossing on Broad and McLemore Streets. To staff it the board hired two black women who met all requirements to teach in Nashville schools, Elizabeth "Lizzie" Lawrence and Channie Patterson, each of whom received an annual salary of $500. The Rev. John G. Mitchell, who was white, served as principal.[9]

The arrangement did not last long. Due to budget restraints, in 1869 the board decided to move its first- and second-graders back to Gun Factory. As a result, Lizzie Lawrence lost her job and did not return to work in city schools. After repeated complaints about its irreparable leaky roof the board closed Gun Factory in 1870 and moved its students and six female teachers to the Trimble School, a four-room, two-story home at 525 South Market Street. Although Belle View and Trimble enrolled more than eight hundred children in 1871, hundreds of youngsters were turned away due to overcrowding. The superintendent refused to open more black schools, claiming "the influx of colored children is so transient that it does not justify the opening of an additional school."[10]

Several African Americans, among them Julia Evans, a former city missionary teacher, applied to work in Nashville public schools, but some did not receive jobs because they could not pass the annual certification test. Even ones who did qualify were turned away because the board refused to mix black and white teaching staffs. In addition, the Nashville City Board of Education deeply resented the presence of teachers who were not from the South. They would, the city's leaders feared, promote social equality by neglecting to abide by rules of racial etiquette that discouraged social interaction between whites and blacks. If the city had to educate African Americans, then the board wanted to control the contents of the education and the educators themselves. The Nashville board's hiring decisions and the retreat of missionary organizations from the North and the federal government's abandonment of African American education in the South meant that by the late 1870s most teachers in black schools were white.[11]

As northern teachers left, African American parents realized that the negative influence of potentially prejudiced southern teachers might outweigh the positive impact of obtaining an education.[12] From the top down, claims of black incompetence patterned the educational arena. In 1871 Nashville school superintendent Samuel Caldwell contended in his annual report that northern teachers created "false enthusiasm" for learning during the first years of emancipation and that due to a lack of attendance and tardiness African Americans could not "be brought up to the standards of white students."[13] Nashville's black leaders saw an intrinsic flaw in a school system that offered to instruct their children but considered them inferior.

As blacks continued to lobby for educational opportunities they encountered a white supremacist attitude among the state's Democratic legislators. When Democrats regained control of Tennessee's government in 1869 they discontinued funding for public education, forcing counties to finance schools with local taxes. Those who supported public education protested, as did African Americans, because such changes threatened the stability of the state's educational system. In response, in 1873 Tennessee became the first southern state to authorize a permanent school fund for public education, which was to be supported by poll and property taxes. African American schools were supposed to receive an equal share of these funds, but the majority of these tax dollars supplemented white schools.[14]

African Americans throughout the rest of the South were also demanding black teachers for black schools. After the 1875 Civil Rights Act failed to enforce public school integration, they soon realized that schools would remain segregated and that black educational facilities would never receive the same funding as their white counterparts. Consequently, black southerners intensified their campaign for African American teachers. Parents wanted instructors who saw unlimited potential in their children and would push them to achieve.[15]

After James C. Napier assumed his seat on the Nashville City Council in 1878 he quickly proposed a resolution "requesting the Board of Education to employ colored teachers for the public schools." The council adopted his resolution, but the Nashville Board of Education restated that it would only hire blacks when enough passed the qualifying examination to staff an entire school. Once again the board justified this policy by claiming that mixing teachers would be an "embarrassment for white faculty," a response reflecting the prevailing attitude toward the education and uplift of African Americans.[16] Basic literacy was enough. The long-range goal was to prepare black students to adapt to the discriminatory social order not transcend or eliminate it. The board considered adult African Americans unworthy to work alongside whites.

Napier also asked the council to form a joint committee with the board to encourage the construction of new facilities for African Americans. The board eventually approved building Meigs Elementary in east Nashville and Pearl Elementary in North Nashville. To address Napier's and the black community's immediate demands, the board agreed in 1879 to open Knowles Elementary School, which was housed in an abandoned Fisk University building at the corner of Hynes and Knowles streets in north Nashville, and hired Scott Washington Crosthwaite as principal and Minnie Lou Scott and Robert White as teachers. Nashville annexed the city of Edgefield and opened Vandaville Elementary School in 1880. It was staffed with black teachers Aaron J. Dodd, Laura L. Douglass, Hester W. East, and John C. Walker.[17]

Black Nashvillians celebrated these appointments, but the board did not alter its policy solely because of their persistent demands. On the contrary, the board realized that it could replace vacating white teachers with African

Americans and pay them significantly less because they had little negotiating power.[18] African American primary school teachers at Knowles received $40 a month whereas whites at other schools received $45. Racialized salary disparities were revealed fully in 1891, when the board published its first official salary schedule for white and black schools. Black elementary or grammar school teachers' salaries ranged from $30 in their first year to $45 by their fourth; white teachers started at $35 and made $50 in their fourth year.

Yet pay discrepancies did not hold back the increase in black teachers and black schools. As great numbers of African Americans met hiring requirements the board could not stick to its assertion that there were not enough qualified blacks to staff black schools. Yearly certification examinations, however, continued to be a problem; some blacks who had proven themselves competent in the classroom were fired after failing the test. In 1887, for example, nineteen out of forty-two African Americans passed the teachers' examination, with W. E. B. Du Bois, a Fisk student, achieving the highest score.[19]

Increased job openings for white teachers at new schools for whites reduced competition for jobs in black ones. The board now had too many qualified applicants for schools for blacks but refused to place those people at schools for whites. During the 1880s the faculties at several black schools in addition to Vandaville changed from white to black: Belle View in 1883, Meigs upon opening in 1883, McKee (at 10 Ewing Street near Church Street) in 1886, and Pearl Elementary in 1887, four years after its establishment. By 1889 Nashville public schools employed fifty-one black teachers and 187 who were white. In order to relieve overcrowding, in 1890 the board opened Carter and Lawrence elementary schools for black students.[20]

Nashville's black community was painfully aware that its schools received fewer financial resources than white schools, and hiring African American teachers, given the other social and political losses during the late nineteenth century, was only a bittersweet victory. As African Americans endeavored to build new lives after Reconstruction, white southerners tried to regain political, cultural, and economic power, and in 1870 the Tennessee legislature imposed poll taxes as a prerequisite for voting. It was an act that significantly undercut black enfranchisement.[21]

A plethora of Jim Crow laws that restricted social interactions between blacks and whites and severely limited access to employment, health care, and public institutions made the role of black teachers all the more critical. In Nashville and elsewhere, African Americans continued to demand black teachers, hoping to protect their children from the damaging psychological impacts of segregation and inferior schools.[22] It was a drive for empowerment rather than an act of acquiescence or accommodation. If school funding was to be unequal, then blacks would still have teachers who could contribute their own cultural capital, time, and money. Those individuals were members of the black community, connected by a critical need to serve the race.

In rural areas, black teachers were scarce or had limited training, but by the end of the 1880s there was an abundance of competent graduates from Fisk and other local colleges in Nashville. They often lived in the same neighborhoods as their students, which afforded opportunities to establish connections with the students' families. As the city's black community invested personal capital to support schools, teachers worked to establish bonds between their school and its surrounding neighborhoods and transform the schools into cultural centers.[23] Black teachers held prominent positions of authority and respect in their communities, and they continued to combat educational inequality.[24]

Nashville's black community knew that hiring and retaining black teachers constituted only part of the effort to expand opportunities for their children. The struggle for better schools was far from over. According to its annual report, in 1884 the board spent $8.55 a year to educate a black student but allocated $12.71 for white ones. Moreover, schools for African Americans tended to be structurally unsound; some, including Vandaville School, were uninhabitable.[25] Perhaps even more damaging, African Americans lacked a sound high school. Meigs offered eighth-grade courses, but black parents wanted the board to provide the same opportunity for their children to take secondary courses as white children had.

Southern government and school officials began to construct high schools for white children but often failed to provide them for African Americans.[26] Nashville's Hume High School opened in 1867, and by the 1880s the city had three high schools for white students. In 1910 only 538 of 54,363 Africans Americans between fifteen and nineteen received public high school educations in Tennessee although 1,296 attended private high schools.[27]

In the mid-1880s African Americans in Nashville pushed the city to open a black high school, a crusade spearheaded by a local parent, Sarah Porter. In 1884 she and several prominent ministers and businesspeople sent a resolution to the board of education: "We who have labored so long and successfully for public education resolve to as speedily as possible consummate permanent high school facilities for the present and rapidly growing class of colored youth who are passing beyond the present school grades and who for the lack of which are forced to close their school lives much earlier than at first contemplated."[28]

When the board made no response, Porter and several parents approached Caldwell's office and attempted to demonstrate their children's academic skills. The superintendent promised to address the issue in an upcoming board meeting. Napier, seven years after his first resolution calling for the employment of black teachers, joined Porter's cause and introduced a resolution at the September 24, 1884, meeting: "Be it resolved that the Board of Education be requested and they are hereby authorized and empowered to rent, lease or purchase without delay a building suitable for school purposes and to employ a sufficient number of teachers for the establishment of a school for colored children who have advanced beyond the grades now taught in the city schools for colored children."[29] Sarah Porter then sent her eldest son, James, to enroll at the all-white Hume High School at the corner of Spruce and Broad Streets in downtown Nashville. School officials refused him, however, and told him to return home. Porter retaliated by purchasing the necessary ninth-grade textbooks for James and sending him back to Hume. "I can't go home," he told officials there, "because my mother sent me here and would not like it if I left."[30] Nevertheless, James was once again sent home.

After her son was repeatedly refused admission to Hume, Porter and prominent black citizens held a mass meeting at Capers Chapel Church, where they agreed to circulate a petition asking for a black high school. The board responded by agreeing in 1886 to add ninth and tenth grades to Meigs Elementary School in east Nashville, with D. N. Crosthwait as principal. Meigs's secondary program began on September 20, 1886, and had three teachers: J. Ira Watson, John M. Turpin, and Lena Terrell Jackson. The curriculum included algebra, geometry, history, geography, Latin, and chemistry as well as other subjects. Seven students composed its first graduating class in 1888.[31]

Meigs's secondary students had to share the facility's limited resources with elementary-school children. In 1898 the board opened Napier Elementary School, named after the city council member, and sent Pearl Elementary School's students there. The board then relocated the high school from Meigs to Pearl, and Pearl became a senior high school. By 1897 ninety-nine students had received diplomas from Pearl. Although the black community celebrated its high school it continued to experience racial inequality. In 1899, for instance, the board spent only $10.45 for each black high school student but provided $32.16 for every white pupil. Pearl's teachers also received less money than their white counterparts. In 1891, according to the annual report of the Nashville Public Schools, African American high school teachers' annual salaries ranged from $62.50 to $72.50 whereas white high school teachers earned between $90 and $120.[32]

In 1897 the board expanded Knowles and closed McKee, which it deemed "totally unfit for a school."[33] Some 388 students graduated from Pearl Senior High School between 1895 and 1913.[34] The campaign to establish a high school for black students reflects the black middle class's ability to mobilize and provide its children with greater educational opportunities. The successful battle to secure a black secondary school was indeed a victory worth celebrating, but the war against inequality raged on. Black schools remained underfunded, and African American teachers fell victim to discriminatory pay schedules.

In 1901 Nashville, as the capital of Tennessee, faced a new century filled with promise of progressive growth. The city was known as the Athens of the South because of its thirteen universities and colleges, which included Vanderbilt and Fisk. Its population of 80,865 included 30,044 blacks, and there were eleven schools for whites and seven for blacks; of a total of 18,101 students being educated, 4,988 were African Americans.[35] Although Nashville officials promoted the capitol as a modern city of the New South, its educational, economic, political, and social structures reflected new efforts to enforce legal racial segregation in all facets of urban life.

Black schools throughout Tennessee, including Nashville, reflected the southern white distaste for black educational progress and a refusal to adhere to the separate-but-equal mandate of the Supreme Court's *Plessy v. Ferguson* decision.[36] According to James D. Anderson, after African Americans pushed for common school education in the South during Reconstruction, poor whites called for free public schools, and state money designated to support African American schools went to white facilities. Even after white Democrats regained political power they were convinced that educating blacks would disrupt the economic structure and social order. Nevertheless, by the end of Reconstruction these leaders, in order to aid in the region's economic and social growth, reluctantly conceded to offering some kind of basic schooling for African Americans. Few, if any, southern schools for blacks received funding and materials equal to those of white schools, and some rural blacks had no access at all to organized education.[37]

Cities promised the best opportunities for blacks who sought an education, but boards of education in Nashville and other urban areas faced the economic burden of maintaining a dual system. In the case of black schools they economized and constructed new ones as infrequently as possible. Instead, they often leased dilapidated houses, such as Belle View, that frequently flooded or unsafe buildings such as Knowles, called "Old Deathtrap" because parents feared it might cave in on their children.[38] In a society where women were still considered the weaker sex, it was common for female teachers to be required to maintain coal stoves to heat their classrooms. Some black schools also had open or troughlike latrines that made it difficult for teachers to sustain sanitary conditions.[39]

African American men also worked as teachers and often became principals, but women composed the majority of the faculty in Nashville's segregated schools by the turn of the century. Men filled most teaching positions in the early part of the century, although reformers and activists such as Catharine Beecher maintained that the nurturing and maternal qualities of women fitted them to be excellent teachers. In her efforts to convince women to teach Native Americans in the West, Beecher helped popularize and promote the field of teaching among middle-class women. Whether filled with a desire for service or merely in need of employment, these women viewed teaching as a way to support themselves and expand their roles as caretakers outside their homes. By the 1880s women were being encouraged to become teachers. The feminization of the profession was also aided by expanding employment options for men outside the classroom and the tendency of boards to pay women less than men.[40]

The number of African American women teachers grew to outnumber that for men in large part because educated black men could obtain higher-paying positions with the railroads, in the ministry, or in black-owned businesses. Those employed in education were often promoted to administrative positions; all Nashville's black principals, for example, were male. African American men in rural areas had little opportunity to attend school or teach because their labor was needed for the family income. In 1890 there were 7,236 black male teachers employed in the United States, a number that almost equaled the 7,864 women in the profession. By 1910 the number of male teachers remained at 7,743, whereas there were 13,524 black female teachers.[41] By 1912 there were sixty-one black women and fifteen men in Nashville's twelve black schools.[42] For black women, their labor opportunities limited, teaching provided the best avenue to a professional position even though salaries were quite low.

African Americans encouraged women to attend college and become teachers or enter other professions. Most expected to work outside their homes because racial restrictions often limited the economic opportunities of black men. African American parents, such as those of Fisk Jubilee singer and later professor Ella Sheppard Moore, wanted their young daughters to become teachers in order to help pull the families out of poverty. The young women were also encouraged to attend college and become professionals in order to avoid the possibility of harassment from white bosses should they work as domestics.[43]

Women who entered the work force relied on training and their self-perceptions as professionals to develop strategies to counter discrimination and injustice. At Nashville's early private schools, which included Fisk University, Central Tennessee College, and Roger Williams University, and later at the city's public institutions such as Tennessee Agricultural and Industrial State Normal School, they learned that their mission included not only preparing students for upward mobility but also behaving as positive representations of African American womanhood. The charge to improve the image of black women and serve the race attracted women to a field that offered status, respect, and honor.

As the demand for African American teachers increased in the South during Reconstruction missionary associations developed the first black institutions of higher learning in Nashville. Fisk founders, Union Army veterans, and Freedmen's Bureau officers John Ogden, Erastus M. Cravath, and Edward P. Smith requested in 1866 that the American Missionary Association (AMA) open a normal school for blacks. Ogden maintained that spending $100,000 of the association's money on training people to teach "would do much more towards educating freedmen of the South than three times that sum spent in supporting northern teachers."[44]

The AMA approved the plan but provided no funds at first. Undaunted, Ogden, Cravath, and Smith offered to raise $4,000 each toward the $16,000 needed to purchase land for the project. Before they began, however, the AMA joined with the Freedmen's Bureau to buy property; eventually, the

AMA even reimbursed the founders' donations. Gen. Clinton Fisk, assistant commissioner of the Freedmen's Bureau for Tennessee and Kentucky, helped locate buildings for the school and donated thousands of dollars. For his efforts, the founders named the school after him, and the Fisk Free School opened in 1866.[45]

When Fisk opened its doors on January 9, more than two hundred men, women, and children were waiting to enroll. The school was housed in a former Union Army hospital barracks in north Nashville. Five hundred students had registered in its daytime elementary program by February, and a hundred attended classes at night. Fisk enrolled more than nine hundred children and adults during its first few months, but thousands more were turned away due to space limitations.[46] Ogden lamented in 1866 that although the school flourished it still lacked appropriate funding. Moreover, he was frustrated that African Americans needed to donate to a private institution in order to obtain educations when others could attend free schools. "They are now looking with a great deal of hope for the establishment of schools under legal sanction," he asserted. "As soon as possible—I think the primary schools, at least in large cities should be supported by the state, which will make a large demand for colored teachers."[47]

For all of its early difficulties Fisk proved indispensable for the black community. The experience of Emma Grisham, a former slave, was but one example of its value. She could only attend Fisk for a short time before her father removed her to work as a domestic. Nevertheless, she sent her daughter to Fisk, and the daughter, Martha, eventually became a Nashville public school teacher in 1893. Proud of the daughter's accomplishment, Grisham told a Works Progress Administration interviewer, "She buy dis place and we live tergedder. We hab good health en both ez happy. I hab a 'oman kum eve'y Monday and wash for us."[48] The Fisk Free School promised to instruct newly freed African Americans, transform them into productive Christian citizens. It also produced well-trained teachers who provided leadership to thousands of former slaves.

After black public schools opened in 1867 Fisk discontinued its elementary program to focus on training teachers in a normal program. Renamed Fisk University that same year, it offered basic secondary courses as well as classes in botany, geometry, chemistry, algebra, and natural history. Due to rising costs, in 1869 Fisk began charging tuition that ranged from $9 to $12 a year. In addition to the academic courses in its secondary, normal, and theology departments, from 1867 to 1874 it also offered manual-labor classes. In addition the school provided a small model elementary school for daily, hands-on training for the normal students. In 1871 Fisk enrolled its first students in a three-year, college-level program.[49]

To augment the AMA's limited financing the university used students to raise funds as well as promote spirituals. The Fisk Jubilee Singers, who became internationally known, entertained audiences across the United States and throughout Europe.[50] Although some students from elite backgrounds attended the school during the 1870s several supported themselves and often worked during the summers to pay for their tuition. Some began to teach before they finished training and opened summer schools in rural areas in order to gain tuition money and experience.

Fisk University represented an educational mecca for blacks, but many of Nashville's African American students encountered almost insurmountable struggles to secure a seat in the city's overcrowded public schools. The success of Fisk students led to anger and frustration among those who considered obtaining a college degree an impossible dream. For some, the students constituted an exclusive black elite that looked down on poor African Americans. Envy sometimes caused a schism between Fiskites and the city's working-class African Americans, so the university encouraged students to do charitable service in the community and thus build better relations. In later years Fisk would become a center for sociology and social work centered on African Americans.[51]

Local whites also resented Fisk students, but for very different reasons. During the school's first year, poor white boys from the downtown Broad Street "bottoms," where there were no nearby schools for white children, became, as one Fisk teacher sarcastically commented, "so incensed at the thoughts of 'niggers' learning to read" that they often threw stones at Fisk students.[52] After local officials failed to help quiet the situation Fisk teachers escorted their students in an attempt to protect them. The harassment stopped but only after officers of the Freedmen's Bureau officers threatened to arrest those responsible.[53] The school's presence and its image of African American academic success continued, however, to unnerve local whites who wanted blacks to remain in subservient positions.

White Nashvillians who feared black progress had good reason to be apprehensive about Fisk. The presence of local universities and colleges helped strengthen the black community by providing young people opportunities to become professionals without leaving the city. As Booker T. Washington, the nationally known and internationally renowned president of Tuskegee

Institute, observed in a 1910 article, "The Fisk students seem to have but one object in view, that of preparing themselves for service to their race . . . I find that considerably more than half of them have gone out into different parts of the South as teachers. In my recent trips through southern states, I have met, and almost without exception, I have found that they are leading useful and honorable lives."[54] By 1915 Fisk graduates composed more than half of the blacks who worked in the Nashville public schools.[55]

Fisk was not the only school catering to Nashville's growing African American population; missionary societies established several other institutions from which black teachers and professionals emerged. With support from the Freedmen's Bureau, the Methodist Episcopal Church founded a school for freed people in 1865, which in 1867 was renamed Central Tennessee College. The institution offered normal school courses and in 1876 opened its medical department, which by 1915 would become Meharry Medical College. During the 1880s the school expanded to offer degrees in law, pharmacy, dentistry, and industrial education. Central Tennessee College, renamed Walden University in 1900, experienced a devastating dormitory fire in 1903 that killed twelve students. That tragedy and the naming of a black president, Edward White, in 1915 led to a loss in white support for the university. Three years later Walden University became a junior college and moved to a smaller campus offering normal school courses. Given its stiff competition from schools such as Fisk and Tennessee A&I and dwindling foundation support, Walden closed in 1929; Meharry Medical School, however, continued and is still in operation.[56]

In 1867 the American Baptist Home Mission Society opened the Nashville Normal and Theological Institute, which promised to train African Americans for the ministry and teaching. By 1877 the school was granting the A.B. degree, and it reorganized as Roger Williams University in 1883. The institution offered courses in Latin, Greek, English, mathematics, science, history, civics, Bible physiology, and teacher training. After the American Home Mission cut support and several years of funding losses, Roger Williams moved to Memphis in 1929 and merged with Howe Institute. The new facility was eventually named LeMoyne-Owen College.[57]

Primarily from the North and Midwest, the white faculty of these colleges faced ostracism and isolation from the local white community. Southern whites often refused to rent to professors or invite them to social or cultural events. Freedmen's school and missionary teachers, and their black students who opened their own schools, risked their lives to teach African

Americans. When a hundred members of the Ku Klux Klan rode down Nashville's Church Street to frighten blacks and Republicans in 1868 it was but one example of the violence occurring throughout the state. In Memphis, whites burned twelve freedmen's schools in 1866; two years later, two Fisk students were whipped after opening a summer school.[58] Tennessee's governor William G. Brownlow, a former Union supporter, advised the Fisk faculty to avoid offending the community because "without federal troops, black pupils would not be able to occupy the school room a week, not a week."[59] Some teachers left Fisk to seek safer surroundings, but in 1870 its ten remaining teachers vowed to continue their religious mission to teach. Adam Spence, Fisk's president, looked to his faith to remain committed to the cause: "O to make this school a fountain of good influence, of piety, of burning devotion for Christ. I believe it were be so made."[60]

With neither minimal support from local white residents nor help from impoverished blacks, Fisk and the city's other private African American colleges depended on religious organizations, which in turn relied on donations from northern whites who shared many of the racist viewpoints of their southern counterparts. Consequently, schools had to reassure such donors and white southerners that they were not educating students to incite social revolution but only to progress within the restrictions of the existing society. Nevertheless, by stressing hard work, thrift, and piety as well as a classical education, Fisk and Nashville's other black private universities taught students that they could expand the boundaries of segregation by achieving economic and professional success.

Numerous individual examples demonstrate Fisk's influence on black women teachers and the influence they in turn had on students. Minnie Lou Scott, for example, born in 1860, graduated from Fisk University's Normal School in 1877. After becoming a teacher at Knowles Elementary School in 1879 and marrying Knowles's principal, Scott W. Crosthwaite, she became an administrator at Fisk and a suffrage activist.[61] She was later Fisk's registrar and a trustee of the school during the 1930s. Throughout her career Crosthwaite served as a professional role model for women who wished to aspire to middle-class status by becoming teachers.

Similarly, Lena Terrell Jackson, a native of Sumner County, Tennessee, was also a powerful force in Nashville's black community. Born in 1865, she attended local public schools; after working for two years in rural Tennessee, she graduated from Fisk University in 1885 with a B.A. degree. Later that year she joined the Meigs faculty and eventually taught Latin at Pearl Senior High School.[62] She was a teacher for more than fifty years in Nashville, retiring in 1942. During the 1930s, principal John Galloway reported that "Miss Jackson is an old teacher, yet she is almost as energetic as a young woman. Children and her fellow teachers respect her. They seek her counsel and advice. She is an excellent teacher."[63] A strict disciplinarian, her former students viewed Lena Jackson with reverence and respect. When recalling her uncanny ability to catch misbehaving students, one alumnus humorously recalled that she could "see the spots on a pony in the back of her classes in the dark with her eyes closed."[64] In addition to insisting that pupils master Latin, Jackson also advised females on how to act properly. Sadie Madry, a student in the late 1920s who then taught elementary school, fondly remembers that the very prim and proper Jackson reminded them to refrain from wearing tight dresses and skirts.[65] In the 1940s her former students and peers honored the retiring teacher's decades of service to Pearl by naming its chapter of the National Honor Society after her.[66]

By the turn of the century Fisk University offered a classical liberal arts curriculum, and students studied the same subjects as their counterparts did at white liberal arts colleges. The program's strongest advocate was the Harvard University–trained scholar W. E. B. Du Bois.[67] Born in 1868, the 1888 Fisk graduate spent his childhood in Great Barrington, Massachusetts. It was his belief that "education and work are levers to uplift a people. Work alone will not do it unless inspired by the right ideals and guided by intelligence. Education must not simply teach work—it must teach life."[68]

Although aware that the majority of African Americans remained in the laboring classes, Du Bois promoted the idea of training the top ("talented tenth") of the black population so they could lead their brothers and sisters to higher economic status. This group, he suggested, bore the overwhelming responsibility of aiding the other, struggling, 90 percent. Armed with a strong liberal arts education, members of the talented tenth were to convey knowledge as teachers, heal as doctors and nurses, defend the rights of the downtrodden as lawyers, and provide jobs and services to their communities as business professionals.[69] While spending two summers teaching in Lebanon, a small Tennessee town some fifty miles from Nashville, Du Bois learned firsthand about the educational inequities in the South and immortalized his experiences in *The Souls of Black Folk* (1903). Throughout his long career Du Bois continually encouraged African Americans to push for better social conditions rather than accept society as it was.[70]

Although Fisk University and the city's other private colleges continued to produce classically schooled African American teachers there remained a shortage of instructors in rural areas. Many blacks wanted a low-cost, state-funded institution of higher learning at which they could be trained as educators. After Tennessee received federal funds from the Morrill Act to open normal schools in 1909, Tennessee's legislature passed a general education bill allocating funding for four normal, or teacher-training, schools, three for whites and one for African Americans.[71] In an attempt to alleviate white concerns that a classically educated black teacher would preach social equality, James C. Napier, now registrar of the U.S. Treasury, maintained along with other black leaders in Tennessee that a normal school could offer industrial training to future black teachers. What they failed to mention, however, was that the new school's other mission included training those capable of teaching liberal arts courses.[72]

Blacks in Chattanooga vied to have the normal college in their city, but Nashville emerged as the victor and received the $40,000 in bond funds. Black leaders negotiated with the city's mayor, Hillary House, a Democrat and political boss known to do anything and everything to get elected, whether offering bribes or paying blacks' poll taxes. Nashville's black community used their cultural capital in a collective effort to receive city bond funds. Although the white normal schools received almost $35,000 each from the state, the general assembly designated only half that amount for the black normal college; black Nashvillians donated more than $10,000 to support the facility.

Proposing to "educate and train teachers for the public schools of the state," Tennessee Agricultural and Industrial State Normal School for Negroes opened in 1912 with a predominately black faculty of ten and 247 students; a summer session for teachers began on June 19, with more than 250 teachers in attendance.[73] Fall classes began on September 16. A year later Napier used his influence to convince the general assembly to pass legislation to ensure that Tennessee A&I State Normal School received an equitable share of the annual $12,000 Morrill funds.[74] Nevertheless, the state continued to provide less money to A&I than it did the other normal schools.

During its early years A&I attempted to remedy some of the inadequacies in the state's black public schools by offering elementary and secondary education in addition to normal school courses. The school's bulletin also announced a model training school program for student teachers, with classes for grades one through eight. A&I students could pursue either of two tracks, academic (high school) or normal (two-year teacher training). Only high school or A&I academic department graduates could enroll in the school's normal program. Students in the two-year, thirty-six-week program had to choose to study agriculture, business, home economics, industrial trades, or teaching. A graduate, according to the bulletin, could teach in any of the state's public schools for five years before taking a qualifying examination. While A&I students in the academic program took secondary subjects, the normal program's courses ranged from psychology to school management. The institution also offered courses in cooking, sewing, and how to run reading circles. Wishing to further their education, many working teachers took summer courses. Some 1,008 students enrolled in A&I's 1914 summer session. That same year the bulletin reported that Nashville women composed half of the twenty-two members of the first normal school graduating class.

William Jasper Hale, a high school administrator from Chattanooga, became A&I's first principal, but the legislature refused to give him the title and status of president granted to leaders of the state's normal schools for whites. Hale received the position because he worked tirelessly, but to no avail, to locate the normal school in his city. Although he was not a native of Nashville, the city's black community finally accepted him after he married Hattie Hodgkins, a graduate of Pearl High School and Fisk University.[75]

During the early years, students at A&I made many sacrifices. They were poorly housed and had limited resources—often it was necessary to carry their own chairs to class. In addition to the regular duties involved in maintaining the grounds and buildings, the students also had to serve as wait staff when state officials or other prominent whites visited.[76] Even teachers had to help. As Hale described their efforts in preparation for the school's first summer session, "The teachers, without one exception put on their old clothes, scrubbed, washed windows, carried out rubbish and did other tasks of like nature necessary to get the two completed buildings in shape for the opening. This represented the very thing that the state school was designed to teach, that labor was necessary and honorable."[77] A&I students did not dwell on the lack of supplies and facilities, however, but on the future opportunities garnered from receiving a low-cost education. They only had to pay a $2 fee, and many worked their way through school. A&I's alumni were well aware of the rare opportunity they possessed as normal school graduates.

With his school's survival depending upon the whims of the state legislature, Principal Hale advocated Booker T. Washington's industrial educational model because it placated whites while still providing some higher educational opportunities.[78] Washington, in turn, promoted the views of his mentor Samuel Armstrong, president of Hampton Institute. Industrial education promised to prepare students to adapt to a segregated environment that had limited job opportunities.[79] As Washington put his educational philosophy when speaking to a graduating class at Fisk, "Young ladies do all the good for your race that you can, but if you can't find a school to teach [in], put into practice some of the things you have learned in the Domestic Science department, do plain sewing, go out cooking, accept serving, adopt nursing, take up housework or do anything else that is decent and honorable to make an honest living."[80] Armstrong's philosophy, which Washington voiced, stressed that whites should have lower expectations regarding black progress, claiming, "A few centuries ago my people were led from the wilds of Africa and suddenly dropped into the very highest type of civilization." The statement reassured southern whites that educated blacks would be "civilized" residents and not agitate for voting rights or social equality.[81]

Just as public schools in the North were designed to Americanize recent immigrants, northern philanthropists believed that pubic schools could direct blacks to accept lowly positions in the South's prevailing racial order. Representatives from the General Education Board (GEB), the Anna T. Jeanes Foundation, the Phillip Slater Fund, and Joseph Rosenwald Foundation as well as other philanthropists embraced the Hampton model and promised to direct their efforts to expanding industrial education-base normal schools.[82] As the philanthropist William H. Baldwin asserted, "The potential economic value of the Negro population properly educated is infinite and incalculable. . . . He will fill the more menial positions; do the heavy work, at less wages than the American white man or any foreign race that has come to our shores."[83] Many white southerners, however, remained skeptical of the power of industrial education to create a docile labor force and did not stress such training in segregated public schools where the curriculum was limited. The few high schools available to African Americans, such as Pearl, offered courses in Latin.[84]

Scholars and critics of the ever-pragmatic and powerful Washington called him an accommodationalist because he did not openly advocate social equality, yet his ideology did not bar him from serving on the boards of philanthropic organizations, where he fought a discreet campaign to allocate funding to liberal arts colleges such as Fisk. Serving on Fisk's board from 1909 to 1915, Washington even enrolled his own son at the institution. A complex man, he acted as a powerful behind-the-scenes advocate.[85] In a speech in 1910 he actually contradicted what had been his position on education when he lauded classical education for African Americans: "The Negro teacher or the Negro doctor ought to have just as sound, just as complete and just as thorough an education as the white man who performs the same work or shares the same responsibilities." Washington did not openly promote including African Americans into the social fabric of white southern society, but white philanthropists and leaders often welcomed him at political gatherings.[86] Perhaps it was necessary to be pragmatic when advocating industrial education in the South, where a black man could be lynched for looking a white person directly in the eye. Washington's ability to support black liberal arts colleges quietly while advocating for a more acceptable type of limited industrial education provided a model for other black college presidents and teachers who depended on southern legislatures and white philanthropists for funding and material.

Washington promoted industrial education, but most of the South's private black colleges, including Fisk, continued to offer courses in the liberal arts. Based upon the goals of missionary teachers, the schools wished to train instructors who would promote Christian values among students and help them become community leaders. J. G. Merrill, Fisk's president, made that position clear in 1904 when he contended, "It is the purpose of the faculty to send forth no one who is unworthy of confidence or incapacitated to be a leader of those who have never had the opportunities afforded at Fisk."[87]

Students at Tennessee A&I State Normal School took domestic courses but did not attend college merely to train for work as future laborers. Many obtained jobs at Pearl High School and the city's other schools, where they challenged students to rise above the positions society had designated for them. Most black teachers in the South knew they would study and work under unequal conditions, yet a restrictive industrial education was better than no education at all. At normal schools like Tennessee A&I, students learned that successful teachers had two identities. One placated the white power structure to secure more materials for students; another expressed the mission to help pupils overcome boundaries placed upon them. With the opening of Tennessee A&I, Nashville's future teachers had two excellent options for a higher education: a traditional liberal arts university and an industrial normal school.

Although African American teachers remained at the middle of an ideological struggle between proponents of industrial education and those who advocated classical curriculums, they chose tenets from both philosophies that best served their needs. Black Nashvillians were also selective about whether they supported Washington and Du Bois's ideas. James C. Napier did not agree with Washington's views regarding black political rights, but he and several other African American leaders supported the Wizard of Tuskegee's ideas encouraging black business development. He did not endorse Du Bois either. Although he considered him an excellent speaker, Napier maintained that he "failed to utter a single word of advice or counsel touching the practical side of the life which these young people will soon have to face." Napier denied the need to debate industrial against classical education. "Both," he concluded, "are honestly striving for the same end."[88]

Ironically, Tennessee A&I found itself defended by Du Bois after a federally sponsored study found it academically inferior to local colleges such as Fisk, which offered a university program, and even the state's white normal schools. In 1917 educator Thomas Jesse Jones conducted a survey on behalf of the Bureau of the Interior and found that the school offered only secondary-level courses and did not meet accreditation standards for curriculum, department size, number of professors with advanced degrees, and library content. Moreover, the A&I secondary or high school only met elementary school standards, and the normal program should have been designated as a secondary or high school institution.[89] Du Bois discounted Jones's study, "What he is criticizing then is the [blacks'] wish to go to college and their endeavor to support and maintain even poor college departments. It is this General Education Board [a philanthropic foundation that supported industrial education] that is spending more money today in helping Negroes learn how to can vegetables than in helping them to go through college."[90]

Jones's study reflected one of the problems inherent in industrial education: teaching students how to "toil with their hands" limited opportunities to learn more academic subjects. Many who were poorly educated needed additional academic help rather than classes in the domestic arts. By the 1920s, liberal-arts advocates maintained that industrial education had failed in its mission to train a new corps of teachers because its graduates did not learn enough to obtain positions in public schools. A&I's normal school graduates could find jobs, but the large number who returned to summer workshops reflected the desire for further knowledge.[91]

Ever in need of additional funds, A&I sought donations from foundations that promoted Booker T. Washington and industrial education. Tennessee became the first southern state to receive funding from the General

Education Board for African Americans. With its state headquarters on A&I's campus, the GEB appointed Samuel Leonard Smith as its first black agent to supervise the foundation's efforts among African Americans in the state. Organized in 1907, the Anna T. Jeanes Foundation funded the salaries of teachers working in rural areas, and several A&I graduates became Jeanes teachers, including Carrie Dunn Denney, the sister of Nashville teacher Lillian Dunn Thomas, who worked in Davidson County. Their duties extended far beyond teaching academic subjects; they traveled into remote rural communities to instruct residents in such life skills as gardening, cooking, sewing, and housing construction. In 1911 the Rosenwald Foundation provided supplementary funds to help construct black schools, but in reality African Americans often donated most of the money. The first black Rosenwald building agent in Tennessee, Robert Clay, also based his office on the A&I campus.

With the construction of new schools throughout the South the demand for A&I graduates became even greater.[92] The teachers went into communities where poor people suffered the burden of double taxation, paying for white institutions while supporting schools of their own.[93]

As A&I received college status in 1922 its academic program became more rigorous: a four-year course schedule of English, mathematics, history, elementary sciences, education, psychology, agriculture, botany, Latin, and bookkeeping. By their junior or senior years students specialized or majored in certain subjects. Although a college, A&I still offered industrial courses, and student efforts in growing produce and raising animals on the school's farm yielded much of their food supply.[94]

Nationally known black leaders and intellectuals such as Washington and Du Bois espoused different theories for educational progress, but black teachers had to translate philosophy into practice. Whether drawing primarily from Washington's theories or Du Bois's, they agreed that it was imperative to form a stable, steady, and growing middle class. The primary goal of industrial education was to train African Americans to mold students into a subservient class. White people considered industrial education as a way to maintain the current social order and limit potential job competition, but black leaders viewed it as a beginning toward a broader education. As members of Du Bois's talented tenth, teachers were thought to have a special responsibility to help the race achieve social equality. "It has, however, been in the furnishing of teachers that the Negro college has found its peculiar function," Du Bois observed. "The furnishing of five million and more of ignorant people with teachers of their own race and blood, in one generation, was not only a very difficult undertaking, but a very important one, in that it placed before the eyes of almost every Negro child an attainable ideal."[95]

Notwithstanding their opposing views, both Washington and Du Bois considered attaining middle-class economic status to be essential for the race's progress, whether achieved by learning a trade and opening a successful business or by studying the sciences and becoming a doctor. Despite facing the daily realities of working in schools that were segregated and unequal to those for whites, black women teachers accepted the mandate to serve as representatives of professional success. "The Negro teacher" in the city, Washington suggested, "has the responsibility to a much larger extent than the white teacher . . . of showing, by the results of his teaching, the value of the kind of education that he is giving his pupils."[96]

As Fisk University and Tennessee A&I students graduated and accepted positions in the city schools they, along with most of Nashville's black leadership, supported Washington's concept of self-help in economic development and community service. These educators also followed Du Bois's talented tenth philosophy in the classroom as they taught chemistry and Latin at Pearl High School despite the lack of resources and materials. In their daily routines and educational philosophies Nashville's black women teachers drew on the ideas of both Washington and Du Bois to carry out the mission of instilling middle-class respectability and racial uplift.

Many black women teachers were normal school or college students when they formed perceptions of middle-class respectability and the appropriate roles for professionals. They had been instructed to serve by precept and example, believing they should be feminine and genteel outside the classroom yet, as teachers, defy stereotypes regarding women's work, intelligence, and strength.[97] The women at Tennessee A&I and other African American colleges learned that a professional teacher's role included meeting the social and cultural demands of the black community. An A&I school bulletin of 1913, for example, claimed, "We endeavor to make the home life of those residing in the institution pleasant and profitable both to themselves and to the communities to which they will return. Habits of tidiness and taste in the arrangement and care of the rooms are inculcated."[98]

Female students learned to maintain a proper home, put on teas and galas, and teach in schools where roofs leaked and stoves spewed debris.

In addition to academic subjects the schools offered domestic courses, not only to provide students with a skill but also to ensure they would be good housekeepers, something essential to achieving middle-class respectability. Given their low salaries, black teachers were rarely able to afford domestic help and thus took care of their own homes in addition to their responsibilities as teachers. They taught domestic skills to families as well as students, information that enabled the women to support themselves should teaching positions not be available.[99]

A&I and other black schools offered classical subjects as well as domestic courses. Universities such as Fisk endeavored to prove the competency of black teachers by displaying their intellectual acumen in and out the classroom. Linda Perkins maintains that although "rural areas of the South attracted the least-prepared teachers, the opposite was true of urban areas." Some districts did hire grammar-school graduates or else refused to hire competent teachers, but Nashville's black urban professional instructors were exceptions to that practice.[100]

One of the most important duties of a professional teacher had nothing to do with classrooms or textbooks. Black women teachers had to present themselves as visual representations of achievement. Nashville's black institutions of higher learning trained them not only to behave like professionals but also to look like them. "Special attention is given to our girls in order to train them in matters pertaining to dress, health, behavior, physical development and the simple rules of good manners," read one A&I promotional pamphlet from the early twentieth century.[101]

The African American community demanded that its teachers portray themselves as leaders, which included dressing as if they received adequate pay and worked in comfortable surroundings. Whether they sewed their own clothes or wore a few key pieces, the women considered conservative attire and good manners as critical to garnering respect and assistance from their communities and possibly from the white power structure. Wages were low, but dressing well reinforced their identities as middle-class professionals. Working-class women, by comparison, often looked forward to dressing stylishly for church or social functions as a way of reclaiming an identity apart from their jobs. For them, what they wore for work did not embody who they were. In contrast, black women teachers longed to be recognized for what they wore to work. Indeed, professional dress served as the urban teacher's uniform.[102]

In behavior, dress, and manners teachers were supposed to represent the ideal lady to students and community. As Ozana Vineyard, a student at Tennessee A&I, described the women on his campus in 1929, "They are perfect in every sense. Modest enough to be real young ladies: Now understand me, I don't mean false modesty. I mean that portion of modesty, which goes to make up the character of real womanhood. Not any of them are far below Venus in physical makeup and all are certainly well dressed."[103] By maintaining an image of piety and respectability the women could also inspire students to become professionals; community approval of their moral character helped teachers withstand discrimination from the white members of the profession.[104]

Of course, the real test of the professional urban teacher occurred in the classroom. By 1912 twelve black schools enrolled some five thousand African American students in Nashville:[105] Local leaders continued to ask the board of education to construct more schools, and Parent Teacher Associations, churches, and other organizations also raised funds for the equipment and material white schools received through the system. In 1913 parents formed the Knowles School Alliance to petition the board for sanitary drinking water for their children, but they were willing to pay for the water themselves if the board did not respond.[106]

During the early twentieth century the board continued to improve educational opportunities for whites while largely neglecting the black community. A lunchroom program was begun, and in the early 1910s the board also decided to fire all black janitors and replace them with white men. In addition, the board ruled that all teachers working for three years no longer had to be reelected annually; they also now worked on a twelve-month salary schedule.[107] Perhaps more substantially, the board approved the construction of a new secondary school for whites although the only black high school in middle Tennessee, Pearl, had become severely overcrowded.

After repeated complaints from black parents, in 1915 the board of education did authorize a new building for black students, which opened the next year on Sixteenth Avenue North and Grant Street in north Nashville. The new facility thrilled the city's black community, but it was less than pleased with Nashville's politicians, who had promised that money from the board's recent $2 million bond drive would support black schools. Only $65,000 went to Pearl, although $250,000 went to the new white high school. The new Pearl added the twelfth grade and courses in home economics and mechanical arts.[108]

One of only three black public high schools in Tennessee at the time, Pearl was a rare jewel in Nashville's black education system. States throughout the South continued to construct white high schools, but Tennessee stood out because, as of 1915, the other states, including Mississippi, Georgia, and North Carolina, had yet to construct any four-year public high schools for blacks. In those states African American students had to attend private institutions or go elsewhere to receive a secondary education. Southern school boards and northern philanthropists advocated building black elementary schools, but due to fears of labor competition they had little desire to encourage secondary education.[109]

Students who wanted to attend high school migrated from rural areas to Nashville, but most local black teenagers could not attend Pearl due to economic restrictions and overcrowding. Even though the school had an enrollment of almost two hundred, sixty males and 136 females in 1915, more than four thousand black children of high school age lived in Nashville alone.[110] Pearl represented educational excellence but was also the symbol of an unattainable middle-class ideal for the majority of black youths who faced the world of work after the eighth grade.

Although the majority of southern states and rural towns refused to provide funding for black secondary schools and northern philanthropists offered to support industrial schools in rural areas only, classical education dominated Pearl's curriculum. Students had to take three years of Lena T. Jackson's Latin class as well as advanced courses in mathematics and history to graduate. Physics, chemistry, and physical geography were also required subjects. Black city leaders pushed for the board to provide funding for more industrial courses at Pearl, but those courses remained secondary to the liberal arts curriculum.[111] Pearl prepared students to attend college, not work as laborers. Several faculty members were Fisk graduates, and the school's staff served as the elite among Nashville's black teachers.

During the late 1910s and early 1920s black schools began to offer split sessions, and teachers worked in shifts with morning and afternoon groups. Superintendent Henri Carlton Weber attempted to cut costs by increasing class sizes and lifting the hiring ban on married teachers. He also initiated a "cadet teacher" program; one could be hired without much experience, with no college education, and at a lower salary than first-year teachers. After four years of classroom success cadet teachers were promoted to the regular staff. In 1921 black teachers earned about 80 percent of white teachers, who made from $75 to $85; cadets were paid $50. In an effort to better use buildings, the board began in 1922 to operate both white and black schools throughout the year, which divided the academic calendar into four twelve-week terms. Although they once led the state in salaries, the city's teachers now taught forty-eight weeks and were paid less than colleagues in Memphis, Knoxville, and Chattanooga, who taught fewer weeks of the year.[112]

Aside from the obstacles of poverty and discrimination, black teachers worked in a society that deemed them and their students inferior. As Stephanie Shaw shows, they battled the effects of racial inequalities by forming and participating in professional organizations. The teachers also hoped such groups would raise their status in the rest of the community, provide opportunities to address collectively changes in requirements, and discuss new instruction techniques.[113]

In 1907 black teachers formed the Colored Library Association to discuss professional issues and raise funds for books. The city had no black library. Reflective of the times, the white teachers' library association received $100 annually from the board but the African American association received only $50. Black teachers in Nashville and its surrounding Davidson County later formed the Middle Tennessee Colored Teachers Association in 1912, an affiliate of the state teachers' association. At their second annual conference they called for more teachers to participate, and the city's black newspaper, the *Nashville Globe*, summarized the event's highpoints: "Out of probably five hundred teachers about two hundred attended this meeting. It is to be regretted that more were not present. . . . However, those who were present, proved that they were interested in the work they are attempting to do. Every paper read and every expression made centered around the truth that the school teachers in this association realize that the destiny of the race lies largely in their hands."[114] In 1923 Nashville's black teachers also established the Teachers' Benefit Association, which offered low-cost summer loans to educators. In addition to addressing black schools' financial needs, the organizations presented opportunities for fellowship in a comfortable setting.

One of the primary duties of a professional teacher was public service. Teachers, as Sharon Harley contends, "thought that they had a special responsibility to serve the community that only they as educated, unmarried women could fulfill."[115] During the late nineteenth and early twentieth centuries they became community leaders, establishing clubs and organizations and working with religious organizations to help better the race. During the 1890s, for instance, black women worked as assistant teachers at the Nashville chapter of the Women's Baptist Home Mission Society, a national organization that worked with black churches to sponsor mothers' groups. It also provided religious-themed educational material for black children.[116]

The call to service was at the forefront of teachers' efforts throughout the Jim Crow era. In 1896 African American women formed the National Association of Colored Women (NACW), which became a powerful national umbrella association for charitable, civic, and social clubs. In 1897 Nashville's clubwomen hosted the first NACW convention.[117] Several officers of the NACW, including Fisk graduate Margaret Murray Washington, once worked as teachers. Moreover, many members, including Belle View teacher Frankie Pierce, a member of the NACW-affiliated Phillis Wheatley Club and later founder of the Nashville Federation of Colored Women's Clubs, taught in the public schools.[118]

Black women educators also joined with the wives of dentists and business leaders to compose the majority of Nashville's Phillis Wheatley Club, named in honor of the eighteenth-century African American poet. From its founding in 1895 to when it disbanded in 1920, the club supported a day-care center, raised money for the sick and needy, and campaigned for equipment for Pearl High School.[119] Teachers also participated in many other women's clubs in Nashville, among them the Women's Day Home Club, Ladies Christian Aid Society, Woman's Supply Club, Busy Bee Club, and Progressive Sewing Circle. The teaching philosophies of most women easily meshed with club principles; each emphasized moral responsibility, middle-class respectability, and the vital importance of schooling.[120]

Clubwomen focused a great deal of energy on encouraging mothers to impart moral values to their children. The clubs also emphasized good housekeeping as a sign of proper upbringing and virtue. Teachers, as surrogate mothers, shared the responsibility of instilling those ideals in their pupils.[121] They expanded their motherly role when helping educate parents about domestic issues. At a 1913 meeting of the NACW in Nashville, Margaret Murray Washington, wife of Booker T. Washington, called for teachers to form mother's clubs: "Schoolteachers should come in contact with the children's parents, and if there is not a mothers' meeting organized in the community where they teach, they should call the mothers together and organize them. The subject: 'At what age shall I allow my daughter to receive company?'—Subjects like this and similar subjects, as, what our children should wear, what they should eat, and where they should go are discussed in this department. This helps to improve our homes."[122] Nashville's teachers responded enthusiastically to aid parents in forming associations that raised funds and supported activities at their children's schools.

The clubwomen did not want women to learn housekeeping skills merely to obtain work as servants but rather to improve home life and communities. If women had to become domestics, training could result in higher wages. Learning housekeeping arts could help students better instruct their sisters in procedures that would prevent disease and provide a better home life. As intellectuals, they also stressed the need to learn academics.

After Emancipation, black women sought to dispel slavery's negative, overly sexualized stereotypes by asserting the right to assume a ladylike status. In promoting such virtues as piety, chastity, and modesty among working-class black women, teachers, whether they served the community decades later as clubwomen or talked to female students in the classroom, hoped to alleviate some of the risks of sexual harassment and mistreatment that all African American women faced and receive much-desired admiration and respect from whites and male members of their own community. While changing one's behavior and attitudes to gain acceptance by white society seemed superficial at best, clubwomen saw it as a practical plan.[123]

Scholars of the black clubwomen's movement contend that it adopted some of the stereotypical attitudes of the larger society when it suggested that African American women assume the responsibility of eliminating white prejudice and disrespect by improving their own morals and behavior.[124] Critics also argue that such efforts to correct the behavior of the poor aggravated class tensions. These arguments have merit, but historians also acknowledge the detrimental impact of racism and white American middle-class culture on the women's views. As members of a larger society, they could not avoid internalizing some of the stereotypical representations thrust upon them. Nevertheless, they considered self-improvement to be the best way to progress when political and legal remedies proved ineffectual.[125] They often adopted middle-class attitudes but accepted those ideas in an attempt to prove themselves worthy to whites.

Washington, president of the NACW, also maintained that teachers were natural leaders for organizations because of their ability to garner community support.[126] Advocating the common goals of Christian charity and promoting a proper moral home, Nashville's black women teachers also looked outside of their communities to seek assistance, sometimes from white religious and civic organizations.[127] Black female reformers attempted throughout the

South to build bridges with progressive white women in order to achieve common goals such as settlement work or suffrage. The white organizations continued to be segregated, but black teachers were willing to follow whatever avenue they needed to in order to better their race. Women were a driving force behind progressivism in the South, and that was true in Nashville. The city's chapter of the General Federation of Women's Clubs, a white organization, for example, worked in several areas, including juvenile delinquency, settlement house work, and public health.[128]

When Fisk graduate and former teacher Sally Hill Sawyer asked Estelle Haskin, director of community-service programs for the Methodist Episcopal Church, to open a settlement house for black children in Nashville, Sawyer described the appalling conditions of the poor girls and boys left to wander the streets while their parents worked. Haskin, a leader in the social gospel movement, then asked the Methodist Episcopal District for help. In 1913 the district provided funds to open Bethlehem House, later renamed Bethlehem Center, in the basement of St. Andrews Presbyterian Church. Sawyer was named its first house mother. The Department of Social Science at Fisk worked closely with Bethlehem House from its inception, requiring sociology students to be there four hours a week. In addition to providing a kindergarten, Bethlehem House served more than three hundred families during its first years by hosting two boys' clubs, a Sunday children's hour, and a mothers' club and by offering courses in sewing and domestic science.[129]

Notwithstanding their focus on improving black home life and their efforts to form coalitions with whites, African American women leaders—and blacks in general—assumed the primary responsibility of supporting their communities. During the so-called Progressive Era, black women in the South watched as the charitable and religious groups of their white counterparts successfully petitioned local and state governments for programs and laws to protect children and those who were sick and poor. Few of the laws, however, applied to African Americans. Glenda Gilmore maintains that despite the obstacles they faced, black women sought to institute similar types of reforms but did not benefit as much as white women from the financial support, publicity, or political protection of husbands.[130]

As the United States entered the late 1910s and early 1920s, especially the era of World War I, black women attempted to remedy social problems by working with white women when possible. If whites would not join them, however, they continued their mission of uplift by working within their own communities to support parallel charitable organizations.

After more than a thousand black soldiers left to "make the world safe for democracy" during World War I, the *Nashville Globe* expressed the belief that "the war had brought to the Negro a better chance for national self-expression than any event in history."[131] Many in the city's black community hoped the war, especially the contributions of African Americans abroad and at home to the war, would bring much-needed changes in race relations within the United States. Many in the community rallied to support soldiers and their families. Clubwomen fixed lunches for the black soldiers who traveled by train to Camp Meade, Maryland, for training, and teachers bought liberty bonds and participated in separate black chapters of service organizations such as the Red Cross, which provided flags and cigarettes for the departing soldiers. Bethlehem House, relocated to a building at Eighth and Cedar Streets, joined in by serving as the headquarters for black Red Cross workers during the war.[132]

Although in much of the rural South most African Americans were completely disenfranchised by the turn of the century, black Nashvillians continued to vote as long as they paid their poll taxes. Even if they did exercise the franchise, the passage of a law in 1883 created citywide, instead of ward, voting, which severely limited black political power. As a result, no blacks held office from 1883 to 1911, when Solomon Parker Harris, an attorney, won a seat on the city council. He was not reelected, though, and blacks remained outside public office until the 1950s.[133]

Elsa Barkley Brown maintains that although black women could not vote they viewed the political process as a communal effort and assumed the right to offer opinions and participate in the political process. Having the vote in Nashville did not substantially change the lives of African Americans, but it did offer them limited power with which to influence public officials. Black woman suffrage workers believed that if they increased voter numbers with women exempt from paying poll taxes there could be greater voting power in obtaining more economic and medical resources and changing the negative laws that affected the educational system.[134]

A number of black teachers in Nashville joined the suffrage drive. Nashville's black suffrage leaders—doctors Josie Wells and Mattie Coleman and teachers Frankie Pierce and Minnie Lou Crosthwaite—spoke at citywide debates as well as to students and other interested persons, about the necessity for female suffrage. They wanted to vote because they wanted help address such issues as juvenile delinquency and the establishment of schools for way-ward children. After the Tennessee General Assembly ratified the Nineteenth Amendment by one vote, black women's organizations continued to work with white groups to encourage women at the poles. Coleman and a white suf-fragette sponsored a workshop in August 1919 to teach women about voting. In that year some 1,300 of 6,007 registered women voters in Nashville were black. A year later more than 2,500 black women had registered.[135] As strong advocates for suffrage, Nashville's black women leaders such as Crosthwaite even challenged conservative antisuffrage Washington supporters. "I cannot agree with them on this question," Crosthwaite declared, "because I am so sick and tired of dodging and parleying over things I know to be right."[136]

Although the Young Women's Christian Association (YWCA) began a nationwide campaign to help female migrants and aid in the war effort by establishing centers to help servicemen and their families, the organiza-tion's women leaders also traveled throughout the South to establish black chapters.[137] Founded June 1, 1919, in the Napier Court Building, the Blue Triangle chapter of the YWCA served as an employment center for black women and a boardinghouse for migrants. It also housed Fisk students. Nashville's black branches of the YMCA and YWCA were among the few places in the city where African Americans could stay. The YWCA also provided after-school recreational services for children and sponsored the Girl Reserves for young area junior high and high school girls with Pearl Senior High School faculty advisors.[138]

The Great Migration affected Nashville's black population but not sub-stantially. Although thousands of African Americans left the rural South during the war to seek better job opportunities and escape pervasive rac-ism, Nashville's black population decreased only slightly—from 36,523 to 35,633.[139] A 1917 study of black migration showed that domestic servants who reportedly preferred "to till their own gardens instead of working at the prevailing wage" composed the largest numbers of migrants.[140] The migration from South to North was matched by the black migration of rural to urban as many African Americans from rural areas moved to Nashville.

Migration north carried few benefits for black women teachers. Salaries there and in the Midwest were higher for Nashville's domestic workers and manual laborers; relocation to the North for teachers could also mean a loss of stature and perhaps even fewer employment opportunities. It was almost impossible for black teachers to secure work in predominantly white neigh-borhood schools, although most northern public school systems did not implement legal segregation. Departure for Nashville teachers also meant possibly losing their special status in the community as local Fisk or A&I alumna. Most teachers remained in the city, and educators from other parts of the state readily replaced those ventured North.

After the war, Nashville had a marked increase in the number of organizations dedicated to fighting for social justice. Black women teachers supported community organizations such as the Nashville chapter of the National League on Urban Conditions among Negroes, founded in 1912 to foster black business development, and the National Association for the Advancement of Colored People (NAACP), which came to Nashville in 1919 when James C. Napier, businessman Robert Mayfield, and ninety-two others organized a branch there. An interracial organization whose purpose was the legal elimination of racial discrimination, the NAACP was created by W. E. B. Du Bois and other leading progressives in 1909 without the approval and support of Booker T. Washington. After Washington's death in 1915, Du Bois could promote the organization freely without the encumbrance of Washington. Napier and A&I president William Hale also participated in the Commission of Interracial Cooperation (CIC), an organization of African American and white city leaders that attempted to alleviate racial tensions before they erupted into violence.[141]

White and black women in Nashville used their new political power to institute the social reforms they had long advocated. Frankie Pierce, for example, received support from the Tennessee League of Women Voters to open a home for wayward girls, who were often sent to prison because of a lack of proper accommodations. After obtaining state funds in 1923 she opened the Tennessee Vocational School for Colored Girls in Nashville.[142] Clubwomen of both races sought to remedy the social ills of a progressive-era society by constructing homes for wayward boys and girls. Whether the women were black or white, their collective work was successful in providing some social services for African Americans, but it was only a small remedy to counter the general lack of financial assistance or legal protection blacks received from local and state governments.[143]

⌐⌐

The debate over woman suffrage raged after World War I, and white retaliation against increasing black protest exploded throughout the nation in 1919. Lynchings, violence in St. Louis and other major cities, the rebirth of the Ku Klux Klan, and increasing segregation dispelled any notion that blacks should expect democracy at home after fighting for it in Europe. In response, the "New Negro" concept emerged among returning veterans and urban African Americans. This philosophy abandoned the accommodation-ist ideals of Washingtonians to stress political, cultural, and social equality. According to its promoters, the image of the subservient, docile, ignorant, and simple black was offensive and did not reflect African American beauty and culture. Instead, the New Negro image described a strong, confident, educated, and culturally astute black man or woman. Subscribers to the New Negro movement expressed appreciation for African American culture through art, music, and literature.[144] While African American organizations and intellectuals debated how to define or use the concept, black colleges in the South continued to stress the philosophy of racial uplift and served as parents to students. Those at Fisk and other black colleges, however, sought to incorporate much of the New Negro philosophy into their educational and social ideas and actions.[145]

In the midst of this new era northern philanthropists recognized the growing black opposition to industrial education and offered full funding to a few liberal arts colleges. They believed that doing so would eliminate smaller colleges and help centralize black education. Fisk and Howard University in Washington, D.C., were two of the designated schools, and Fisk's president, Fayette McKenzie, received financial pledges from white city leaders as well. Although he excelled in raising money for the school, he did so by courting white favor, and many Fisk students resented him for that.

The autocratic McKenzie established strict rules regarding behavior and dress, curtailed student organizing and expression, and sacrificed black dig-nity by suggesting to white donors that he was perfectly satisfied to reinforce segregation. Unlike the accommodating students of the past, however, those at Fisk demanded change, and they appealed to outspoken alumni such as Du Bois for help. Du Bois supported the students against McKenzie, claiming in a commencement speech at Fisk:

> I have said that these things are taking place at Fisk, mainly through ig-norance. . . . But there is, I confess, one other reason, a reason so sinister and so unfortunate that I hesitate to mention it: . . . And it is possible that for a million dollars these authorities of Fisk University had been asked to either openly or by implication to sell to the white South the control of this institution. It is not the first time that this Corrupt Bargain of this kind has been attempted. Its earlier form at Hampton and Tuskegee included an understanding that these institutions were not to do college work and that they were to furnish servants for white people.[146]

The campus erupted when President McKenzie had several student leaders arrested for protesting in 1925. The majority of students embarked on a semester-long boycott to protest the lack of freedom at the university. Their activism resulted in McKenzie's resignation and gave students a larger role in campus government and autonomy over student publications. It also led to the establishment of sororities, fraternities, and social organizations at Fisk.[147] The call for McKenzie's resignation incensed the philanthropic community, though, and many organizations rescinded funding offers. Students at other African American colleges also began to reject some of their schools' paternalistic regulations and demanded more autonomy.

Unlike McKenzie, Fisk's new president, Thomas E. Jones, could meet student demands while placating the philanthropic community, and some funding was restored. Although students of the 1920s—who would populate Nashville's elementary and secondary school faculties in years to come—did not abandon the ideology of racial uplift, they attempted to redefine it in the era of the New Negro by fighting for more independence.[148] As Minerva Johnson Hawkins, who taught history at Pearl High School and participated in the 1925 Fisk boycott, recalls the causes of the strike: "There was not much opportunity for self-expression and there was no student government. Students were regimented and of course, we had never known anything else and it prevailed everywhere so we accepted it. But eventually we began to realize that there were restrictions that inhibited our own personal inner-selves. It was hard to explain, but we were aware of that." Hawkins remembers the new atmosphere on campus as being one in which students had more power over their lives.[149]

Women exercised their new freedom by joining and forming chapters of national black sororities and clubs. They had an advocate in Du Bois, who maintained, "The sororities offer scholarships and prizes to colored graduates. Fisk University has no right autocratically and without consultation with or listening to the advice of students, parents and alumni to ban these powerful and influential organizations and cut their graduates off from the best fellowship for life."[150] In essence, Fisk women defined liberty as being able not only to gain leadership skills but also to form sisterhoods in exclusive organizations.

African American sororities and fraternities reinforced the importance of middle-class values and structures for budding black teachers. Established to provide more social and cultural interactions for black college women, the organizations also connected students who had similar values and class status. The two largest African American Greek sororities, Alpha Kappa Alpha and Delta Sigma Theta, began at Howard University in Washington, D.C., in 1908 and 1913, respectively. Delta Sigma Theta Sorority formed the Alpha Beta chapter at Fisk in 1926, and Alpha Kappa Alpha formed its Pi chapter at Fisk a year later.[151]

Fisk and Tennessee A&I trained future teachers to become professionals in community uplift, but participation in exclusive sororities and clubs reinforced their middle-class identities. The women knew their positions called for them to help the less fortunate, but some balanced responsibilities as community leaders with a desire to enjoy the social pleasures of middle-class life and escape the daily duties of being a role model. A sorority was an ideal place to do so. By the 1930s other national sororities had formed chapters at Fisk and A&I, including Zeta Phi Beta and Sigma Gamma Rho, an organization founded by seven black Indiana teachers in 1922.

Membership requirements for black sororities overtly called for scholastic achievement and strong moral character, yet some were just as likely to select members based on skin color and beauty. Unfortunately, although such displays of internalized racism permeated the black community, determining membership based on those factors falsely suggested that women who looked white and had straight hair were smarter and more beautiful than their darker sisters. Other divisive factors, such as popularity, reputation, family background, and economic status, were also used to reject or select members.[152] Alongside sororities, certain clubs also chose members based on shade of skin color; some organizations would be designated as being for brown-skinned or darker-skinned women. Lillian Dunn Thomas, who taught home economics, participated in the Alba Rosa Club, known to prefer only "pretty brown-skin girls."[153]

Sororities and clubs also considered behavior when choosing candidates. The sororities wanted women who looked and behaved like ladies, dressed modestly, spoke proper English, and were sexually chaste. Alpha Kappa Alpha member Virginia Westbrook, a former English teacher and graduate of Tennessee A&I, has defined what she considers a proper AKA: "A lady in my lifetime and still when I use the term 'lady,' I don't use it often—is a person who stands out, who is different from all of the others. Who has something about her that tells you that she likes herself and she wants you to like her, but she isn't trying to be like everyone in the crowd, but stand above the crowd."[154]

Greek organizations and clubs controlled and maintained most of the social and cultural activities on Nashville's college campuses, but African American women have conflicting memories of sorority life. As a sorority officer, Thelma Baker Baxter participated in parties and public events such as parades and "Greek Sunday," at which all fraternal organizations performed for students. Sorority members frequently won homecoming queen titles and other student leadership positions. "Back then," she asserts, "if you weren't in a sorority or fraternity you hadn't arrived. Some say that the sororities went according to looks. But I have seen some mighty sad [not pretty] looking Greeks. If they got in, it wasn't for that."[155]

Others who attended college between the 1920s and the 1940s, such as Lillie Bowman, downplayed the role of Greek organizations in that experience. Bowman maintains that one "didn't need sororities to be popular." For Bowman, the experience of attending A&I itself raised her self-esteem. The child of laborers who dreamed of sending her to college, Bowman, who was an assistant principal, remembers her father's response when his employer chastised her for saying thank you instead of thank you ma'am, the common response given to whites during segregation. "My father said, 'I will say the thank you ma'ams,'" she fondly recalls. "'I am sending you to college so that you don't have to say thank you ma'am. That is why I am polishing this brass so that you won't have to say thank you ma'am.' I walked off that porch and held my head up high."[156]

From their inception sororities offered scholarships and donated money to charities although lavish sorority parties evoked the stereotype of frivolous elitism. Nevertheless, the Great Depression diminished most extravagant sorority social activities and increased the focus on community-service programming. By the middle of the decade sororities and local chapters of national black women's organizations had begun to lobby state and federal governments to better race relations; they also sponsored health clinics and traveling libraries in the rural South.[157] Sororities supported notions of middle-class propriety and exclusiveness and also provided opportunities for young women to develop community leadership skills and create lifelong bonds of friendship and sisterhood.

Members in these organizations continued to perform community service even though their efforts could not address all the enormous financial needs of depression-era blacks. Friendship, community connections, and benevolence went hand in hand, according to Sadie Madry. As she shared her reason for joining Zeta Phi Beta, another national sorority founded at Howard University, she attested to the importance of social connections among teachers and students. "The people I liked were Zetas. Mrs. Hale, the [A&I] president's wife was a Zeta. One of my teachers from Pearl High was a Zeta. I wanted to be just like those ladies." As Minerva Hawkins, a Delta active in the sorority for more than seventy years and at one point a regional director, observes, "There's nothing else I would ever be."[158] The sorority experience seemed to parallel the sense of inclusion and superiority that the women felt as teachers, by 1930 only 4 percent of the city's black female adult working population.[159]

⌇⌇

The social, political, and community lessons that black women teachers learned as students in the early twentieth century played a central role in their efforts during the 1930s. When the Great Depression hit Nashville, teachers saw relatives, friends, and students' parents lose jobs, businesses, and homes.[160] The depression constituted a crisis for the city's black women teachers; between 1920 and 1940 only 5.4 percent of the local black population was employed in that profession or any other. The more than 79 percent of Nashville's blacks who were domestics and laborers sank to even greater depths of poverty, and by 1934 roughly 25 percent of male African American heads of households could not find employment.[161]

The depression aggravated conditions in the city's schools by intensifying problems in cost expenditures and teacher-student ratios. The appropriations of those hard years failed to meet the needs of a growing student population. Even before the depression, a 1927 study of cost expenditures per student had shown that Nashville schools ranked last among those of fifty other American cities. Several evaluations, national as well as state, revealed the city as having the highest student-teacher ratio among similar cities in the United States.[162]

During the 1930s African Americans in Nashville were forced to confront the depth of educational disparities in new and profound ways. In 1931 the city's school board hired Peabody College of Education professor Frank Bauchman to conduct another survey of its schools. His report described the system's weaknesses as well as blatant inconsistencies in the funding and facilities of black schools, where teachers often had more than forty-seven students per class. None of the city's fourteen black schools were ranked as good; one rated as fair, five were unsatisfactory, and eight were declared unusable. African American first- and second-graders attended elementary school for half days or in split sessions, and many school buildings were in poor shape. Few had lunchrooms or gymnasiums, and the majority had no central heating. Twelve of the fourteen black schools, in fact, still used unsightly and unsanitary open-pit latrines.[163]

Bauchman directed much attention to the overcrowding at Pearl Senior High School, where classes met in the library and on the auditorium's balcony. Pearl also received little funding for vocational education and musical instruction and had inadequate library facilities. Bauchman suggested that the city address the problem by constructing a hundred new classrooms for black children. He also noted that a high percentage of the children did not meet academic requirements, entered school late, or frequently missed school and subsequently failed.[164]

Overcrowding and underfunding exacerbated the difficulties of teaching for many black women, and some had difficulty managing their classrooms. In an attempt to maintain control, some who were new or frustrated went too far, Novella Bass remembers, and others carried their prejudices about skin color into the classroom. Yet as these women saw students failing or leaving school they continued to use whatever resources available—from donating money to supplying the students with old coats—to keep pupils in school.[165]

When state funding was cut during the depression, the Nashville City School System was forced to review its buildings and programs. The board responded by suspending summer school, which had provided additional income for black teachers. Although the women had performed community service with limited support from governmental institutions in the past, this time they joined many others in the nation by turning to the federal government for assistance.

In 1936 the Nashville City Board of Education received funds from the Public Works Administration to build new schools, and it decided to use most of the federal money to build what became East High School for whites. It also allocated money to construct a new Pearl High School at Seventeenth Avenue North and Jo Johnston Avenue in north Nashville. Throughout the twentieth century the city's black residents had regularly requested a new school; Pearl still operated in split sessions. Designed by the local black architectural firm of McKissack and McKissack, the new high school was a modern structure that many African Americans embraced with pride and admiration. The same architects also constructed Ford Greene Elementary School, which opened in 1937.

During the economic crisis the teachers, still the city's largest group of professionals, continued to expand the idea of middle-class status beyond economic level to include educational status, community service, and participation in exclusive organizations. Although they worked under substandard conditions and with desperately poor students, the women continued to advise their pupils that success required an education. Despite financial challenges, some black teachers attempted to retain their middle-class identity by participating in exclusive clubs.

Although working-class blacks used the social arena to escape from the dictates of white society, African American middle-class women were proud of patterning their activities after white social functions. Whether they attended sorority parties or sponsored debutante balls, they wanted to prove themselves equal to white, middle-class counterparts by staging comparable events. Some scholars criticize the behavior of the segregated black middle-class, asserting that they engaged in superficial socializing, but the activities were used to mask hurt and bolster their collective self-esteem. Although this world to some extent mirrored white social practices, it also supplied a cultural framework in which African American professionals could network among themselves.[166] The desire to strengthen their position as middle-class women by distancing themselves socially from working-class blacks reflected a need to redefine themselves as individuals worthy of respect from the community and from whites as well. Moreover, middle-class blacks often frowned on the social behaviors of the working class, whose actions they thought reinforced negative stereotypes.

Whether dancing to racy songs in blues clubs or praising God during foot-stomping church services, working-class African Americans developed their own cultural spaces where they could escape the daily slights of racism and develop resistance or survival strategies in a welcoming atmosphere. Tera Hunter contends that black women domestics could, by dancing, reclaim their bodies and be free to move as they chose.[167] Most middle-class blacks in Nashville, however, did not perceive the actions of working-class African Americans as liberating or helpful to the race. Some middle-class and working-class black Nashvillians, in fact, socially distanced themselves from one another. Robert Phillips observed that "there are some Negroes who would rather attend dances at A&I, Fisk, or private house parties than attend a public dance at the [working-class-populated] Silver Streak Ballroom." Of movie theaters he added, "The more intellectual and conservative type attend the Ritz while the more boisterous and uncouth type attend the Bijou. The patrons of the Ritz seldom or never attend the Bijou because they object to associating with a group whom they think are of a lower social level than themselves."[168] Yet class differentiation and distinction did not hinder all cross-class alliances among African Americans. Even though Phillips's findings suggest a chasm between working- and middle-class blacks, some African Americans of different social classes worked together in church activities and did build alliances.[169]

Although some teachers and other professionals attempted to operate in a hierarchical society, bonds of race and shared heritage still connected them to the working class. Neighborhoods were racially segregated, moreover, and middle- and working-class African Americans were bound to live close to one another.[170] At times the members of various social classes were so indistinguishable that educators had trouble discerning who was part of which economic and status group. Tommie Morton-Young, a writer and former teacher who grew up in Nashville during the 1930s, describes a resentful classmate scratching her after school because she seemed to be the teacher's favorite. When she reported the attack to the principal, who had mistakenly assumed she was a physician's daughter, he promised he would severely punish the bully. Unfortunately, after learning that Morton-Young's father was not a doctor he dismissed her but did not discipline the other girl.[171]

Although some teachers and administrators used class and skin color to differentiate between students, working and middle class blacks ultimately depended upon each other. In a discriminatory society in which one's educational status and conduct influenced the dimensions of black middle-class life the status of African American teachers depended upon approval of the working class. If a woman did not act like a teacher in behavior and attitude she could lose community respect and thus status. Teachers had to perform as if they deserved their positions on pedestals.[172]

As Gwendolyn Vincent, who taught reading, remembers, "When I was growing up teachers were held in very high esteem. They were the last word in promoting excellence and high morals." Ruth Young, who taught biology in later years, added, "Teachers served as role models. There were certain things [as a teacher] you had to practice and that was just it and you did it because you were there."[173] By maintaining a perception of success and what Shaw refers to as "socially responsible individualism," which called for creating a distant but visible role in the community, African American teachers maintained their position and thereby the trust and respect of parents.[174]

During the depression, local white charitable organizations discouraged blacks from applying for aid, and the inadequately funded city welfare commission could not meet the needs of the poor. Consequently, African American teachers helped by donating to their communities through their churches. Although some scholars characterize the black elite as unsympathetic and claim it discarded its mandate to help those less fortunate to focus on social climbing, most of Nashville's black women teachers never abandoned the mission to serve.[175] They used their positions as members of exclusive organizations and as leaders of social groups to perform charity work.

The Alpha Beta chapter of the National Sorority Phi Delta Kappa serves as a case in point. A teachers' sorority, founded in 1940 by fourteen instructors, its members engaged in fellowship and professional development yet still cared for their communities. Phi Delta Kappa sponsored a children's recreation room at Hubbard Hospital, offered scholarships, and helped bring prominent speakers to Nashville. As a former president of her local Zeta Phi Beta sorority chapter, Sadie Madry helped organize the "Stork's Nest," on Jefferson Street, a place that offered children's clothing and food to indigent mothers.[176]

Teachers followed other avenues for community action as well. By volunteering at Hubbard, Nashville's only black hospital, or attending board meetings at the local YWCA or the Bethlehem House black women teachers not only helped the community but also networked and enjoyed the company of other like-minded colleagues. The ability to raise funds or organize financially successful activities also indicated middle-class status for it provided an arena in which to undertake benevolent roles.[177]

Although these women embodied accomplishment within their own communities, white society often treated them with minimal politeness. In most instances whites ignored class differences among African Americans, and consequently some black women professionals cherished any courtesies they received from whites. They relished receiving better treatment because they interpreted recognition, albeit small, of their status. Ironically, the African American community's efforts to elevate teachers to a superior position resulted in some professionals thinking they were entitled to a certain level of respect and treatment not due those with lesser educations.

In the late 1930s Charles Johnson, a prominent sociologist, head of Fisk University's School of Social Research, and later president of the university, conducted a multicity study of segregation in the United States. As one of the Nashville researchers, Edmonia White Grant, a former teacher, investigated and recorded how some of Nashville's most popular retail establishments treated African American customers. Laced throughout her case study are personal comments that reveal her social and economic status and her attitude toward whites and poorer blacks. Although she intended to act as an objective observer, Grant often chastised store clerks who refused to let her try on clothes or failed to wait on her in a timely manner. She also reported that she usually shopped at the more expensive stores, where clerks treated her with more respect.[178] As a professional African American woman she was proud of her ability to choose where she spent her money.[179]

Reflecting some of the attitudes of her counterparts, Grant was intensely conscious of class and status appearances. She did not scold clerks for failing to address properly another shopper dressed in maid's clothing. To Grant, working-class blacks did not deserve the same social dignities as middle-class African Americans. In an era when most southern whites avoided addressing black women by their last names or their titles, Grant contended that teachers who made the mistake of mentioning their first names deserved to be insulted. She said of another teacher, "She used the form expected from the lower-class Negro and received the treatment accorded this group."[180]

Grant's behavior reveals the problematic side of basing black progress on class. Although she sometimes received cordial treatment, other African Americans who did not dress in professional attire did not. Her appearance and behavior prevented her, in some respects, from receiving poor service. Without the presentation of middle-class status, Grant would be considered just another poor black woman. Her research disclosed much more about race and class in Nashville than she probably intended, for although it added to knowledge of racial structures and attitudes in Nashville it also displayed the negative aspects of classism within the African American community.

Middle-class status, however, was always precarious for African Americans, especially those women who taught. Although Grant stated that she only shopped at Nashville's better clothing stores during the 1930s, as a Rosenwald Fellow in 1942 she had no problem writing to the foundation for more money because "she was a widow with a child and was in 'dire financial straits.'"[181] Her plea reflected a common dilemma among teachers and other black professionals during the Jim Crow era: Projecting a middle-class image was just as important as actually being middle class. Unfortunately, salaries did not always support that lifestyle.

During the depression, some African American teachers worked during the summer to supplement their incomes and earn enough to maintain a middle-class standing. The necessity of assuming jobs usually held by working-class women suggests that the dividing line was slim indeed. Teachers' excursions into the laboring world did not diminish their position in the community, though. Educators sometimes worked for whites in subordinate positions, but they were still teachers and community leaders in their own neighborhoods. As long as they portrayed themselves as professionals they could maintain their places as role models in black society, regardless of temporary financial setbacks. As Novella Bass put it, "No one advertised that they worked as a maid during the summer. Some teachers received referrals for summer work from their parents' white employers."[182] Teachers married to working-class men were sometimes the only professional in their households or entire families.[183] Bass's father encouraged her to continue teaching while she attended Fisk University because his business ventures as a barber and in real estate were suffering. Even if teachers could not satisfy middle-class economic requirements they were still responsible for meeting community standards regarding demeanor and behavior.[184]

Although much looked bleak for black women teachers amid the Great Depression, they, their schools, and their community had come a long way since the years immediately following the Civil War. When Alfred Menefee and other black leaders first petitioned the board of education to hire black teachers in 1868, those instructors bore the enormous responsibility of ensuring the mental well-being of their students and helping them learn in a society that offered little financial or cultural support. Nashville's black teachers entered into an unwritten contract with the black community. The educators promised to serve the city's children, and the community assured the teachers in return that they would receive professional status. Nashville was unique in the United States, in part because Fisk University and Tennessee Agricultural and Industrial State Normal School, the two primary institutions of higher education for African Americans, worked out the discipline's larger struggles of the day. African Americans in Nashville found creative ways to fuse Washington's educational philosophy with Du Bois's, and they remained committed to educating children in even the most difficult of times. Placed within the larger burden of educating students in a system designed to circumscribe their intelligence, black women knew that their duties continued after school and worked in organizations that helped the community. Adapting self-help and the concepts of the talented tenth to their own environments, and working with or without the help of white people, Nashville's black teachers became leaders in efforts of racial uplift.

After more than forty years of teaching in the city's schools, by the 1930s they were overwhelmed as mounting poverty engulfed the city. Yet they were teachers, and they continued to struggle to retain their middle-class status and identity. During World War II and the cold war the teachers redefined their educational mission in an effort to promote the "American way of life" to students who seldom experienced the fruits of democracy. Black teachers were often in the forefront in the NAACP's movement for social justice only to see their status transformed by the push for integration in later years.

TWO

"The Living Symbols of Democracy": World War II and the Cold War

In 1942 the NAACP sued the Nashville City Board of Education on behalf of local black teachers over the issue of equal salaries. They were ecstatic when the NAACP won. Upon receiving her first paycheck from Ford Greene Elementary School after the ruling, Sadie Madry could not contain her excitement. "I shouted," she recalls. "It was more money than I had ever seen in my life!"[1] Part of a larger campaign by the national NAACP to end salary inequities, the Nashville case inspired teachers and provided some evidence that the freedom and democracy for which American troops were fighting abroad might be realized at home. World War II, in fact, provided a critical social and ideological backdrop for the U.S. civil rights struggle.

Throughout the war and during the first decade of the cold war that followed the nation called on educators, both white and black, to promote the principles of patriotism. In Nashville, African American women taught the merits of democracy, but they stressed elements of it that whites tended to downplay—racial tolerance and equality. Outside their classrooms they actively tried to influence recognition of racial equality and joined the NAACP in attacking discrimination.

Black teachers across the nation realized that aligning with the NAACP and its push for integration could damage their professional reputations, but commitment to their vocation led them to support the larger struggle in order to help black children. They still worked in segregated schools, but they continued to teach, although they did so quietly, that equality is the true foundation of democracy.

⌐⌐

As part of its program to dismantle educational inequities during the 1930s and 1940s the NAACP sued school boards that maintained separate and discriminatory salary scales for teachers based on race. Its first full effort to secure equal pay for black teachers was in Montgomery County, Maryland. On behalf of William Gibbs, a principal as well as a teacher, the NAACP petitioned the Montgomery County Board of Education to equalize salaries. After the board refused its request, the NAACP filed a writ of mandamus to equalize salaries. The board eventually acquiesced and developed a single-salary schedule in 1936.

Although successful in Montgomery County, the NAACP's victory in *Mills v. Board of Education of Anne Arundel County* (1939) helped further the organization's goals of setting a precedent for future lawsuits. In *Mills*, the federal district court ruled that the Anne Arundel County Board of Education's unequal faculty pay levels were based solely on the race of its teachers, not their differences in achievement and experience.[2] Following that triumph, Thurgood Marshall, the chief lawyer for the NAACP, scored wins in several other Maryland counties and then fought for salary equal-ization throughout the nation. Teachers in Norfolk, Virginia, filed suit for equal salaries shortly after the *Mills* decision, and in 1940 the Fourth Circuit Court of Appeals ruled in *Alston et al. v. School Board of the City of Norfolk, Virginia* that paying black teachers less than whites was a clear violation of the Fourteenth Amendment.[3] All in all, from 1939 to 1947 the NAACP successfully won twenty-seven of thirty-one salary equalization cases across the South.[4]

The NAACP viewed public school teachers as ideal plaintiffs with whom to assault racial discrimination because teachers, as employees of the govern-ment, were supposed to receive equal treatment under the law. Moreover, the discrepancies between the salaries of black and white teachers were blatantly unfair and vividly displayed that "separate" was far from "equal" in American education. These cases constituted an important element in the NAACP's broad campaign against discrimination, which included suing for blacks to gain entry into white professional and graduate schools at southern public universities and equalizing educational opportunities in segregated public schools. The NAACP hoped that by winning these equalization cases it could eliminate the policy of paying blacks less than whites for doing the same work. Marshall and others also hoped that such a change would affect teachers and the entire African American work force.[5]

Pay disparities between white and black teachers were obvious during the middle of the twentieth century. African Americans who had the same educational background and experience as whites and taught at the same grade level received lower pay than white faculty. In 1931, for instance, the average teacher's yearly salary in seventeen southern states was $900 for whites and $410 for African Americans. In 1935 the average was $833 for whites and $510 for blacks; that same year, Tennessee paid white teachers $752 a year, and blacks received only $520. In Georgia, white teachers earned $709 annually and blacks made $282.[6]

The NAACP first considered a salary-equalization suit in Nashville in the mid-1930s. In 1935 the NAACP's lawyer Charles Houston, the key developer of the organization's strategy to dismantle segregation wrote to three black attorneys in the city to inquire whether teachers and the rest of the local black community were interested in pushing for salary equalization. Although several Fisk professors, including education specialist Horace Mann Bond, expressed interest, a Nashville attorney, Z. Alexander Looby, lamented that few local teachers seemed inclined to do so. "I am sorry to say there is no agitation in Nashville or Tennessee on the part of school teachers for equal salaries," he responded to Houston. "I would be interested in handling such a case, but not in making any efforts to obtain a client."[7]

A native of Antigua, Looby joined the Nashville community in 1926 as a professor of economics at Fisk University. A graduate of Howard University and Columbia University Law School, he started his Nashville practice in 1928 and became a member of the NAACP's legal committee in 1932. By 1939 Looby and the city's black teachers had begun to formulate strategies to obtain equal salaries, and one of their first steps was to address the issue with the city council, and the council decided to refer the matter to the school board. School officials maintained that there were not enough funds to bring all teachers' salaries to the same level, but the city council, supported by Mayor Thomas Cummings, passed a resolution requesting that the board "take steps toward equalizing the pay as soon as it is financially possible."[8] According to Looby, however, the mayor's gesture was insincere. "Cummings expressed himself as being in favor of equal salaries but the board of education is against it," Looby pointed out. "Yet, he appoints the board. This is their way of passing the buck."[9] After losing votes in several predominately black wards in the previous election, Cummings may have verbally supported the measure merely to appease black voters.[10]

NAACP leaders hoped that a precedent in the Nashville school district would help African Americans throughout the state. In 1940 Charles Houston declined an invitation from a West Tennessee teachers' group to bring a salary equalization suit there on the grounds that they were too intimidated by Memphis mayor William "Boss" Crump's powerful political machine. Houston told the teachers, however, that "NAACP field organizer Daisy Lampkin's membership campaigns in Nashville, Chattanooga, and Knoxville may prepare the ground for more courageous action in the future."[11]

The plaintiffs sometimes paid a painful price for salary equalization. Local school boards vehemently resisted granting equal salaries and often intimidated, threatened, and fired possible plaintiffs. Many black teachers were concerned that the NAACP and local teacher associations were unable to protect plaintiffs and secure their employment.[12] Consequently, the NAACP developed strategies to overcome apprehension by filing suits only in areas where teachers' organizations were unified and willing to support the case. The association also required that the credentials and qualifications of plaintiffs be equal or superior to those of whites and suggested that local teacher associations provide compensation for the plaintiffs.[13]

Although the NAACP may have considered Tennessee teachers too frightened to take legal action, in March of 1941 the Mountain City Teachers Association of Chattanooga took decisive action and demanded that the city's board of education equalize salaries, filing suit after the board denied their request. W. Henry Elmore, a local black attorney, represented the plaintiffs, and in less than six months they won their case.[14]

Encouraged by the success in Chattanooga, Looby brought action on behalf of Nashville's black teachers after efforts to secure equal salaries there failed. Harold Thomas, who taught at an elementary school, agreed to serve as a plaintiff. Born in 1905, Thomas earned B.A. and M.S. degrees from Fisk University and possessed a Collegiate Professional Certificate, the highest credential issued by the Tennessee Board of Education. He joined the teaching staff at Pearl in 1935. On April 12, 1941, the Nashville NAACP filed *Harold Thomas v. Louis H. Hibbits et al.* in U.S. District Court. The lead defendant, Hibbits, was president of the board of education for Nashville city schools. City attorney W. C. Cherry and the Memphis Board of Education's attorney Marion Evans served as counsel for Hibbits and the school board. The case came to trial in February 1942, with Thurgood Marshall serving as the NAACP's special counsel and Looby as Thomas's local attorney.[15]

The widespread practice of paying African American teachers significantly less than their white counterparts reflected larger disparities in the city's segregated educational system. A teacher's salary was based on several factors, including certificate test score, type of degree, experience, and grade level taught.[16] Officially, that was a fair and impartial way to pay the teachers, but race influenced their compensation as well and was a deciding factor for African Americans. No amount of teaching experience or education enabled them to earn as much as whites, a fact that frustrated them. Mildred Freeman, who taught at Pearl High School, cited pay inequities as a blatant example of prejudice: "Do you know that Negro teachers in Nashville are better prepared than white teachers? Yet, we don't get the same salary they get. . . . The older teachers are afraid to say anything about it because they are afraid of losing their jobs," Freeman further explained. "The younger teachers are beginning to talk about equalization of salaries. There are some white people who believe in equal salaries for Negro teachers and I think we will get it eventually."[17] In 1940 salaries in Nashville ranged from $95 to $115 a month for African American teachers and $120 to $170 for those who were white.[18] A white elementary school teacher with only a year of teaching experience, in fact, took home a higher salary than a black high school instructor who had taught for four years.

Bound to a discriminatory pay scale, African American women teachers attempted to manipulate the system by acquiring the highest levels of education possible. In the summers they took and completed correspondence courses and enrolled in graduate summer classes at northern universities. Education provided a way for career advancement and improved compensation. In effect, the pay disparity made the teachers far more academically

Table 1. Nashville Teacher Salaries, 1940, by Years of Employment

	Elementary School		High School	
	1 Year	4 Years	1 Year	4 Years
White	$120	$135	$140	$170
Black	$ 95	$110	$100	$115

Source: Annual Report, Nashville City Schools, 1940.

accomplished than their white counterparts. By 1937, for instance, more than 72 percent of black elementary teachers in Nashville city schools had completed at least two or more years of college whereas only 42 percent of white teachers had done so.[19]

Racialized pay disparity was at the center of the NAACP's case. Thomas's attorneys pointed out that the board paid lower salaries to black teachers who had commensurate qualifications, experience, and duties as reflected by the fact that Thomas received $110 a month whereas a white teacher with the same credentials and experience earned $135. The plaintiffs stated that the school board based these salary differentials solely on color and, as in previous cases, maintained that this practice violated the Fourteenth Amendment. The defendants responded by suggesting that the board based salaries on the race of the children who attended the school, not its teachers. Judge Elmer Davies dismissed that argument by stating the board had recently adopted a new salary schedule for both white and black schools, "which is just another way of saying that it would have a separate schedule for white teachers and colored teachers, in as much as only white teachers are employed in the white schools and colored teachers in the colored schools."

Hibbits's defense team employed a host of other justifications as well. They claimed that the board paid unequal salaries because black teachers had few other avenues of professional employment, and, therefore the board could hire them at the lowest possible wages. "That is the trouble here," Hibbits testified. "We can get all of the Negro teachers that we want. We have trouble in getting enough white teachers, what with the war going on." The defense also contended that African Americans had a lower standard of living and did not require as much pay as white teachers. Thurgood Marshall shattered the arguments of the defense, especially when he asked Nashville school superintendent W. A. Bass, also named as a defendant, if he had ever visited a black teacher's house to see whether that person's standard of living was indeed lower. Bass responded that he could not verify the statements and had only heard them from others. The defense also suggested that it did not have enough funds to equalize salaries and would have to use money designated for building improvements. The defense countered that having African American teachers work at white schools would lower costs.[20]

Judge Davies dismissed the defense arguments and agreed with the NAACP that the Fourteenth Amendment had been violated. On July 28, 1942, Davies issued a ruling:

The Court is unable to reconcile these theories with the true facts in this case, and therefore finds that the studied and consistent policy of the Board of Education of the City of Nashville is to pay its colored teachers salaries, which are considerably lower than salaries paid to white teachers, although eligibility qualifications and experience required the same for both white and colored teachers. Moreover, that the sole reason for this difference is because of the race and color of the colored teachers.[21]

Davies granted a declaratory judgment and an injunction to restrain the Nashville City Board of Education from discriminating in the payment of salaries solely on the grounds of race or color.[22]

African American teachers in Nashville exalted in their court victory, and Sadie Madry was especially grateful to Looby and the NAACP. "Mr. Looby, he was a man who stood tall," she maintains. "Mr. Looby introduced the program and Thurgood [Marshall] came to Nashville. I was a young teacher then; they won the case. I was one of the first black teachers that got an equal salary. We were being treated as first-class citizens. Mr. Looby had more brains and power in his head than all of [the people] in Nashville, Tennessee."[23]

Success in the courtroom did not end the struggle for equal pay, though, and African American teachers did not uniformly agree on the best course of action. As Marshall and the NAACP tried cases in several states the NAACP combated economic and cultural justifications for maintaining salary inequality. Victory in Nashville helped undermine some of the prevalent arguments that salary differences were based on economic conditions such as lack of funds or the living conditions of blacks. Black teachers, the NAACP argued, deserved equality, and it was the system's responsibility to figure out how to achieve it.

Nevertheless, although the NAACP won most of its cases some school boards throughout the South retaliated by threatening to lower the salaries of white teachers or by demanding raised municipal taxes to pay for the needed funds. Boards in Virginia and other areas circumvented raising black teachers' salaries by reclassifying those instructors to lower positions or firing them. Districts in Arkansas and South Carolina defended differentiated pay scales by claiming that salaries were based on test results rather than race. States also implemented pay schedules based on merit, including subjective criteria such as attitude and personality, as a way to pay blacks lower salaries. These schemes, especially ones that used testing to determine salary level, were powerful tools in delaying pay equalization and, later, desegregation. Teachers themselves also had differing opinions concerning the best response to unequal pay. In several teacher-salary cases in Louisiana and Florida, for instance, disunity and impatience among the teachers negatively affected cases.[24]

Yet in Nashville the *Thomas* case marked a watershed for African American teachers, who had grappled for decades with the notion of inferiority implied by the board's unequal pay scale. Their salaries suggested that they were, despite education level or experience, still inferior to white teachers. The board instilled fear in many during the trial through threats of funding cuts for black schools or job loss. Harold Thomas and Lillian Dunn, also a Nashville teacher, married in 1946. Several of his colleagues, she recalls, encouraged him to proceed with the case despite the threats directed toward him and at other teachers.[25]

With the exception of three members, the Teachers' Benefit Association voted to allow its name to be used in the case, and none of its members voted against filing suit. Looby met with teachers to raise money, and most of Nashville's black community participated in the cause. "I remember we went to meetings and invited our friends to go," Bass says. "I remember my father and mother went with me. The only ones didn't go were those who were really scared to death or didn't give a damn."[26]

Although the teachers' association provided financial support it is not clear whether Thomas had the support of all other teachers. After his death in 1968, the *780 Countdown*, a local black newspaper, noted that he received little open support from his peers. Moreover, "Teachers were the direct beneficiaries of a battle Thomas is said to have stood virtually alone in waging."[27] In a 1939 interview, Mildred Freeman maintained that many older teachers feared legal action. Novella Bass also acknowledged that Thomas lacked universal support, something she considered to be another mark of his heroism: "Mr. Thomas had the God given strength to serve as a plaintiff. I am sure that others thought about, but nobody had dared touch that thing. My sister was teaching at the same school with him. He had to decide if I lose my job, so be it. It ought not to be."[28]

Many older teachers had only a normal degree, and some feared they would lose their jobs or pensions if they supported the case or served as plaintiffs. Earlier NAACP losses in breaking segregation barriers, especially at the University of Tennessee at Knoxville in 1936, may have also dampened teachers' enthusiasm. Yet even those who refrained from publicly endorsing Thomas and the trial privately supported him by offering words of encouragement.[29]

As mentioned in the suit, black teachers sought jobs in Nashville because higher pay and more social opportunities were there than in rural areas. A 1935 analysis of Tennessee schools found that the Nashville city school system paid black teachers a higher salary than they received in the county schools surrounding Nashville. More than 65 percent of the city's African American elementary teachers earned more than $100 per month, whereas more than 85 percent of those who worked outside the city limits in Davidson County received only $60. In part, the difference was due to state legislation in 1933; slashing the Tennessee education budget caused school closings, teacher layoffs, and salary cuts in rural areas. The reduction was not as adverse in Nashville as in surrounding counties because the city also received federal funding and relied on income garnered from sales taxes on luxury items.[30]

Nashville's black women teachers had a number of reasons to avoid public support for Thomas. Although the city discriminated by race in pay scales it did not do so by sex. Because of their educational attainment, therefore, many of the city's black female elementary teachers earned more than their male counterparts. Consequently, some did not openly support Thomas because they feared having to find work in a lower-paying school system. In addition, women may not have openly backed Thomas because they did not want to lose their professional status. By defining themselves through family roles, home life, and community activities, African American women created identities beyond their positions as domestic or service workers.[31] Service-position work was something they did just to pay their bills.[32] Teaching, in contrast, was integral to, and defined, their social, cultural, and individual personalities.

Nevertheless, although the plaintiff in *Thomas v. Hibbits et al.* was male, it was women, 83 percent of the 114 black teachers of Nashville, who reaped the largest benefits from the NAACP's legal triumph.[33] They were now on the same financial footing as their white counterparts. Although new positions were available for black women in social work and other professions, the *Thomas* case was an important victory because teaching remained the best avenue of employment for professional women. They now had legal recognition that they were equal to and as competent as white teachers. Openly supporting the case might have threatened their positions, but receiving equal salaries reinforced their status in the community.

Nashville's black teachers were not the only winners in the salary equalization fight. All had to obtain a teaching certificate, but salary schedules varied among high school, junior high, and elementary school teachers, with elementary instructors receiving the lowest pay. When the city had to ask the state for funds for pay equalization for blacks, representatives from the city's white teacher association successfully secured additional money to establish a single salary schedule for all teachers in 1943. If it was illegal to base salaries on race, they pointed out, it was just as unlawful to discriminate by grade level. Most whites did not support their black colleagues, but African American teachers' efforts at economic parity benefited all in the system, in large part because the board threatened to lower salaries if they won.[34]

Factors such as increased educational attainment levels and teacher vacancies during World War II also helped close the gap between salaries for white and black teachers, whether in Nashville or throughout the nation. In 1936 African American teachers in Nashville earned 39 percent less than their white counterparts, but by 1950 they earned only 21 percent less. Although they still took home only 79 percent of the salaries that white teachers enjoyed, their gains were impressive. Nationally, the average annual earnings for black teachers climbed to 82 percent of white salaries during the 1940s, and by 1954 some in Nashville earned more than white women because they had better educational credentials and more experience.[35]

World War II created a culture of patriotism and increased economic prosperity in Nashville. Although thousands of black Nashvillians joined the Armed Forces for patriotic reasons, those who remained in the United States faced an ongoing battle against discrimination. The city welcomed defense-related companies by offering them financial incentives and programs to train workers, but the local business community, government, and schools consistently blocked African Americans' attempts to secure job training and obtain defense-related positions. Nashville's black community retaliated by pressuring business and government officials for full enactment of the democratic ideals they endorsed and promoting the importance of having all members of society contribute to national defense.

During the war, the NAACP and other civil rights groups deployed government propaganda of democracy and freedom to further the attack against racism. To counter blatant discrimination in the nation's defense industries, the veteran civil rights and labor leader A. Phillip Randolph threatened to lead thousands of protesting blacks on a march at the Capitol. President Franklin D. Roosevelt responded by enacting Executive Order

8802, which promised to eliminate employment discrimination in defense-related plants. The order also established the Fair Employment Practices Committee (FEPC) to monitor discriminatory practices and discipline businesses that hired by means of racial categories.[36]

African Americans in Nashville supported the war effort and focused principally on the safety of family and friends who were overseas. In segregated America they had to protect their own. Participation in the war effort reflected the paradox of living in a society that espoused equality but denied it to millions of citizens.

As black women teachers sold victory bonds and attended USO dances they saw the war transform their city. New industries sprang up, and others expanded to meet the country's needs. Already the fiftieth-largest city in defense production, Nashville grew even more in 1940 when Vultee Aircraft brought seven thousand new jobs to the area to build bombers. Wartime advertising asked women to serve their country by joining the labor force. Although they often received lower wages than their male counterparts, salaries at Vultee were higher than those offered in service positions.[37]

Despite protests resulting from local blacks and federal inquiries, however, the Vultee plant hired no African American workers for production jobs. When FEPC officials questioned those discriminatory hiring practices, Vultee responded that it could not find trained blacks and blamed the local board of education for failing to graduate skilled students. Vultee provided the board with $10,000 to create training schools, and one was opened at the all-white Hume-Fogg High School. A closed-shop factory, Vultee also maintained that no blacks were union members, and the local chapter of the International Association of Machinists did not admit blacks. The FEPC issued a cease and desist order for Vultee to stop its discriminatory practices, but the order could not be enforced.[38]

Vultee management stated even before the war that it would never hire African Americans in factory positions, and Pearl High School principal J. A. Galloway and the black community had to battle board of education officials and business leaders to obtain equal training opportunities. Hume-Fogg vocational students learned aircraft assembly and radio communications techniques in order to work at Vultee's plant and elsewhere. By contrast, Pearl offered no such courses although it did offer classes in sheet metal, auto mechanics, gas forging, and electronics.[39] In 1943 the board finally opened the Pearl High School War Production Welding School, located separately from the school at Sixteenth Avenue North and Ireland Street, but the majority of its graduates had to obtain jobs outside Nashville.

In spite of these obstacles, employment opportunities for black women improved during the war years. As the home-front economy boomed, some demanded higher wages from employers; others abandoned domestic jobs altogether to search for more profitable work.[40] Ironically, while white women in Nashville heeded the call of "Rosie the Riveter" and left their homes to join the labor force, some black women welcomed the opportunity to leave domestic employment and become homemakers. Their husbands' military wages, $50 a month, were quite enough to make doing so possible.[41] Others sought jobs as waitresses, as service staff workers, and in a host of businesses that catered to soldiers. Many moved to cities in the North, Midwest, and South to work in the defense industries. More than 250,000 women in the United States left domestic work during the war years. In Nashville, the number who worked in private households declined by almost half, falling from eight thousand in 1940 to 5,800 in 1950.[42]

The wartime economy also generated more career opportunities for black women in cosmetology and retail. Pearl's vocational training programs offered courses in hairdressing so female students could obtain better-paying jobs and eventually their own businesses. The training opportunities for women in Nashville reinforced the city's segregated society. The board of education's Distributive Education and War Production Program offered courses in retailing for white women, but the YWCA's Blue Triangle Branch only offered waitressing and food service courses for African Americans. It was necessary to take the courses at the local YWCA because Pearl High School did not have space or equipment for actual demonstration work.[43]

Although new positions emerged in business, government, social work, and nursing, the education profession remained the most accessible way for black women to attain middle-class status in Nashville.[44] Employment shortages provided opportunities for African American women teachers such as Ivanetta Davis, who became the principal of Clifton Elementary School, to obtain leadership roles in schools and organizations. In 1944 the board of education eliminated half-day sessions for second-grade elementary students and hired more teachers to meet the demand. Only two of the eighteen African Americans hired in city schools were men.[45] Women teachers now had the opportunity to break gender barriers and acquire more decision-making power in their schools. Whether, like Davis, they assumed more administrative posts or served on board committees as Minerva Hawkins did, their influence extended to the entire school.

The women continued as community leaders during the war by being active in the local Girls Service Organization (GSO), the United Service Organizations (USO), and other organizations dedicated to helping soldiers and their families. Carter-Lawrence Elementary School teacher and GSO leader Phynetta Nellis and her singing group made more than 380 trips to army camps and local USO parties in order to perform for soldiers. At a surprise party to celebrate her efforts she modestly commented, "I don't know why they honor me. My girls, who have gone through all kinds of weather and given up all civilian entertainment for the entertainment of servicemen, are the real ones who deserve the honor." In 1944 the prominent clubwoman Frankie Pierce and *Nashville Globe and Independent* editor Henry Boyd sponsored a campaign to raise $5,000 for the Red Cross. Teachers also helped the black-owned Citizen's Bank sell more than $700,000 in government bonds and other securities to the local African American community.[46]

Segregation and racism continued to mock the nation's call for unity. More than five thousand black men, a third of the entire black male population of Nashville, served in World War II, and African American men composed 15 percent of the twenty-two thousand Davidson County males in military service.[47] As in other urban centers, however, white Nashvillians resented black men who wore military uniforms. A race riot nearly occurred in 1943 after a white police officer arrested a black military policeman for the public display of his weapon. After that incident black MPs were stationed only in African American neighborhoods.[48]

Although surrounded by sweeping economic and social change Nashville's black schools reaped few rewards from wartime prosperity other than more vocational education courses. Teaching conditions were still substandard. The city built three new elementary and junior high schools for blacks in 1939, but wartime limitations on building materials prevented school construction during the 1940s despite severe overcrowding. The classroom populations in eight of the twelve black schools exceeded fifty-five students per teacher; three such oversized classes were at Pearl High School.[49] Moreover, although the *Thomas* case equalized teachers' salaries, financial disparities based on race continued. In 1942 Nashville city schools spent $33.68 for each white high school student but only $18.85 for each African American one.[50]

Although painfully aware of these inequalities, African American administrators and teachers led campaigns within their schools to support the war. Addressing the Middle Tennessee Colored Teachers' Association (MTCTA) in 1942, Mary L. Williams encouraged them to remain faithful to the nation. "In spite of all the bitterness that wells up in our hearts we must be loyal to the ideals of government while we fight the unfair practices of government officials," she urged.[51]

Many black teachers realized their students were entering society at a tumultuous time. Fathers and loved ones were away fighting, families were relocating, and in some cases students were inducted the day they graduated. African American Education professor Eunice Matthew stated in 1943 that "a sense of security and emotional stability is the first need of every child during these times."[52] Teachers, too, felt the war's impact when loved ones left for service. Ella Thompson had to temporarily quit teaching home economics at Pearl High School so she could run her husband's dry-cleaning business while he was away. "I have a husband in service," she told Superintendent Bass. "He has a little business here and I'm trying to work and keep it open so he will have something to do when he comes home."[53]

As some of their students ventured off to war, teachers and parents shared a profound responsibility to protect the emotional and physical well-being of those who remained. Only ten days after the Japanese attack on Pearl Harbor, the board of education informed teachers and parents what to do in the case of an air raid in Tennessee. "We don't need to be caught napping again, anywhere or anytime. We are not going to say again—it can't happen here," the directive of December 17, 1941, began, reflecting the panic of much of the nation. "Don't rush around. Don't worry. But Act! These are simple precautions. Read them again. Think how you will apply them to your school. Then take the necessary action today. Parents! If an air raid should come while your children are away at school, see to your own safety. Stay home. Go to your refuge room. Do not try to reach the school. The number one rule is to stay off the streets. Do not try to telephone. The wires must be kept clear for the police and fire department."[54]

Nashville's black teachers brought the war effort into their classrooms in numerous ways. An article in the June 1942 *Broadcaster* encouraged them to "grasp every opportunity to instill into our pupils love and devotion to Old Glory and to make them conscious of the duties as well as the privileges of good citizenship." And that is what they did throughout the war. In 1944, for example, black schools raised more than $30,000 by selling stamps and war bonds. By creating contests among schools, the teachers fostered a competitive spirit in support of the nation.[55]

Student clubs such as the Junior Service Academy, Girl Reserves, and Junior Red Cross, also sponsored fund-raising activities. African American children initiated letter-writing campaigns, donated reading material, and entertained soldiers at the YMCA; the youngsters at Peebles Elementary School even collected pennies to buy cigarettes for soldiers. Frances Reeds, who was young during the war years, later became a teacher. She remembers that she "became more conscious of patriotism and what the war meant to Americans." The June 1942 *Broadcaster* also mentioned that teachers "should grasp every opportunity to instill into our pupils love and devotion to Old Glory and to make them conscious of the duties as well as the privileges of good citizenship."[56]

As their professional associations stressed the inclusion of patriotism into the curriculum, African American female teachers provided opportunities for children to envision a world of racial equality and understanding. At Pearl High School, home economics teacher Lillian Dunn Thomas held Hawaiian Day in her class, and Callisto Bell's high school Spanish class watched filmstrips of her studies in Mexico. When Nashville's education officials implemented a character development program called "Going Our Way," local teachers seized the opportunity to promote belief in tolerance. Ford Greene Elementary School students participated in monthly music programs that stressed accepting other cultures, and the city's teachers were part of national programs that underscored racial and ethnic understanding and activism.[57]

The black women educators linked the war abroad with racial justice at home. In 1945 Edmonia Grant, a former teacher and researcher for Charles S. Johnson at Fisk University, became the director of education for the American Missionary Association. With an office on the Fisk campus, she worked to eliminate racial prejudice by developing campaigns such as the "Races of Mankind" series.[58] In addition to working with college students, Grant lectured at some local black schools; in February 1945 she gave an address during Win the War, Win the Peace Week at Cameron Junior High School.[59] A year later Grant became the program secretary of the National Council of the National Board of the YWCA. In that capacity she created a poster program, "Sincerely Yours," which focused on the issues that affected minorities. African American colleges and public schools across the nation received the poster-letters, and Grant advised students to respond by writing to their representatives in Congress. Under a greeting to the fictional "Dear Marion and Jack" the letters described a plethora of issues that included employment and political concerns and also linked the war and racial discrimination:

> Dear Marion and Jack,
> Since you are studying the Tolan-Pepper-Kilgore Bill so carefully, I am not surprised that you ask me about the Anti-Poll Tax Bill. For these two bills are closely related. We can't mobilize our total re-sources as long as ten-million American citizens are disfranchised by means of a poll tax. In seven southern states, six million white and four million Negro citizens do not have a free voice in their govern-ment. Because we believe in the Christian principle of the equality of all people, we shall continue to try to extend political democracy to all Americans. You can help by writing a letter to the representatives in Congress in your district asking them to sign discharge Petition No. 3 which will bring the Anti-Poll Tax Bill (H.R. 7) to the floor for a vote.
>
> Sincerely Yours,
> Edmonia[60]

Grant's poignant efforts encouraging students to fight against the poll-tax and promote positive race relations among young people, illustrates African American efforts to connect the war's promise of democracy over fascism to their own fight for equality.

Nashville's local black institutions of higher learning also benefited from growing African American expectations of social equality during and after the war. In 1942 Fisk initiated its Race Relations Institute, to be led by Johnson, a sociologist. The annual three-week conference invited white and black scholars; representatives from local, state, and national organizations; and public leaders in human relations to discuss racial problems in an integrated environment.[61] By 1945, after the Rosenwald Foundation's Edwin Embree, a white northerner, claimed that "uppity white people would have to take care else they might be slapped down by the darker races of the world," Nashville's white leaders began to pressure Fisk's white president, Thomas Jones, to cancel the institute. Johnson refused the president's request, and Jones unexpectedly resigned. In 1946 Johnson became the university's first African American president.[62] Over the years the institute had an integral role in race relations in Nashville and nationally as well.

As a state-funded institution, Tennessee A&I could not openly sponsor any like the Race Relations Institute, but the school nevertheless prospered after the war. Greater tax revenues caused a financial surplus, thus generating greater funds for higher education statewide, and in 1947 $3.5 million was appropriated for the expansion of A&I. It was the third in a series of improvements since Walter S. Davis was hired as president in 1943. Following his inauguration, the faculty increased from thirty-two, including two who had a Ph.D., to 121, twenty-one of whom held a Ph.D., by 1947. Davis's administration organized the college into a university format with graduate programs and an increased budget for salaries and laboratory supplies.[63]

Attempts to equalize facilities at Tennessee A&I also benefited from the NAACP's continued legal actions after the late 1930s to force the University of Tennessee at Knoxville to accept blacks in its professional and graduate schools. The Tennessee State Board of Education expanded funding to Tennessee A&I in an effort to circumvent the growing push to desegregate the South's public universities. As greater numbers of blacks refused to take scholarships to out-of-state private graduate and professional schools and filed suit to attend in-state universities, southern states suddenly funneled money into black schools to create or strengthen those graduate and professional programs. In 1950, after cases such as *Sweatt v. Painter* and *McLaurin v. Oklahoma State Regents for Higher Education* succeeded in opening graduate schools to blacks, the NAACP sued for four plaintiffs, and federal courts ordered the University of Tennessee at Knoxville to desegregate its graduate and professional programs.[64]

Created in 1943, Tennessee A&I's graduate program in education incorporated America's emphasis on democracy by stressing "improvement of citizenship" as a teaching objective. One of the elementary education department's main goals, moreover, was to "train teachers in social understanding of our democratic culture." Student teachers put educational theories to practical use through observation, participation, and remedial teaching at Ford Greene. One of the new teachers' goals was to instill tolerance in students in order to promote feelings of self-esteem and worth.[65]

Unfortunately, democracy and equality remained little more than theories for most black Nashvillians. State and local governments established programs to aid citizens during the depression and support the war effort, but those efforts seldom acknowledged the needs of African Americans unless forced to do so by legal action. Black Nashvillians faced obstructions at every turn when they attempted to exercise their rights as citizens. As one example, they boycotted the local V-J Day parade when officials instructed the triumphant black veterans to march at its rear and in segregated units.[66]

In addition to African Americans' complaints, local newspapers such as the *Nashville Tennessean* campaigned to abolish the poll tax by claiming that it promoted bossism and political corruption. Wealthy politicians could buy votes by paying the poll taxes for poor citizens. After the tax was discontinued in Nashville in 1947, African Americans organized voter registration drives. After fighting in a war that liberated millions they were less willing to accept the racial status quo of the United States.

In 1946 Coyness L. Ennix, an African American lawyer in Nashville, formed the Solid Block, an independent organization that called for blacks from all walks of life to pool their collective political power by creating a mass of voters and supporting black-owned businesses. The organization also wanted more black representation on the police force and city council and in the fire department and school administration. By 1949 the Solid Block could boast of several achievements: The city had been pushed into hiring several black police officers, $1 million in state funds was obtained for a boys' industrial school, and enough votes were secured to pass a school bond issue that benefited black schools. The Solid Block organization attracted young people impatient with the progress of race relations in Nashville, and it invigorated the efforts of the city's existing organizations to eliminate injustice.[67]

In response to blacks' growing political power and block voting, Nashville's Democratic city government redesigned election districts and created several wards in which African Americans were in a majority in 1949. Redistricting ensured that at least one African American would win election from his or her ward. Although the wards hindered black Nashvillians' ability to vote as a block, many relished the possibility of electing an African American to the city council. Memberships in political organizations increased, and in 1951 attorneys Alexander Looby and Robert E. Lillard were elected to the council.[68]

The city's black teachers' association responded by becoming more involved in city politics and contributing to the local chapter of the NAACP.[69] The teachers, members of the City Federation of Colored Women's Clubs, joined with the male City-County Negro Democratic League to promote voting and civic education, and by 1950 the twelve-year-old coalition had enrolled more than six thousand members.[70] As Charles S. Johnson observed, "There is a great deal of objective evidence that his [African American] attitude is increasingly becoming one of protest. . . . We have, then, in the South, on the one hand, a situation in which the great majority of Negroes are becoming increasingly dissatisfied with the present pattern of race relations and want a change. . . . Yet, most southern whites could not contemplate making any adjustments at all."[71] Nashville's African American teachers could use postwar political and economic successes to promote their claim that America's democratic freedoms were attainable.

During the cold war, the African Americans at local and national levels sought to expose injustices and flaws in American democracy. The nation patriotically supported its veterans from World War II, but the heroes now also included those who fought on foreign shores or ferreted out communist spies or government detractors at home. With communism viewed as a threat, teachers were charged with instilling a love of democracy and free enterprise among students. In such perilous times, anxious university administrators fired thousands of liberal-thinking professors, and school officials prohibited educators from teaching literature that ranged from the classic *Robin Hood* to the work of D. H. Lawrence. Those who refused to advance the prevailing anticommunist philosophy could lose their jobs or even face criminal charges.[72]

In the nineteenth century, northern teachers, blacks as well as whites, packed their bags and traveled south to help educate newly freed slaves. At the turn of the century, educators had another mandate: Americanize the nation's growing immigrant population. A wave of anticommunist hysteria swept the nation after World War II, and every public institution from post offices to public schools heeded the mandate to promote democracy and protect society from communist spies and sympathizers. Exhibiting patriotism became an important job requirement for teachers in cold war America. School systems across the nation asked teachers and administrators to develop curriculum and programs to promote democracy in an effort to instill hatred and distrust of communists. According to W. A. Bass, "Russian communism is sending its emissaries into our midst, seeking out troubled areas, and undertaking to supplant democracy with communism. It uses any means at its disposal to disturb and to destroy, to disorganize, and to disrupt both small and large elements of our population. It renounces all faith in God. It undermines and destroys the home and morality. Its methods are both hypocritical and deceitful. We should meet this challenge head-on through appropriate teaching with fidelity to fact."[73]

Black teachers serving in a segregated system and society had little power for public defiance or to contradict local curriculum dictates. They were repeatedly instructed to teach students to appreciate democracy although they did not live in a racially democratic society. In his 1948 address to the board of education, for instance, Bass called for teachers to "develop in the children a zeal for American democracy." He also asked them to "make pupils intellectually and emotionally aware of the individual and the collective rights, privileges, responsibilities, and opportunities which our democracy offers and guarantees."

In board–sponsored segregated seminars and at local universities, African American teachers and college students listened to impassioned speeches concerning the necessity of teaching democratic ideals. In 1949 Bass addressed future elementary teachers at Tennessee A&I and remarked, "One of the fundamental tasks of the modern teacher is to bring the pupils to an appreciation of the superiority of democracy. Every child has the right to grow, to develop, and to become outstanding citizens in this—the greatest country of them all—and the job of the schoolteacher and more especially of the elementary school teacher is to see that each pupil has his opportunity."[74]

As the superintendent of schools, Bass's sanctimonious praise of democracy, especially that "it guarantees and protects the rights of minorities against the majority," smacked of outright hypocrisy to many black educators and students. In reality, Bass's definition of democracy did not apply to African American teachers or pupils at all. The superintendent called for elementary school faculty of both races to teach how to live and work together with mutual respect for the rights and privileges of others but in their own respective segregated schools of course. He also instructed all high school teachers to educate students about the significance of landmark documents such as the Constitution.

The board of education, however, made no effort to suggest that instructors teach respect for others across racial lines. The *Nashville Globe and Independent* attacked the local schools' annual celebration of Brotherhood Week for such blatant duplicity. According to the newspaper, the real themes of Brotherhood Week as practiced by segregated schools should state, "We believe in the brotherhood of all members of the white race and their affiliates. . . . We believe also, in the brotherhood of the colored brothers, one to the other and not otherwise. When the celebration was finished, a report could be made, showing the result achieved by both the white and the colored divisions of the brotherhood, within their separate and distinct zones of operation, AND NOT OTHERWISE."[75]

African American teachers had the difficult task of transforming the rhetoric into concepts students could accept. They had to develop a democratic ideology that suggested students should aspire to achieve despite discrimination and prejudice and that the fruits of democracy belonged to no single race.

Although the board selected several black teachers from Pearl to develop a program to promote "democratic living" along with white instructors from Howard High School, it was clear the educators approached democracy differently. The white speakers at several teacher workshops in 1946 conveyed a practical message: Students must become active participants of democracy by reading newspapers and studying public issues. In contrast, the black lecturers told their audience that "democracy is a concept with several basic premises; the equality of all men under the law and the right of all men to liberty—political, economic, social, artistic and civil."[76]

While white teachers emphasized the tools needed to promote democracy blacks stressed that it should be equated with freedom. Most white students had already experienced the benefits of democracy and could look forward to full participation in a free society, but democracy was a more abstract term for the city's black children. In order to reach them, African American teachers used the tenets of democracy to generate hope and self-esteem. [77] Moreover, Nashville's black women teachers expanded discussions of democracy to call on students to develop strategies to improve daily life. According to Eunice Matthew, "Some objectives sought in educating for democratic living in the United States include the ability to recognize significant problems; to think intelligently about social problems, and to plan for action on these problems."[78]

As women who faced the double prejudice of race and gender, the teachers may have seemed to be unlikely subjects to teach egalitarianism. Yet as William J. Faulkner, an African American himself and a dean and minister at Fisk, has suggested, "Teachers should be the living symbols of democracy, because it takes a great personality to inspire a child to become a great man or woman."[79] To many, black teachers embodied equality's potential, and African American women educators represented the ability to rise above the low expectations of society in general. They wanted students to know that America's democratic ideals might make it possible to change their personal situations. The teachers understood the limits of American democracy but attempted to balance the oppressive reality of daily life with hope that the nation was poised for change.

The women took advantage of the call to promote democracy by teaching that to be prejudiced is to be antidemocratic. "The best test of democracy is in the way in which we treat our fellow men," observed Eunice Matthew.[80] As Elsie M. Lewis expressed this position, "Name calling carries with it danger. No teacher should allow a pupil to call a person 'dago,' 'wop,' 'greaser,' 'Jap,' 'slant-eye' or 'nigger.' Time is better spent correcting such wrong attitudes of boys and girls than correcting papers in arithmetic and spelling."[81] White teachers also received lesson plans that stressed tolerance and acceptance of other cultures, but their material failed to denounce, or even address, the racism between African Americans and whites. Black women teachers, however, used tools given by the board to promote patriotic nationalism and suggest that racial equality is the true American ideal.

They focused on helping students to avoid conflicts, whether with whites or each other. In 1946 the Teachers' Benefit Association sponsored the publication of *How to Belong*, a booklet that suggested a code of conduct and provided advice on proper decorum and interpersonal skills. The association's focus on children's behavior offers insight into the larger community's growing concern about juvenile delinquency. Whites tended to attribute the increase in youth crime and misbehavior to the fact that more mothers worked outside their homes.[82] The creation of the booklet also indicated that African American teachers wanted to ensure that their students behaved properly and maintained appearances that were acceptable to society in general. Correct behavior would not only assist students in keeping friendships but also help protect the older ones from police brutality and enable them to obtain employment.[83]

Some black teachers were concerned about discrimination and prejudice at a variety of levels and were even willing to speak out against divisions within the black community. In 1948, for instance, Idabelle Yeiser, a professor of education, explained to the annual session of the Tennessee Negro Education Association the importance of refusing discrimination of any kind: "We as a race are demanding certain things, certain equalities, but as we demand we must examine ourselves to see whether or not we are giving what we ask for. Suppose prejudice keeps people from uniting. We as teachers must aid these youth in getting rid of prejudices such as color both within the race and without it. Some hate others because they are fairer. Some hate others because they are darker." Yeiser also warned against religious and class prejudice as well as men disliking women as their superior officers or barring them from certain jobs."[84]

During the late 1940s and early 1950s those who spoke at the state association's annual conferences frequently discussed the importance of relating education and democracy, but they rarely rebuked the United States directly for racism and discrimination. *The Broadcaster* officially supported equalizing educational opportunities in state schools, but discussions of pending school desegregation cases or racial inequities seldom dominated the journal's contents. Authentic free speech brought the possibility of repercussion. It was perilous for government employees to speak negatively about the nation. Complaining about discrimination suggested that one was not patriotic or possibly a communist sympathizer. Although blacks were disappointed at the progress of race relations in America, the Tennessee Negro Education Association, which represented the state's African American teachers, used *The Broadcaster* to focus on patriotism. The publication also, presumably, eased the minds of the white establishment.[85]

Ironically, as black women teachers espoused racial unity and freedom from their desks in underfunded segregated schools, the United States was promoting the capitalistic "democratic American way of life" to people of color in formerly colonized nations. In cold war rhetoric, everyone was free and equal. When young black people soon decided to question why the philosophy of democracy did not reflect reality, their efforts to correct the discrepancies by participating in the civil rights movement often embarrassed the government.[86]

As words such as *equality, freedom,* and *democracy* became the official themes of the Nashville public schools, *discrimination, deprivation,* and *inequality* continued to describe the educational environment for the city's black students. In 1947 the board closed the eighty-year-old Belle View School, which had eight teachers and an enrollment of more than three hundred. The building had been in poor physical shape for years. When Novella Bass taught there in the 1930s Belle View would flood whenever it rained and need to be closed until the water was removed. "It was," the *Nashville Globe and Independent* reported, "the most horrible excuse for a school that existed anywhere in the city. . . . That old stove used to heat the school cracked and hot coals flew across the room. Fortunately, students were at recess at the time and no injuries resulted." Instead of building a new school, the board decided to send students to three different elementary schools. The decision indicated, the *Globe and Independent* observed, the racism that marred the board of education: "While there are some fair minded and God fearing members on the board of education, there also are those who are set in their determination to keep colored children from getting treatment equal to that provided for white pupils."[87]

Overcrowding became an even bigger problem after 1947, when the number of students in the city's black schools rose after the state legislature increased the mandatory education age from sixteen to seventeen. After hearing complaints concerning the high rate of illiteracy among soldiers, the legislature hoped that extending the dropout age would improve literacy rates. Teachers had to report attendance records to the state, and truancy laws were enforced.[88]

African American women teachers in Nashville now had an even greater responsibility to ensure that their students remained in school.[89] In response to the increased enrollment, the board submitted a bond issue to the citizens authorizing $4 million to improve and build new schools; approximately $1 million would be allocated to the black schools to construct new additions. The board appropriated no funds, however, for a new elementary school to replace Belle View.[90]

The wartime experience and contradictions in Nashville led to a new spirit of militancy among black youths. Young men and women were reaching maturity in a country that promoted itself as the "home of the free" while simultaneously circumscribing the lives of African Americans. Although they attended segregated schools that were inferior to those for whites, their teachers encouraged them to view themselves as equal to anyone. When opportunities presented themselves students acted on what they learned in school and demanded democracy. In 1947 the Southern Negro Youth Congress, a radical, interracial organization that helped young people unionize and resist labor inequities, formed a Nashville chapter. In the 1940s Nashville's African American community had celebrated victories such as the teacher-salary equalization case; by the early 1950s their quiet determination had exploded into a full-scale assault upon segregation.

⌐⌐

As Nashville's African American teachers pushed for genuine democracy and equality in the United States amid the dangers of the cold war and racism, the NAACP took up the issue of educational segregation with renewed vigor. During the war it attacked discrimination in America's industries and in the military. Although its membership and funding increased during the war, the organization was in a precarious position because some whites considered its protests un-American. Beginning in the 1930s, the lawyers and leaders of the NAACP grappled with whether to gain equal educational opportunities within the existing segregated system or attempt to force the courts to eliminate racial segregation in education. In 1931 Nathan Margold, a white attorney for the NAACP, reported that the struggle to equalize schools in hundreds of segregated districts would require extensive financial and legal resources. To bring suit for equalization would leave the door open for districts to retain segregation, he continued, and higher taxes and fewer funds for white schools would result. None of this would please white parents or taxpayers. Instead, Margold called on the NAACP to launch an all-out assault on school segregation. The organization might force education officials to adhere to the law and still negotiate separate but genuinely equal schools for African Americans.[91]

The debate over the direction of the NAACP led to the resignation of one of its veteran leaders. In the midst of the Great Depression, W. E. B. Du Bois wanted the organization to fight for economic remedies. He also urged blacks to pool their collective financial resources in order to do so. Segregation could be an opportunity for collective development rather than an indication of inferiority. Du Bois, moreover, did not consider litigation the most effective way to end racial discrimination in education. "A separate Negro school, where children are treated like human beings, trained by teachers of their own race, who know what it means to be black . . . is infinitely better than making our boys and girls doormats to be spit and trampled upon," he maintained in 1935. "To sum it up is this: theoretically, the Negro needs neither segregated schools, nor mixed schools. What he needs is education."[92]

Yet Du Bois's viewpoint was a minority one within the NAACP and contrary to the new direction and focus of the organization led by Charles H. Houston, the former dean of Howard University's law school. Houston saw the NAACP as a driving force to end segregation, first in education by setting legal precedents that would eventually lead to *Plessy v. Ferguson* being overturned. After resigning in 1934, Du Bois returned to the NAACP in 1944 as director of special research but left again four years later because of growing conflicts about the organization's focus.

The NAACP now turned much of its intellectual, legal, and financial resources to attack racial segregation in education. After the experiences garnered from the teacher' salary equalization cases, most leaders of the organization agreed with Margold and thought that suing to equalize educational facilities on a case-by-case basis would be financially taxing, time-consuming, and only marginally successful. Moreover, it was difficult to find plaintiffs and generate widespread community support. Houston's protégée Thurgood Marshall and his legal defense team decided to seek a Supreme Court ruling to end segregation, which would eliminate the necessity of trying cases in individual cities and counties.[93]

Other black leaders took different approaches. Texas journalist and lawyer Carter Wesley maintained that southern school boards might offer funds to equalize segregated schools if compelled, but black children's lives might be in danger if they attended white schools. He and his supporters endorsed a dual approach that focussed on equalization as well as desegregation. Some black Texans supported Wesley, but the NAACP's legal defense fund dismissed his ideas. Marshall and his colleagues branded Wesley a sell-out and hindrance to black progress. Such harsh criticism silenced other dissenters, but Wesley remained undaunted. Marshall's response to him was that "equalization could be the default result of trying to end segregation but one should not settle for existing in a discriminatory system."[94]

If intellectuals and prominent people such as Du Bois and Wesley remained unheeded, then the opinions of the thousands of black teachers apprehensive about desegregation would have equal difficulty changing the NAACP's course.[95] During the war, the National Association of Teachers in Colored Schools, later renamed the American Teachers Association (ATA), an organization composed of black college presidents, faculty, principals, and teachers, supported the initiative to obtain equal facilities. In addition to publicly stating that it advocated racial equality in schools, it waged a national campaign for accrediting organizations to judge black high schools by the same standards as those for whites, hoping to pressure white school systems for more money and emphasizing the disparities in funding and buildings. The ATA also supported the NAACP's campaign for educational equality and contributed $16,000 to its legal defense fund.[96]

Cognizant of the leadership roles black teachers held both nationally and in their communities, Marshall and his colleagues considered it a challenge to convince them to support the campaign for total desegregation. The NAACP had learned a great deal about the politics of garnering local support from the successes and failures of salary equalization cases.[97] Although black teachers supported the quest for equality within the segregated system, they were apprehensive about a potential loss of jobs and autonomy if public schools desegregated. Gross inadequacies prevailed in segregated schools, but at least black administrators had the power to control day-to-day activities.

African American teachers had good reasons to be wary of desegregation. Many male teachers feared it would lead to their unemployment because of the presumed unwillingness of whites to allow a black man to teach white girls. As employees of the segregated schools, black women teachers also had more incentive to urge equal facilities than to urge desegregation. They were also guided by colleagues and gained support from students' families and the community. Moreover, they were at the pinnacle of female economic success. Integration could result in mistreatment by white colleagues, demotion, or loss of employment.

Nashville's black community realized that their schools, although inadequate, were still superior in facilities and funding to segregated schools in surrounding towns and counties. Yet they did not hesitate to complain about inequities within the system.[98] In 1953 the board denied funding to build a new junior high school for students who lived in north Nashville between Jefferson and Eleventh Streets. The *Nashville Globe and Independent* complained bitterly over that decision:

> Every day the authorities discriminate against the children and teachers of Wharton School. They are planting in the minds of both pupils and teachers a feeling that they are supposed to accept a status of inferiority, and like it. Plainly the authorities may force the school children and their teachers to obey an order to occupy a school that merely qualifies as "good enough for Negroes," according to old time traditions, but it is certain they will not make either the teachers or the pupils endure the discrimination happily.[99]

Tennessee's first public school desegregation case did not come from Nashville but from Clinton, a small town in rural East Tennessee.[100] In 1949 Wynona McSwain and several other black parents pressured the local board of education to fund the travel and tuition costs they incurred when sending their children almost forty miles to attend Austin High School in Knoxville. Because the local high school did not accept blacks, McSwain claimed that it cost from $40 to $100 a year to send her children to school. The board refused the mother's request. Consequently, in 1950 five black high school students attempted to enroll in the all-white Clinton High School. The principal, unsurprisingly, refused them. Three months later McSwain asked the NAACP to sue the Anderson County school system on behalf of her daughter, Joeathrea, and five other plaintiffs. The NAACP accepted the case and contended that the segregated school system did not provide equal educational facilities. In 1952 the federal district court ruled in favor of the board. The NAACP appealed to the U.S. Sixth Circuit Court of Appeals in Cincinnati, asking for desegregation of the schools.[101]

As the cases moved forward, Nashville's black women teachers continued to work within the system to advance professionally. In 1953, eight years after Teachers' Benefit Association secretary Bessie Dixon first petitioned the board of education in 1945 to appoint blacks to the Teachers' Panel, two African Americans, J. K. Petway, principal of Meigs Junior High School, and Mrs. M. K. Robinson, who taught at Pearl High School, were added to this select three-member panel, increasing it to five. The panel did not have voting privileges but it did have authority to influence policy, and it represented the views of the teaching corps to the board. Before Petway and Robinson were appointed, African American teachers had no voice on the panel.[102] It was a short-lived victory, however, because the board quickly enacted regulations that reduced the panel's influence. The accomplishment might have seemed ineffectual when compared to a legal decision, but it reassured many of Nashville's black teachers that they could progress in small but significant steps by working within the system.[103]

In addition to Clinton, the residents of Clarendon, South Carolina, and Topeka, Kansas, asked the NAACP to file desegregation suits against their local school systems, and the Court decided to combine five of them under the name *Brown v. Board of Education of Topeka Kansas.* The NAACP's lawyers selected testimony from social scientists and psychological experts to support the claim that segregation damaged African American children. During the early 1950s, the NAACP used psychological evidence from the research of the prominent child psychologists Kenneth and Mamie Clark to suggest that black children had poor self-esteem because they attended schools in inferior segregated environments. In the Clarks' tests, which made use of black dolls and white ones, African American elementary-school children preferred the white dolls.[104] In addition, they attributed negative characteristics to black dolls and positive characteristics to white ones. The evidence played a vital role in the *Brown* case because it suggested that even if the all-black schools were equal to schools for whites they would still be damaging to the self-esteem of black children.

The results also seemed to indicate that the efforts of black teachers' to raise their students' self-esteem had little positive impact on psychological development. That was bound to be frustrating news to those who had worked so hard to overcome the negative effects of segregation. As Derrick Bell notes, when attacking educational segregation the NAACP, and civil rights leaders in general, downplayed the important role of African American teachers in the educational development of black children.[105] The lawyers needed to convince the Supreme Court, however, and not the teachers, so no positive aspects of segregated schools were mentioned. Evidence that teachers had successfully educated students under substandard conditions would not convey the point that segregation was inherently unequal.[106]

Scholarly studies have shown that the Clarks' doll studies were flawed, but they served the purpose of Marshall's legal team. Had the Clarks studied children at Pearl High School after years of attendance at all-black schools their results might have been different.[107] Many African American schools were inferior, and Pearl received fewer materials than its white counterparts, but those who attended schools like Pearl gained a great deal of self-esteem. Although students at all-black schools offered numerous complaints about their education, ranging from torn textbooks to lack of curriculum choices, they rarely, if ever, considered the schools completely inferior. Their teachers' battles against educational and material inequities were ongoing, and they developed parallel programs and opportunities for their students. Ola Hudson, who was an administrator and also taught home economics, remembers the students, teachers, and parents as being very close. "We were a community," she recalls fondly. "We were all black, all striving for equality. We worked really hard to be sure despite where they were that we still gave the children the best that we could give."[108]

Of course, black teachers could not overcome all obstacles thrust upon them by segregation and oppression. Most students, however, believed them to be caring and that they demanded excellence in spite of discrimination. African Americans, who experienced segregation frequently, contended that their schools' nurturing environment helped them develop positive self-concepts and the sense of community. Lillian Dunn Thomas, a former teacher comments, "It was like they belonged to us and they [would] tell us how they [now] tell their children how lovely you [teachers] all were and how we respected you all [teachers] as our parents."[109]

From the Great Depression to the early 1950s, African American teachers experienced significant changes. In Nashville, they obtained equal salaries, at least in theory, to their white counterparts; they supported the nation during World War II; and they had deployed theories of democracy and freedom in new ways throughout the decades. With the *Brown* decision, though, they would once again have to readjust. After their salaries were equalized, the city's black teachers had little incentive to leave their communities and teach white children. Others refrained from protesting the negative implications of the *Brown* decision because they did not want to suggest that black children should not have opportunities to attend better schools. As teachers, they had always told students that they were equal to white children, and they could not deny their pupils the opportunity to prove their excellence in integrated schools. Beginning with *Brown v. Board of Education*, black women teachers developed yet another definition of racial uplift. It involved sacrificing their status and positions in the community to better the lives of African American children.

THREE

"We Are Ready Whenever They Are": *Brown* and the Civil Rights Movement

Some of Nashville's black teachers were excited when they first learned of the May 17, 1954, *Brown v. Board of Education of Topeka, Kansas* decision because black children would no longer have to attend schools that lacked curriculum choices and materials. Others welcomed the ruling outlawing racial segregation in schools but doubted that integration would ever occur. Some were concerned about losing their jobs. Almost a month later, on June 10, 1954, the Nashville branch of the NAACP vowed to protect jobs when it submitted a document from the Atlanta branch to the local board of education. The branch declared that "the fullest resources of the association, including the legal staff, the research staff, and educational specialists on the staff will be utilized to insure that there will be no discrimination against teachers as a result of integration."[1]

Despite their fears, most of Nashville's African American teachers supported integration and its promise of better education for black children. They were, as education professor William Gandy maintained, "Negroes first, and teachers second."[2] Whether the teachers looked on *Brown* with anticipation or trepidation, they were resigned to their fate. "It didn't matter to me," Lillian Dunn Thomas commented of the decision.[3] She was a teacher and would continue to do her job.

While white officials in segregated states expressed outrage at the *Brown* decision and took measures to evade compliance, Tennessee politicians responded in a variety of ways, ranging from disgust to reluctant acceptance. Nashville's mayor Ben West, for instance, stated publicly, "All of our citizens are entitled to the opportunity of an education and I am sure our Board of Education will protect all in this right."[4]

Nevertheless, Nashville's white education officials responded to the *Brown* decision in a manner similar to many southern school boards and passively resisted the ruling. Coyness Ennix, an attorney and the board's only black member, later said, "After you've had segregated schools for a hundred years and you've been saying they're separate but equal, you're not going to all of a sudden say, 'I've been wrong all this time.'"[5] Although often referred to as the "Athens of the South," Nashville, with a population of approximately 174,000 that included more than fifty-eight thousand African Americans, was still racially segregated. The local NAACP filed suit against the board of education in 1955, and in 1957 the U.S. Sixth District Court forced the board to develop a model for integration. The model, known as the Nashville plan, was a gradual, grade-per-year program that was so successful in delaying public school desegregation that other school systems in cities such as Dallas and Houston implemented it later.[6]

While they supported the Nashville NAACP's legal battles to end school segregation the city's African American teachers and administrators worked to provide a positive student environment by trying to obtain better facilities and materials in the segregated schools. During the years immediately following the *Brown* decision the board allocated funds to construct new black schools, remodel older ones, and hire more black teachers. It was ironic that the Supreme Court's declaration that segregated schools were inherently unequal and therefore unconstitutional soon led public school systems in southern towns and cities to begin construction of state-of-the-art institutions for blacks.

In the midst of dealing with school segregation and integration issues, Nashville's teachers had a new set of concerns in the early 1960s. The city's black college and high school students took the civil rights movement into their own hands through sit-ins and marches. Some of the black teachers supported them and often took them to protest meetings, nervously waiting to drive them home safely. The responses of African American women teachers to the civil rights movement and *Brown* decision show they remained committed, through it all, to the students. A host of black Nashvillians continued to work simultaneously to maintain equal educational facilities for all children, the retention of black teachers, and school integration.

Although images of black children attempting to integrate schools are more familiar, white parents in Nashville were the first to test the *Brown* decision and challenge the state's 1901 school segregation law that prohibited teaching or attending schools with those of another race.[7] After two white Fisk University professors and their wives, Lee and Grace Lorch and Robert and Gertrude Rempfer, asked the board of education to register their children at all-black Pearl Elementary School, the board notified them in June that the applications would be discussed at an undetermined date. On September 7 the two academics registered the children at Pearl, which Lorch's friend, Principal M. E. Tipton, reluctantly refused to allow.[8]

Long-time civil rights activists, the professors participated in a number of human rights causes and viewed their actions in response to *Brown* as part of their hopes for an integrated society. A state vice president of the NAACP, Lorch claimed that he and Rempfer wanted to demonstrate "an atmosphere of peaceful compliance with the *Brown* decision and to show that there was white support for it."[9] The board dismissed the request of their lawyer, Z. Alexander Looby, to permit the white children to attend Pearl Elementary and refused to discuss the issue of integration. The board later maintained that it denied Looby's subsequent October request to allow the white children to enroll in a black school because it did not want to implement a plan before the Court's decision in *Brown II*. The veteran civil rights lawyer responded that he would have to "take other steps."[10]

In the middle of the controversy emerging from the June 8, 1955, *Brown II* ruling, which ambiguously stated that schools must integrate "with all deliberate speed," the board of education suddenly took an interest in studying the issue.[11] A day after the Supreme Court's decision, School Superintendent William Bass suggested that the nine-member appointed board establish a committee to examine school integration. The board subsequently created a four-member instruction committee that excluded Coyness Ennix. The committee held numerous meetings with university scholars, white teachers' associations, and Parent Teacher Associations (PTAs) to collect information. It also studied integration plans from other states.[12]

The committee seemed intent on moving the process of integration slowly. It ignored the request of Meredith William Day, the Nashville NAACP president, to comply with the wishes of several parents who had signed a petition asking that their children be allowed to attend formerly segregated schools. Instead, on August 11, 1955, the committee reported that "it would not be in the best interest of the schools to undertake implementation of the court's decision during the school year 1955–1956. There are too many unresolved problems for this course of action to be initiated now."[13]

The committee also claimed it could not propose a specific plan for school integration until it conducted and analyzed extensive studies, among them a complete census of school facilities, determining the age-grade distribution of the city's school-aged children, changing the athletic policy, altering the curricula, selecting teachers to work in integrated schools, and developing an orientation plan for teachers and principals.[14] Despite those widespread plans, however, the board was in no hurry to desegregate. The process, a stalling technique, provided time to determine how to meet the white community's demands while adhering to the law. The board was under enormous pressure from white parents, community members, state and local government officials, and the press to defy *Brown* and maintain the dual school system. What seemed the best action was no action at all.[15]

Looby's threat to take other measures reflected the NAACP's frustration with the delaying tactics. After gaining consent from black parents who lived in areas near white schools, on September 1, 1955, the NAACP sent tenth-grader Robert Kelley, whose father, Alfred Z. Kelley, was a barber, and twenty other high school, junior high school, and elementary students to enroll in white schools.[16] The Kelley family lived on Gallatin Road, which was within walking distance to all-white East High School, but Robert had to catch a bus across town, at his own expense, to attend all-black Pearl High School. When Robert Kelley and six other black students arrived at East, its principal William H. Oliver, who became school superintendent in 1958, told them that the board prohibited him from enrolling African Americans. Robert Kelley recalled that day with understatement: "Like the beginning of any new school year for students our age, we were excited and anxious—but on that particular morning, unsure of what to expect. I remember specifically arriving at East High and seeing the large crowd of concerned persons; some were not too amicable."[17]

Albert Shaw, a former high school mathematics and science teacher and one of the students who tried to enroll, remembered the occasion in vivid detail and with pain: "As we walked into East High School, students ran out of their classrooms and started yelling and screaming 'Niggers you don't belong here, Get out!' and the teachers did nothing. I was very afraid. I was sort of relieved that they didn't let us in. We didn't know what would have happened to us."[18]

The rebuffed students, Alfred Kelley, and the lawyers retreated through the jeering crowd. After the younger children also failed to gain admittance to white elementary and junior high schools Thurgood Marshall, Looby, and his law partner Avon Williams Jr. filed a class-action suit on September 23 against the Nashville City Board of Education in *Robert W. Kelley v. Board of Education*.[19] An active member of the NAACP, Kelley allowed his son to serve as a plaintiff because he, a business owner, did not fear the loss of employment. The names of Shaw's parents and the other plaintiffs would not be disclosed in order to protect their jobs. The class-action suit involved twenty black children and the Rempfers' two white children, Jean and Richard, who now wished to go to Pearl Elementary and Washington Junior High Schools.[20]

After the NAACP filed the *Kelley* suit the board redoubled efforts to improve black schools. Previously, it had refused the black community's requests to build new institutions, maintaining time and again that the "threat of desegregation may make Negro schools obsolete."[21] Faced with a local legal challenge, however, the board switched gears and tried to appease African Americans who wished for better educational facilities. In 1955 it approved funding for the new Wharton Junior High School. The neighborhood north of Jefferson Street between Eleventh Avenue North and Eighteenth Avenue North, where Wharton was to be located, had lobbied for a new school for years.[22]

Since the 1890s Pearl Senior High School had been the city's only secondary institution for blacks, and by the late 1950s overcrowding there was severe. In response, the board authorized the expansion of Cameron Elementary and Junior High School to include secondary education. Cameron Senior High School opened in the fall of 1956, and many African Americans were thrilled. Charleene Spencer, a former high school history teacher, remembers her student years at the new school with joy: "Cameron was great! It was only three years old. I was in the third graduating class. I knew some of the teachers from my church." Compared to the Catholic school that Spencer had attended before, "Cameron was better equipped as a public school. It had many more things. Our alumni association has raised over $32,000 for scholarships."[23]

The board of education also authorized funding to expand Meigs School in east Nashville to include secondary grades. Now the city had three high

Albert Shaw, teaching at East High School, 1975.
(Courtesy of Albert Shaw)

Exterior of East High School, which Albert Shaw and others tried to integrate in 1955. They were not admitted. (Courtesy of Albert Shaw)

Lillian Dunn Thomas, shown near a flower arrangement at the dinette section of her classroom at Pearl Senior High School, had returned in 1955 from studying flower arranging in Japan. (Courtesy of Lillian Dunn Thomas)

Gwendolyn Vincent. (Courtesy of Gwendolyn Vincent)

Donzell Johnson (far left) with students from Hunters Lane High School at a Model Metro Government conference in Nashville during the early 1990s. The photograph was taken in the city council chambers and in front of vice-mayor's desk. (Courtesy of Donzell Johnson)

schools for African Americans. Students who once had to travel across town could attend schools in their neighborhoods or closer to their homes. As Lillie Bowman, a former teacher at Meigs, comments, "Meigs was a neighborhood school in all senses of the word. We knew the kids, and we knew the parents. Right now when they see us they run up and hug us."[24]

The neighborhoods surrounding Cameron and Meigs had lacked a secondary school, so faculties there had to develop bonds with parents to foster a supportive environment. Helen Young, who taught home economics at Cameron, remembers that they had help generate support by ensuring that parents and neighbors knew about school events and performances. Cameron's new teachers instilled in their students the desire to prove that their school was not inferior, and soon, according to Young, Cameron students were "getting their share of the prizes and awards."[25] Cameron and Meigs eventually became friendly rivals of Pearl in athletics as well as academics, although the students still only competed in a segregated environment.[26]

The effort to secure more funding for black schools contradicted the NAACP's integrationist goals, but the *Brown* decision gave the black community new power. Nashville's black community supported NAACP efforts while simultaneously seeking to improve the situation of black schools by using the board's desire to avoid integration. In fact, some leaders who thought integration had a better chance if black schools were improved viewed construction of new buildings for African Americans as part of the drive toward integration. New buildings would make white parents more agreeable to sending their children to black institutions.[27] The *Nashville Globe and Independent* articulated the concerns of many readers when it claimed, "When the Negro communities are supplied with better and equal schools there will be many white pupils who will admit that it is just as well to go to a formerly colored school as to a formerly white one."[28]

Black Nashvillians were not alone in attempting to support black schools. Teachers and parents in segregated areas across the nation fought to maintain African American schools, which they considered valuable cultural institutions in their community. Since the inception of Nashville's African American schools in 1867 the city's black residents had pushed for new and improved schools, increased funding, and better materials. Finally, after years of meager gains, there were significant improvements. Nashville's black parents and teachers did not want to abandon the years of cultural capital they had invested in their schools. What they wanted were more options for their children to obtain better educational opportunities, whether by attending a better-equipped white school or a newly improved black one.[29]

Nashville's teachers applauded the news of new school construction not only because it provided more opportunities for the city's black children but also because it promised new jobs, especially at the secondary level. Superintendent W. A. Bass assured the black community in 1956 that "the problem of handling the new schools in colored communities will of course be under the control of colored school teachers, most of them will likely have colored principals, and these arrangements seem destined to meet general satisfaction."[30]

Bass's attempts to curtail interest in integration by improving black schools benefited teachers and students but failed to stop the push for integration. Most realized that the much-needed gains came only because of that threat. In following years the city would continue to improve black schools while it developed plans to hinder integration.

Nashville prided itself on its image as a progressive southern city. Black and white teachers received the same salaries, African Americans sat on the city council, and Nashville was the home of the nationally recognized Race Relations Institute at Fisk University. Yet that image of respectful race relations was fractured after black leaders pushed to force the board of education to implement the *Brown* decision and whites reacted violently. Anti-integrationist groups composed of parents, college professors, businesspeople, and politicians objected to integration. They were not alone. Throughout the South, white politicians, parents, and school officials engaged in concentrated efforts to disobey the edicts of the *Brown* decision. Scholars have termed the movement to disobey the Supreme Court's order as "massive resistance."[31]

By 1956 states all across the South had eradicated local NAACP chapters and evaded the *Brown* decision by enacting new laws and policies, using economic intimidation to threaten black parents and teachers, and looking the other way when segregationists resorted to terrorism. In the years after *Brown*, several states drew up "pupil placement" laws that used arbitrary factors such as morality, attitude, and other criteria to select students for a particular school. Oddly enough, black students never met the "criteria" necessary for white schools. Other states passed legislation to make it illegal to fund systems that desegregated. Some communities closed schools and offered white students grants from state governments in order to attend private schools and avoid compliance.[32]

Coyness Ennix objected to Nashville's instruction committee's 1957 decision to employ a gradual, grade-per-year approach. He wanted to "take three bites of the apple" and desegregate all elementary grades in one year, junior high school grades the next, and secondary grades in the third.[33] In the committee's plan, Nashville's black students could attend white schools starting with the first grade only.

African Americans composed a third of Nashville's thirty-seven thousand school-aged children. Yet the plan also included rezoning the city's school districts so only 155 of 1,409 black first-graders were zoned to white schools. Of that smaller group, 105 received transfers back to black schools. White first-graders zoned to attend black schools could request a transfer to white schools based on racial preference alone.[34] The Rempfers' two children could not participate because they were beyond first grade. After none of the city's white first-graders went to black schools, the *Nashville Globe and Independent* noted, "It was unfortunate that in our first experience with desegregation, no white youngsters were assigned to colored schools. Colored teachers had been alerted to deal kindly in a Christian spirit with the children assigned to them regardless of race. This has been emphasized in several in-service institutes."[35]

Before the fall of 1957 first-grade teachers and their principals attended board-sponsored conferences composed of small groups of black and white teachers, the first time the group had an opportunity to speak formally with one another about integration. They even ate lunch together. That small attempt to build bridges was a rare occurrence, though. After the meetings, when the school year began, teachers went back to their respective segregated schools.[36] Edna Benson, a white member of the board of education, added:

> The attitude of the teachers will be an important factor in preparing the parents of all children to accept and cooperate in the program. Integration to be successful must be gradual, well planned, and each person's feelings respected-so skillfully that they will sincerely feel "we did this ourselves." Considering the fact that beginner pupils usually go along with their older brothers and sisters for protection and the fact that Negro children and parents have pride in their own schools, wholesale shifts of children from Negro to white schools are unlikely. The ingenuity and ability of teachers will be put to more serious tests in integrated classes, but good teachers will accept the challenge and opportunity to improve their professional skills.[37]

In January 1957, U.S. District Judge William E. Miller accepted the board's proposal but ruled that it would have to develop a more comprehensive strategy to integrate subsequent grades by December 31. In response to a petition of six thousand Nashville parents and supporters filed by the Parents' School Preference Committee, a pro-segregationist organization, the board agreed to adopt the committee's plan. Three separate systems would be implemented, one for black students, one for whites, and another school system open to both. Parental preference would determine attendance. Anti-integrationists maintained that this plan granted the parents more freedom and choices for their children. The Tennessee General Assembly approved the plan as the Tennessee School Preference Act in March 1957, but the federal court dismissed it as unconstitutional on September 7, two days before school opened.[38]

In reality, integrating the white schools of Nashville was a trying and violent experience for the African American community. On September 9, 1957, their first day of school, nineteen black six-year-olds walked past angry mobs. Escorted by their parents and local civil rights activists, four of the nineteen were denied admission for administrative reasons. Fifteen black students were enrolling in six previously white elementary schools, so each had fewer than five black students. By the end of the school year only ten of the students remained in integrated schools.[39]

Many white Nashvillians responded aggressively. On the first day of school the police arrested three women for throwing bottles at the black parents and students. Some parents refused to send their children to school after receiving bomb and death threats. Others depended on older siblings to care for their younger children and could not send them to separate schools.[40]

Johnetta Hayes, then chair of the education committee of the Nashville NAACP and president of the Nashville Council of the Tennessee State Congress of Colored PTAs witnessed attempts to integrate as she accompanied parents and their children on that first day of school. "It was unbelievable coming from mature human beings," she remembers. "Crowds of jeering whites met us as we made our way to the school entrance. While policemen stood guard, white parents and their children vented their hate by striking out at the black parents and children."[41]

Although she was threatened, Rosemary Lewis, a former high school teacher, decided to continue to send her child to the all-white Fehr Elementary School. Lewis had recently moved from Pittsburgh and was unprepared for the hateful response she and her son, Calvin, enountered. "They just screamed all kinds of things," she recalls. "Some people would ask, 'Why do you want your child to go to school with mine? Niggers, go home. We'll get you later.' I was in awe of the hatred." Calvin's white teacher nervously told the bewildered boy that the crowd was there to welcome him. Despite the tensions outside the school, Calvin Lewis grew to adore his new teacher, who "stood her ground. She did what she was supposed to do as a good teacher."[42]

Violence escalated during the first days of the school year. Shortly after midnight on September 10 a bomb exploded in Hattie Cotton Elementary School, and all signs pointed to John Kasper, a white supremacist, as being responsible. Earlier that week the police had released Kasper on bond. He had became famous for inciting race riots in Clinton, Tennessee, after the desegregation of that city's white high school in 1956. Relocating to Nashville, Kasper threatened that bombings and lynchings could result if the city sought integration.[43]

No one was hurt from the explosion, but it destroyed part of the school building and resulted in $71,000 in damages and the school being closed for a week. The sole black student at Hattie Cotton did not return. After the bombing, Police Chief Douglass E. Hosse commented, "This has gone beyond a matter of integration. These [segregationists] people have ignored the laws and they have shown no regard for you [whites] or any citizen."[44] Local black ministers such as the activist Kelly Miller Smith responded to the outraged black community's call for retaliation by pointing out that "we can do what some of you want which is to fight them, and we can get a lot of our own people killed. Or we can go forward as planned and try to show them the right way."[45]

The bombing, however, may have hurt the cause of white supremacists more than it helped. Although local segregationists still vehemently opposed school integration and a conservative newspaper, the *Nashville Banner*, promoted Gov. Orval Faubus's defiant reaction to desegregation in Little Rock, Nashville's other newspapers and the city's officials did not wish to tarnish a so-called progressive reputation with violence. The all-white Nashville City Teachers Association, which previously offered little public support for integration, now submitted a resolution in support of the board's efforts. "We join the Board of Education," it stated, "in calling on all people of good will to assist us in making the adjustments in our schools that may be demanded by this monumental change."[46]

Kasper was convicted for disorderly conduct, vagrancy, loitering, and illegal parking. He completed his sentence at the city workhouse and was ordered to stay out of the desegregation process. Nashville's segregationists did not advocate school bombings and other acts of large-scale terrorism, but they still attempted to hinder desegregation efforts by harassing black students and petitioning government officials.[47]

As the integration process continued, members from the Congress of Racial Equality (CORE), NAACP, and the local black PTA initiated walking campaigns in black neighborhoods to encourage parents to send their children to white schools. The groups offered counseling and support, providing escorts for both parents and children. In addition, CORE, led by Anna Holden, a white sociologist and Fisk professor, worked to increase black enrollment in white schools. By the time the organization's members visited them before school began, some parents had already received threatening telephone calls and notes. After the bombing of Hattie Cotton School, CORE members attempted to comfort frightened parents and children by stressing that "the mob was in the minority." One said, "I think the fact that we were an interracial team, from the same organization, did more to influence them than anything else."[48]

Some black parents continued to feel vulnerable. Carl T. Rowan discussed the views of one anonymous parent who withdrew her child from an all-white school after the bombing and said she resented that "Negro professional people replaced segregationists on her phone," imploring her to keep the child in the white school. "I don't remember you offering to come by here and help stand guard," she told the callers. "There were thugs volunteering to guard some Negroes, but not a single doctor or dentist or professional man, not a teacher from Fisk or Meharry or Tennessee State offered us any help during the crisis. I suppose they were afraid someone would bomb their $30,000 homes."[49] Despite such complaints, CORE's membership did include a Meharry Medical School biochemist, a graduate student, and several ministers. The Rev. Kelly Miller Smith enrolled his daughter in a white school.[50] Perhaps the parent who complained thought that the professionals who called her considered integration more important than her child's safety and mental well-being.

In December 1957 the board filed the Parents' Preference Plan with the U.S. District Court, which would allow parents to decide whether their children attended black or white schools. Judge Miller, however, considered the plan too similar to the Tennessee School Preference Act and dismissed it. He mandated that the board develop a new plan that actually integrated schools in a timely fashion.[51] In March, a group of black leaders, including Kelly Miller Smith and Mrs. L. C. Reddick, president of the Nashville Council of Colored PTAs, submitted a letter to the board of education that advocated full school integration. "We feel," they asserted, "that it would benefit the community to accomplish desegregation as quickly as possible so that the process will not be dragged out over a long period of time keeping the public in a state of tension and confusion and giving those who are opposed to compliance a constant field of debate."[52]

In April 1958 the board returned with an extended version of its original gradual proposal, now called the Nashville plan, which integrated a new grade each subsequent year, beginning with the second grade in the fall. The federal court approved the amended plan on June 19, 1958, and thirteen more black second-graders went to white schools, bringing the total to twenty-three. Again, all fifty-five white children zoned to black schools transferred, and black schools remained segregated.[53]

"It seems to me," Roy Wilkins, executive secretary of the NAACP, wrote to Looby, "that both sides should give a little so that the full brunt of desegregation will not fall upon Negro school children's heads. . . . a Negro child who entered the first grade in 1956 will not be eligible to attend a desegregated school until 1968! This is a long time to wait to enjoy a right awarded by the United States Supreme Court in 1954. And some white people persist in saying that the Negroes want to go too fast."[54] The Nashville NAACP appealed the ruling to the U.S. Court of Appeals, Sixth Circuit, but the District Court upheld the Nashville plan a year later on June 17, 1959. Wilkins responded with much frustration:

> Some ultra-conservatives among us may argue that this is a start and we should accept it. . . . But it would be foolish for us, it seems to me, to consent to plans which under the camouflage language of compliance contain the ingredients for perpetuating a racially segregated system. Any plan which begins with the concept of "white" and "Negro" schools and virtually invites parents to maintain that concept is not a desegregation plan, no matter what introductory paragraphs are used to describe it, or the intentions of the board.[55]

The majority of Nashville's black students still sat in all-black classrooms and received instruction from African American teachers even as the national, state, and local debate raged concerning segregation and civil rights activism. The controversy was spurred on by the brutal murder of fourteen-year-old Emmett Till in Mississippi, the successful Montgomery bus boycott, and the desegregation crises in Clinton, Tennessee, and Little Rock, Arkansas.

While black parents, their children, and civil rights lawyers encountered white resistance, black teachers worked within segregated schools to provide an environment in which students could develop in a comfortable and protected all-black world. At a meeting of the Tennessee Education Congress in 1958, James E. Nabrit, a Howard University law professor, stated to the audience of five thousand teachers and administrators that "the fact that the Negro seeks absolute equality and no racial discrimination is not to imply that we wish to lose our identity as Negroes or our traditions." Teachers, he maintained, should teach black history, encourage young people to explore wider horizons, and ensure that students were prepared to adapt to a changing economy.[56] Standing on a foundation of uplift, some teachers thought their responsibility included educating boys and girls politically as well as academically. Jacqueline Jordan Irvine has demonstrated that black teachers practiced "other mothering" and considered helping black children as a way of advancing the race.[57]

Although some of Nashville's segregated schools were in dire need of repair and remained severely overcrowded, those who taught at them continued to create ways to make students proud of the facilities. They developed a process of community bonding or connection that defied the physical and the visible and placed more focus on psychological benefits garnered from attending school. Vanessa Siddle Walker has proposed in her study of a black North Carolina school during segregation that there was no "poverty of spirit" among faculty and students although the schools were severely underfunded.[58] As they passed through the schoolhouse doors, young black children entered an environment in which teachers knew their names, their families, and the specifics of their lives. The same might not be so at predominately white schools.

The teachers attempted to address the collective needs of African Americans by contributing financially to students and schools. Whether they petitioned the board for more material, supported PTA fund-raisers, or bought lunches and clothing for needy students, teachers and principals worked as advocates to help students and parents. As Alice Epperson, a 1962 graduate of Pearl, explains, "The instructors took personal time to enhance our education. I can remember Reverend Richard Ewing spending his summers with math sessions for students. Mrs. E. F. Walker, an English instructor, was very instrumental in encouraging people to write poetry, stories, and participating in a number of contests throughout the city."[59]

The teachers at Pearl and black educators elsewhere helped bolster school pride by supporting functions such as football games and proms and by sponsoring May Day celebrations, when children came dressed in their Sunday best and wrapped streamers around a flagpole. Black teachers took responsibility for creating programs and rituals that not only celebrated their schools but also reinforced the collective self-esteem of students.[60] Thelma Tears, who taught physical education, recalls the Friday co-recreation days at Pearl High School: "All of the classes would be combined and the kids would learn dances such as square dances and calypso. We taught them things that they were not getting [elsewhere]. The kids had to dress up. I saw kids' self-esteem rise so high. When kids dressed their best; they acted their best."[61]

A 1956 newspaper article described a "this is your life" tribute to Myrtle Thompson upon her retirement after thirty-two years. The account provided more evidence that bonds remained strong among black teachers, their students, and their communities. Thompson, a well-known and beloved staff member at Meigs Junior High School, was also active in several church and civic organizations:

> Mrs. Thompson all through her career was a joyful teacher, taking far more interest in her work than even what was required of her. Trips and tours with her pupils, both within the city and to other towns by train; radio broadcasts and other extra-curricular activities, all came under the alert teacher's supervision, much to the delight of her pupils, all of whom she really loved. . . . They [the principal and Thompson both] reciprocate their admiration for each other's devotion to the cause of efficient teaching and community betterment.[62]

As consumerism engulfed the United States during the 1950s African American students began to envision a world in which they could acquire the trappings of material success. Nashville's black educators also continued to underscore the importance of college and motivated students to attend by bringing them to local black colleges for exposure to campus life. Whether informing the students about various academic careers or showing them the kind of houses they could have one day, teachers provided information on how to make the best of opportunities.

Many students felt intense respect for their teachers. Charleene Spencer, for instance, recalled one of her favorites: "It is amazing how people play a part in your life. Ola Hudson [her home economics teacher] took us to restaurants. She wanted women to be self-sufficient. We had Inspiration Day. She and E. C. Reed held a career smorgasbord. One person that really impressed me was my history teacher, E. C. Reed. She used to take us to her home on weekends. She lived in Haynes Heights in a trilevel house. I thought she was the richest, prettiest woman I had ever seen."[63]

African American teachers in Nashville remained committed to racial uplift in all aspects of their work. Pearl High School history teacher Minerva Johnson Hawkins and others incorporated culturally relevant material to supplement daily classroom assignments. During the late 1940s and 1950s, when Tennessee provided scant material on African American history, she created her own curriculum, which included plays on the topic. When Hawkins's students staged a vignette about Reconstruction and the Ku Klux Klan, complete with costumes, the audience erupted in laughter when they saw the students' black hands protruding from Klan robes. It was then that Hawkins realized she had forgotten to tell the actors to wear gloves.[64]

In some cases teachers delved into students' personal lives in order to protect them. Sadie Madry recalls one child who did not want to go home with her mother's boyfriend. "This man came to get this little girl. This little girl didn't want to go home. He was not her father, but her mother's boyfriend." "I don't want to go home with him," the girl told her teacher, and Madry replied, "Get behind me." Then, she adds, "I picked up a stick and I said. 'Mister, if you touch this little girl, you are going to fall down those steps.' He reached anyway and I hit him with that stick. The police took the man away."[65]

Schools remained segregated, but Nashville teachers realized they had to prepare students to live in an integrated society in the future. In previous years, black communities called on teachers to help their children overcome the limitations of living in a segregated society. Now the teachers were responsible for preparing the children to take full advantage of a free nation without racial barriers. Johnetta King Williams, supervisor of Chattanooga's black schools, maintained in 1955 that along with the freedom and opportunities promised by *Brown* there were also new responsibilities: "You have to start young to teach them to love even before they are six or seven." Teachers, she added, must help their young students become "socially literate individuals."[66]

In 1954 more than eighty-two thousand black teachers were at work in segregated schools across the United States. Throughout the following decades they and black administrators suffered job loss, demotion, harassment, or displacement during the desegregation of the nation's schools. Those who lived in smaller cities and rural areas suffered most when their school boards decided to close black schools. Black principals across the South faced being demoted to vice principal or coach, and teachers sometimes received new, and lower-paying, jobs as library aides. They were also discriminated against in grade and classroom assignments.[67]

Some black teachers faced persecution if they belonged to the NAACP. Michael Fultz contends that southern legislatures wanted to break the bonds between teachers and that organization, which, as educated, middle-class professionals, the teachers ardently supported in defiance of racial arguments of white superiority.[68] The Nashville branch feared that Tennessee would enact new restrictions on its members similar to those passed in other states, yet the local NAACP was not to be broken. A successful campaign increased its life memberships from 286 in 1954 to 586 in 1955.[69]

When Morehouse College president Benjamin Mays addressed Nashville teachers at a July 1954 meeting of the American Teachers Association, he confidently argued, "If Negro teachers are competent, if they have tenure . . . then we will have jobs, and we will have schools in which to teach and students to teach."[70] Despite such reassurances, however, black teachers had every good reason to fear for their jobs. At the Middle Tennessee Negro Teachers' Association 1955 meeting in Nashville, the guest speaker, Adam Clayton Powell of New York, advised fighting to protect their positions. "Colored teachers of the South," he told them, "now know that even qualified teachers, even those who have met tests for teaching equally as hard as any white teachers, nevertheless are not assured of holding their positions on equality with white teachers."[71]

Tennessee had one of the strongest tenure laws in the nation. Educators who had performed several years of service did not have to be rehired annually, and they had protection from unfair firing. In 1955, however, the state legislature amended the tenure law so authorities had power to fire teachers deemed inadequate for integrated schools. The *Nashville Globe and Independent* saw clearly that "sudden whole-scale integration could cause discrimination because of the amendment to the teacher tenure law."[72]

Throughout the South, African Americans teachers found themselves under assault. In 1956, a Louisville, Kentucky, school superintendent attacked faculty integration by stating that black teachers, despite their greater experience and college training, were culturally inferior to white ones.[73] By 1957 African American teachers and principals in several states, including Oklahoma and Kentucky, had encountered job loss and harassment.[74]

Nashville teachers voiced their concerns at a state teachers' meeting in 1958. The *Nashville Globe and Independent* reported that they worried about having to be better than white teachers in order to receive equal treatment: "The teachers seem to be majoring in making doubly sure that if and when there is actual, unrestricted integration they themselves, will not be vetoed because of lack of preparation for their teaching jobs."[75] Black teachers knew they might be working at a white school. The token desegregation of several Kentucky school districts in 1957, when a hundred were sent to previously all-white schools, was not encouraging. Although the state labeled the reassignment a success, teachers reported mixed experiences. Some who taught high school were reassigned to elementary schools, those sent to high schools were placed as librarians, and others lost their jobs.[76]

Despite their support for black schools and love of the nurturing environment they had created within them, Nashville's African American teachers publicly endorsed integration. In an open letter to the Tennessee State Board of Education, the state teachers' association reported: "We have carefully noted and examined instances of integration within our state. The Tennessee Education Congress seeks to discover the best means of accomplishing with dispatch the goals of full citizenship as set fourth by our nation."[77]

A powerful segment of the black community, the teachers could have protested school integration and slowed or even halted that process. Instead, they supported the NAACP's efforts, although there were dissenters among them. In a survey of black teachers from other states, some educators suggested that "black leaders should curb their zest for democracy and their anticipation of martyrdom." The principal of the Ehrhardt Negro School in South Carolina, Lewis Butler, contended that "for the Negro teacher and children to be thrust into a most particular situation which will be beset with many perplexing problems and grave consequences, I am of the opinion that the Negro children's educational opportunities will suffer for the next fifty years."[78]

Nevertheless, Nashville's black teachers encouraged the NAACP and vigorously defended themselves as being capable of teaching in integrated schools. As one said, "We will be ready [to desegregate] whenever they are." The *Nashville Globe and Independent* added that they "were ready to make just as enlightened a record in serving the white youngsters assigned to them as any white teacher would make in serving colored children."[79]

Without support from black teachers the city's branch of the NAACP would have found it more difficult to seek desegregation. Although charismatic ministers, courageous student protesters, and voting rights' workers tend to receive the most credit for the civil rights movement of the 1950s and 1960s, educators were critical to the cause and supported the campaign in a host of ways, among them cooperation and sacrifice. As proponents of uplift, and as parents themselves, the educators were responsible for ensuring that black children could attend integrated schools.

Integration had made little headway in Nashville by the late 1950s despite the efforts of teachers, the NAACP, and the African American community. Strict zoning restrictions continued to block the enrollment of black students, segregationists harassed black parents and students, and African American schools improved each year. By the fall of 1958 only twenty-three black first- and second-graders were enrolled in white schools. The next year that number rose to forty-three black students. By the fall of 1960, there were 157 of some three thousand black students who attended desegregated educational institutions.[80]

The majority remained in segregated schools, but some, like the *Kelley* plaintiff and retired elementary school principal Albert Shaw, who was then a student at Tennessee A&I, joined the local civil rights movement. The failure of school integration led Shaw to the crusade. "I remembered back in 1955 when I tried to go to East High School," he says. "The 1954 decision should have integrated everything, but it didn't. I think it was just a matter of saying I am just tired that this decision was handed down and why hasn't Nashville done much with it. It is still totally segregated eight years after the decision. So I wanted to be a part of it."[81]

On February 13, 1960, more than 125 students from Fisk University, Tennessee A&I State College, Vanderbilt University, American Baptist Seminary, Meharry Medical College, and other schools staged sit-ins at three variety-store lunch counters in downtown Nashville. While local activists discussed several types of nonviolent direct action, the students were driven to act after a sit-in by four North Carolina Agricultural and Technical State College students on February 1. Soon the protests developed into a larger movement of sit-ins, marches, and boycotts to integrate the city's restaurants, businesses, and social settings.[82]

Many of the participants attended programs at Fisk University's Race

Relations Institute. In 1958, local ministers and student leaders formed the Nashville Christian Leadership Conference (NCLC) as a branch of Martin Luther King Jr.'s Southern Christian Leadership Conference. In 1959 the Rev. Kelly Miller Smith, and James Lawson, a nonviolent activist and Vanderbilt divinity student from Los Angeles, began holding workshops to coordinate small sit-ins to protest segregation in downtown businesses. Lawson taught the concept of nonviolence, wherein protest stems from a concept of Christian love rather than retaliation. In the workshops, students learned methods of nonviolent direct action and confrontation, a concept developed from the ideas of Gandhi as well as from Christian principles and used to challenge the moral authority of their oppressors even if doing so meant violating the law.[83]

The majority of the leaders of the Nashville student movement were from other cities. Some, such as Fisk student Diane Nash, hailed from midwestern or northern cities and were appalled at the pervasive prejudice in Nashville. Those from the Deep South, however, viewed that city differently. John Lewis who came from Alabama, and Marion Barry, who was born in Mississippi, considered Nashville as a place where racial progress could occur. They led sit-ins, but students native to Nashville participated as well. Leo Lillard recalls why he joined: "All the intellectuals or people who put the sit-ins together were from out of town. Being a Nashvillian, I felt I had clear obligations, clear reasons to put my body on the line, put my mind on the line. It was basically our movement; it was a city movement, even though students from out of town started it." Lawson added, "There was an esprit de corps among us. The students had publicly pledged themselves to a non-violent form of action in mind and spirit. They could rely on each other. They knew they were not alone."[84]

College students and ministers led the sit-ins, but high school and junior high school students participated as well. Virginia Westbrook recalls an unspoken understanding among the teachers and students at Washington Junior High School: "If the college students were going to be protesting, our kids would get up out of the classroom and join them and go downtown to where the protests were going to be. We did not punish them in any way and the board never said anything to us."[85]

As students increased their activism, white supremacists increased the amount of violence. On the morning of April 19, 1960, a bomb rocked the home of Z. Alexander Looby. Along with Avon Williams, Looby had rushed to help the activists by representing them in court and arranging bail.[86]

Their home was destroyed, but Looby and his wife were not hurt. Later that day, some three thousand demonstrators staged a silent march from Fisk downtown to the courthouse square. When they arrived at the courthouse, Diane Nash asked Mayor Ben West: "Do you personally think segregation is immoral?" He replied with honesty that he thought it wrong, and he also asked store owners to integrate.[87] Before the Looby home was bombed, activists had sponsored a successful boycott of downtown stores, beginning right before the Easter weekend. Due to the demonstrations, boycotts, and behind-the-scenes negotiations, on May 10, 1960, the downtown stores agreed to desegregate lunch counters.

At first some local students seemed content with segregated life in Nashville. Ruth Young, a high school biology teacher who was in college during this period, maintains that she did not experience overt prejudice until she began to work. In her world, which was completely segregated, everyone knew where they belonged:

> At TSU [Tennessee A&I] basically everything was all black. I didn't feel any pressures until I started to work. We had pressures from our own kind. We had only been in all black situations. When we rode the city bus everyone on the bus looked alike. A lot of things we needed were right on the campus. At the time, unless you were in a group, you knew that there were boundaries that you didn't cross. [Although] you knew you were prohibited and that angered you to a certain extent, you didn't fight unless you were in a group or crowd.[88]

Activists not from Nashville shook the complacency of some local blacks. The impatience and dissatisfaction with segregation that the outsiders expressed helped encourage students to transform the theory of democracy that their teachers espoused into a workable plan of action. They had absorbed the teachers' promotion of equality but rejected the quiet and subtle methods of their elders. They devised their own plans for change.

Some black teachers agreed with the tenets of the students' movement but not its tactics. Although outwardly conservative, they could not continue to be nonviolent. One teacher, Thelma Tears, claims she would not have been able to accept abuse and punishment from whites. "I did not participate in the civil rights movement," she recalls. "I didn't have the temperament. Those kids trained to learn nonviolence. I think if someone spat on me, I would have spat on him or her back. I was grateful to them. My daughter marched."[89] Being denigrated, insulted, or physically assaulted could have

cracked the veneer of middle-class respectability that the black women teachers assumed, to expose their hurts and make them seem like everyone else.
They could endure discriminatory conditions in the workplace, but some
refused to accept personal abuse by whites without retaliation.

Other teachers were concerned about the risks involved in overt participation, particularly when they perceived the activists' goals as ill-defined and
short-term. Many friends of Donzell Johnson, who taught high school history, were active, but he did not personally advocate sit-ins or marches. A war
veteran who paid his own way through Fisk, Johnson was more concerned
with practical matters such as graduation and financial stability. Charleene
Spencer, who attended Tennessee A&I in the late 1950s and early 1960s,
remembers,

> Lots of people got hurt doing dangerous things. I supported them. I told my
> roommate [a marcher] that I would contribute to her trip [freedom ride].
> I made Kool-Aid and hosted sleep-overs for the marchers. I thought they
> were brave. I just wanted to know after the march were they going to tutor
> [children] so that [they] could make the same grade as [whites] on the ACT?
> What were the economic advantages? I lost friendships because I didn't get
> on the bus. I was never quite sold on the [freedom] ride. I needed verifica-
> tion that it was lasting.[90]

After the *Brown* decision, universities such as Fisk were determined to
prepare students to take advantage of new educational and employment
opportunities.[91] The university never advocated breaking the law, but according to Minerva Johnson Hawkins, who was married to Fisk's treasurer
during the 1950s and 1960s, the university president sent her husband to
post bail for Fisk and Tennessee A&I students who had been arrested. In
May 1960 the *Nashville Globe and Independent* published a letter from the
Fisk faculty, which affirmed, "We support the students who have participated
in recent non-violent sit-in demonstrations at lunch counters in Nashville.
. . . We deplore any academic community which through the threat or use
of suspension or expulsion of students restricts the civil rights of students
who are protesting in peaceful ways against racial discrimination."[92]

Although Fisk University's professors openly supported the protesters, some activists criticized the positions of other universities and their
faculties. As Diane Nash asserted, "The Negro who has received several
college degrees or who has a profession and who can consider himself a
successful and important man will still attest to his own inferiority by coop-
erating with segregation. Why are the faculty members and administrators

of southern Negro colleges not on the picket lines and sitting at the lunch counters?"[93]

Despite Nash's remonstrance, local black residents, including teachers, participated in the movement in their own fashion. Albert Shaw maintained that movement leaders discouraged teachers from demonstrating because they could lose their jobs. Teachers not only feared unemployment but also were deeply concerned about the possibility of violent mistreatment of their students. In addition, they worried about the possibility of being humiliated by whites. They served as communication specialists, meeting organizers, and drivers and also provided financial support. Myra Dixon, a reading specialist, worked part time on Tennessee A&I's campus during the sit-ins and with other teachers provided rides to the activists or sponsored refreshment stands. "I was more or less as I am now a person who counsels and supports," Dixon maintains. "I thought it was a beautiful thing to see them work aggressively as they did." Novella Davis, a librarian at Pearl High School during the movement, recalled her experiences:

> My husband was at Tennessee State and those kids were really into it. He sponsored the student council. We used to transport kids to secret places and have meetings in our house. We faced danger. We had just taken some kids to First Baptist Church and a group of whites in a truck threw rocks. A lot of them [students] got hurt. We went back and picked them up. It was a terrible time. Our children stayed inside the house. People didn't go outside because whites would come through and do things particularly to those people who were seen with the kids.[94]

In April 1960 the members of the Women's Unity League, a middle-class organization to which several teachers belonged, sponsored "Freedom Sunday" talent shows to raise money for the demonstrators' legal defense fund.[95]

Leaders of the civil rights movement and local desegregation activists pushed consistently for African Americans to gain access to white schools, business establishments, and social settings, but most African American female teachers did not risk their status by taking a more active role in that cause. In large part they held back because teaching was one of the few professional and social arenas in which black women had power. Some provided for their families economically, and a loss of employment would have thrust their loved ones into poverty. Integration of local businesses and retail establishments could result in greater economic and social opportunities for Nashville's black middle-class students, but it could also have a negative impact for professional teachers.

Although there was no incidence of teachers being fired due to civil rights participation, LaMona Prince McCarter described the reaction of her mother, a teacher, when her sister asked to march: "The civil rights movement in Nashville started in my junior high school years. My sister asked my mother if she could participate. But because my mother was a teacher, [and] teachers were held in high regard; maybe her job would be at stake. She said that protest was just one avenue; you can do some of your best work by being a good student. She did feel that they would say, 'look at Mrs. Prince's child, Mrs. Prince's daughter was seen out of school,' and her job would be lost from our participation."[96] Unlike African American women teachers, Ruth Young adds, others who participated in the movement had little to lose: "It was real interesting. They tried to use those people that would not be affected such as students, ministers, and blacks who had their own private businesses."[97]

The young activists did, however, inspire Virginia Westbrook and another black teacher to engage in their own personal sit-in: "A fellow teacher and I went downtown and ordered an ice cream cone at a downtown lunch counter even though I could see the newspaper headlines, 'City Teacher Fired for Requesting a Cone of Ice Cream at the Five and Dime.' After we got our ice cream, we sat down at the counter. The girl didn't know what to do. She told us, 'You can't sit here.' I said, Why what's wrong with the chair? I'm fine.' As if I didn't know what she was talking about. Meanwhile we were still licking the ice cream. She asked, 'Why are you still sitting here? I will have to call the police.' We finished, and we left and we didn't pay our dime."[98]

Teachers, moreover, used their economic power to seek freedom. Dorothy Baines first moved to Nashville in the midst of the boycotts. "Those students had guts," she recalls. "I don't know if I could have done it. [During the boycott] I didn't know what was going on. We went into Cain Sloan [department store] to go upstairs. Outside there was a bunch of students who had signs. We came out of the store out of respect for them."[99]

Some activists believed teachers did little to promote civil rights and that they actually advocated for Jim Crow. Although some of Nashville's public school teachers seemed content to remain in their segregated world and refused to risk losing their positions because of open protests, their efforts to motivate, sustain, and support students suggest deep engagement with the movement. They may not have rallied to sit-in and march with students, but they often provided bail or paid attorney fees. Furthermore, by instructing students in the importance of democracy, self-worth, and community value, teachers helped instill the ideals of equality and freedom that the pupils endeavored to put into practice throughout Nashville and the rest of the South.[100]

Although the Nashville student movement successfully desegregated the city's downtown stores, in 1960 only 189 of approximately four thousand African American students attended white schools. In the surrounding Davidson County, the school system was even worse, and there was no formal desegregation plan. The failure to implement public school integration in Davidson County led Henry C. Maxwell, a farmer, to file suit in 1960 against that county's board of education after his two sons and five other black students were refused enrollment at the all-white Antioch and Glencliff High Schools. The federal court ordered Davidson County to integrate grades first through fourth immediately and then to desegregate one grade a year in accordance with the Nashville plan.[101] Nashville and the surrounding Davidson County merged in 1963 to create the Metropolitan Nashville–Davidson County government, and the county and city school systems combined in 1964. Black desegregation activists also decided to combine the *Kelley* and *Maxwell* cases.[102]

By 1964, after four years of nonviolent sit-ins at restaurants, stand-ins at movie theaters, and sleep-ins at hotels, most of the city's businesses had integrated. As the outward appearances of legal segregation were eliminated, white and black professional teachers' organizations combined.[103] The impetus for integration, however, did not lie with African Americans. The two white teacher associations representing educators from city and county schools wished to merge with their black counterparts in order to gain unity in the new consolidated metropolitan government. With consolidation, teachers in Nashville and Davidson County would earn the same beginning salaries. The teachers also wanted a professional growth program.[104]

Some members of Nashville's African American teachers' associations, however, wanted to retain their professional organizations. Apprehensive, they feared that an integrated organization would not fight for black children. They also thought they would lose power and leadership and that their ideas would be ignored. In addition, African American teachers had little reason to expect fairness from their white counterparts. In earlier years, when blacks tried to join the teachers' credit union, they received discourteous and discriminatory treatment. Under pressure from the white associations, however, they did agree to merge. In 1964 the four groups—the City Teachers Association for white teachers, the Middle Tennessee Negro Teachers Association, the white Davidson County Education Association, and the black Davidson County Educators Congress—became the Metropolitan Nashville Education Association (MNEA) by a vote of 2,817 to 169. In 1967 the state teachers' associations combined as well.[105]

During the 1960s the *Brown* decision sparked changes in the circumscribed but comfortable world of black teachers, transforming both professional and personal lives. Once holding a great deal of control in their professional worlds, they now had to abandon their advocacy organization and form a unified front with white teachers who were once their nemeses. Nevertheless, the teachers consented to the merger because they did not want to be perceived as segregationists. "We felt we had no choice," explains Virginia Westbrook.[106]

Although African Americans often lost leadership positions after the mergers they worked to promote the larger goals of the organizations and also tried to protect themselves from discrimination and promote their own interests. Ola Hudson, a former home economics teacher, shared why she joined the MNEA: "You may be an excellent teacher, but the day you join a professional association, you become a consummate professional. The association allows you to grow and opens up new avenues and new ways of doing things."[107]

Ironically, as the civil rights movement celebrated the successful passage of the Civil Rights Act of 1964, some young black Nashvillians began to absorb the tenets of black power and decided to abandon the ideology of nonviolence. In 1964 Pearl High School students and city police engaged in a violent altercation after a protest march, and three years later, in 1967, a riot erupted after a fiery speech by Stokely Carmichael at Vanderbilt University.[108] In response, Avon Williams asserted, "Stokely Carmichael should stay out of here and our people and our community will be better off." But, he added, "At the same time, part of the trouble was the result of the blindness of the white people who have refused for months to see trouble coming."[109] Two years later, in 1969, Rose Park Junior High School teacher J. C. Garrett maintained that black power was the "coming together and pooling of resources to govern those things in the black community which affect the black man. It does not mean separatism."[110]

Although the ideals of black power were discussed in the city, the majority of black leaders still advocated nonviolence. Activists generally worked within the system and behind the scenes to address issues of institutionalized racism. Unlike Birmingham and other southern cities, Nashville desegregated relatively peacefully, and what local leaders termed the "Nashville way" of calm protest was emulated across the South.[111]

Yet the schools had no Nashville way, only the Nashville plan. In 1966, after repeated challenges from the NAACP, the Metropolitan Nashville–Davidson County Board of Education abandoned the "grade-a-year" plan and began to integrate all grades. That had little impact, however, on school demographics. The board did not call for children to be transported from segregated neighborhoods to those in other areas, and the vast majority of black and white parents refused to send their children to school with people of other races.[112] Several years earlier, in 1959, in Washington, D.C., at the Youth March for Integration, some twenty thousand students from across the United States called for enforcement of the *Brown* decision and civil rights legislation, yet there were no local mass demonstrations in Nashville to achieve racially desegregated schools. In later years, ironically, blacks would protest to preserve African American institutions.[113]

In 1968 the assassination of Martin Luther King Jr. in Memphis led to rioting in Nashville as well as in several other cities. Black teachers watched as some of their students responded violently and their community's lawyers fought to make changes that would later alter their destiny. They may have remained in the background while their students stormed out of classrooms to protest, but their behind-the-scenes efforts contributed to the movement's success. The barriers to integrating city schools seemed insurmountable, considering a school board and a community that refused to dismantle segregated schools. Nashville's black teachers responded by keeping on doing their jobs in familiar surroundings. They prepared students to live in an integrated society, but some teachers were not ready for the changes that occurred when they had to function in desegregated schools.

FOUR

"The Only Way We Fought Back Was to Do a Good Job": Public School Integration

When Gwendolyn Vincent arrived at Rosebank Elementary School, a predominately white suburban facility, in the late 1960s she noticed that there were ample supplies of pencils, paper, and books for the children on the first day. "At the black schools," she recalls, the story was quite different. Teachers there had to wait "almost two months before people had what they needed to work with. I couldn't believe [that] in the supply room you could get all the things you need. If a window was broken at Rosebank [her new school], you just had to make one phone call and it was fixed." Although she appreciated the comfort of having materials readily available she felt under intense pressure to succeed. As one of the first African American teachers at Rosebank, she remembers nervous white parents who watched through the classroom doorway. "There were anxieties. Everyone was looking. I had the motivation not only to be prepared, but also to be on my toes."[1]

Vincent's experience at Rosebank Elementary is just one of the stories of the almost 2,500 African American teachers from 1964 to 1971 who integrated into the Nashville school system's teaching staff. As the federal courts directed Nashville's Metropolitan–Davidson County school system to send teachers into unfamiliar surroundings it later called for children to ride buses as part of a new plan to achieve the dream of racial integration. Desegregation, with its opportunities to learn in new environments and make friends across racial lines, affected the city's children, and it also redefined black teachers' roles as workers, status in the community, and identities as women and professionals.

By the late 1960s, Nashville civil rights activists had put down their protest signs after the successful desegregation of downtown restaurants and businesses.[2] Although they waged persistent court battles to desegregate city schools, the board of education had been the victor since the *Kelley* case in 1955. Its plan, which included a gradual phase-in of integration, successfully met federal requirements and simultaneously prevented wholesale desegregation of area schools.[3]

In 1964, the same year as the merger of the Nashville City and Davidson County Boards of Education, John Harris, director of schools for Metropolitan Nashville–Davidson County, quietly called for volunteers and later began to ask certain teachers to work in schools populated by students of the opposite race, either white or African American. Several of the first volunteers taught in the Nashville Education Improvement Project, a five-year pilot program sponsored by the Ford Foundation designed to help "culturally deprived" poor children develop reading skills.[4] Three African Americans, Alyce McDowell, Dorothie Beasley, and Hattie Tears, went to work at white elementary schools, and one white teacher, Jean Smedley, was hired at an African American school.[5]

Although there was no official board policy, the four women had to meet the highest criteria regarding academic achievement, credentials, and classroom experience. Some African American teachers believed the board selected not only the best applicants but also those whose appearance whites would find less threatening. Helen Anne Mayes, another black teacher who volunteered to go to a white school in 1967, maintains that color and class distinctions were part of the board's decision. "They came right down the color scale with those first transfers," she contends. "I have a cousin with blond hair and blue eyes, and she was the first one sent to a white school. Even the custodian didn't know she was black." Then, Mayes adds, "They started getting us a little browner."[6]

The teachers' welcomes ranged from hellos to icy stares. In the late 1960s the board granted Virginia Westbrook permission to transfer from all-black Washington Junior High School to all-white Apollo Junior High School.[7] Westbrook had almost twenty years of teaching experience at Washington when she applied for the transfer and was also married to a college professor. That combination of qualities made her a good candidate in the eyes of the

board. Some children of teachers and other African American professionals attended Washington, which was located near Fisk University in north
Nashville, but many black children from poor families were pupils there as
well. Westbrook often spent her own funds to help students. Emotionally
exhausted, she volunteered to teach at a white school because she wanted
to work in an environment where a teacher had fewer responsibilities outside the classroom. As she explained, "My son didn't want me ever to go to
Apollo. He said the kids at Washington School needed me. I had twenty
years there and I was tired of buying Easter shoes and lunches. I was not only
the teacher, but also the mother. I had my life of that, fighting for equality,
never winning."[8]

In 1968 Roberta Jackson applied for a job in the Metropolitan Nashville
school system. Because of her knowledge of a new technique for teaching the
alphabet she was soon offered, and then hired to fill, a vacated position at
the predominately black Head Elementary School. As the only white teacher
on the faculty, she sought advice from other teachers and soon formed close
friendships with them. After the assassination of Martin Luther King Jr.,
they all "walked hand in hand across the glass-strewn parking lot to our cars
for safety."[9]

When Albert Shaw was a student teacher at Wharton School in the early
1960s, students sensed his inexperience and attempted to take advantage.
In 1968, when one of the two new white teachers resigned from Wharton
because he could not control his rambunctious class, Shaw agreed to help
the remaining teacher by serving as her "protector." He would stand at the
door of her classroom and warn that students who misbehaved would have
to deal with him. The strategy seemed to work, and the teacher stayed.[10]

By 1969, after five years of voluntary faculty desegregation, more than 97
percent of Metropolitan Nashville schools had mixed-race faculties. At best,
however, this was token integration. Fifty-six of 115 white schools had two to
four black teachers, thirty-eight schools had only one, and twenty-one had
no blacks at all. Only five of eighteen African American schools employed
white teachers. Four black schools had four white faculty members each, and
Elliot Elementary School had only one.[11] In Metropolitan Nashville's 142
schools that same year, 11,468 of 23,049 blacks attended formerly all-white
schools but only 376 of 18,893 whites went to previously all-black ones.[12]

A year earlier, in 1968, the Supreme Court ruled in *Green v. County Board
of New Kent County, Virginia* that freedom of choice plans placed unfair burden on black children to transfer. School districts, the Court declared, must

dismantle segregation by "root and branch," which meant desegregating the entire system, including faculties.[13] In 1968, in *Alexander v. Holmes County Board of Education*, the Court also decided that schools in Holmes County, Mississippi, had to undergo immediate desegregation and that the county had to operate a unitary or racially balanced education system.[14] Drawing on the *Green* ruling, the U.S. Fifth District Court, in *Singleton v. Jackson Municipal Separate School District*, established the "Singleton ratio," which ordered desegregation based on the percentage of blacks and whites in a district. If a school system was 80 percent white and 20 percent black, then every school was mandated to have that same white-to-black student ratio. The Court furthered these decisions in *U.S. Supreme Court v. Montgomery Board of Education* by reversing an Alabama Court of Appeals ruling and calling for immediate integration of educational faculties.[15]

Standing on the legal precedents set by these rulings, Avon Williams Jr., now a Tennessee state senator, argued on the behalf of the plaintiffs in *Kelley*, most of whom were adult, that schools remained segregated. Williams believed that the board of education's plan to construct large comprehensive-vocational high schools in Nashville's suburbs reinforced segregation and white flight by offering white students the opportunity to attend new schools.[16] There were no plans to remodel or construct inner-city schools for black students. On November 6, 1969, Williams requested that District Court Judge William Miller place a temporary restraining order and halt the Metropolitan Nashville school system from new construction until it submitted a full-scale desegregation plan to achieve a unitary school system. Judge Miller found in favor of the *Kelley* plaintiffs. He ordered the board to develop a new plan, denied new school construction funds, and suspended the case to wait for the Supreme Court's impending ruling in *Swann v. Charlotte–Mecklenburg County, North Carolina*.[17]

After Williams's successful appeal to the Sixth U.S. Circuit Court of Appeals for Miller to lift the stay, in July 1970 the judge, citing the fact that Metropolitan Nashville's school zones hindered desegregation, ordered the board to submit a plan within thirty days for the complete desegregation of students and faculty for the upcoming 1970–71 school year. Using the wording of *Montgomery*, he ruled, "It is well recognized that faculty and staff integration is an important aspect of the basic task of achieving a public school system wholly free from racial discrimination. In order to implement this mandate, the court concludes that in the instant case [*sic*] faculties must be fully integrated."[18]

Filed on August 19, the board's new plan included new school zoning areas, construction, student and faculty integration.[19] Following the Singleton ratio, every Metropolitan Nashville school now had to have a faculty that was approximately 20 percent African American and 80 percent white, which was similar to the district's racial population. After teachers submitted three school preferences, the board then reviewed teacher's subject area, age, grade-level experience, and present school assignment before placing the teacher.[20] The board transferred 1,164 out of 4,010 teachers in 1970 and reassigned 1,240 more the following year.[21] African American teachers made up the majority of transfers.

To facilitate the process, the Metropolitan Nashville school system received a federal Emergency School Assistance Act (ESAA) grant of $565,000 to help hire staff and develop material to facilitate the desegregation process. Congress created the ESAA in 1970 to offer funding for programming and materials in newly desegregated schools. To help teachers adjust, they were offered a one-day summer workshop on August 24, at which principals offered orientations for their respective schools.[22] In-service workshops dealing with faculty integration were developed later, but the August workshop covered the usual adjustment issues and offered little advice for teachers transferring to new environments.[23]

As the Metropolitan Nashville Board of Education accepted the mandate to integrate faculties it also sought an acceptable plan to exclude busing. In the fall of 1970 the board hired five education consultants to help develop the plan. The key component of the Building and School Improvement Study (BASIS) was development of "great" or comprehensive high schools. Such schools, the study suggested, would facilitate desegregation by offering a multitude of attractive courses and programs and enrolling students from smaller African American and white secondary schools. Those smaller high schools would then close and later reopen as middle schools. Judge Miller accepted the board's plan for faculty integration but delayed student desegregation until the board could bring in a more feasible plan. After reviewing the board's two plans in December, Judge L. Clure Morton, who replaced Miller as the presiding judge after he received an appointment to the Sixth Circuit Court of Appeals, dismissed them as "only a token effort." Morton then asked the Department of Health, Education, and Welfare (HEW) to design a new plan.[24]

After Judge Morton took this action, Nashville City Councilman Casey Jenkins, an antibusing spokesperson, led an angry pack of more than five hundred white parents to protest at the HEW hearings. After they blocked the courthouse doors for several hours and only a few protesters were arrested, NAACP attorney Williams complained, "What would have happened if this had been a black mob? They would have called the National Guard." Some 2,500 enraged white parents had met the night before at War Memorial Auditorium to voice outrage over the new plans.[25]

Jenkins sponsored an antibusing resolution in the council and urged whites to keep their children away from schools. "Busing deprives us of our freedom of expression, of our freedom of hope, of our freedom of choice, of our property rights, and our civil rights, and we will not stand busing of our children to create racial balance," Jenkins announced. "Busing is not a problem between black or white. Busing is not a problem of integration or desegregation. Busing is discrimination against all the people."[26] Other protests included a March 16 meeting at which nine hundred people signed a petition to "stop the busing of children out of their environment." The day before, parents who lived in neighboring Madison had decided to boycott their schools, and 43 percent of the pupils there were absent.[27]

Amid the chaos the HEW team continued to review the board's plan. In April 1971 the Supreme Court ruled in *Swann v. Charlotte-Mecklenburg County, North Carolina* that public school systems could use busing to achieve racial balance.[28] Issued during a conservative backlash in the Nixon-led federal government, *Swann* attempted to eliminate the effects of neighborhood segregation on school desegregation. Several school systems, including Nashville and Charlotte, offered plans that placed the burden on the individual who wanted to attend a desegregated school, and little actual integration resulted. *Swann* allowed school systems to bus children away from their neighborhoods and attend schools with children of other races. Of course, white and black students had been bused for decades to attend segregated schools not within walking distance, but now they would travel solely to achieve racial balance. *Swann* also called for pairing or clustering black and white schools and incorporated earlier rulings that held that each school should have a racial composition similar to the school district as a whole.

With clear directions from the Supreme Court, the HEW team decided to adopt measures similar to those recommended in Charlotte for Metropolitan Nashville's school system in the 1971–72 academic year. Finally, some seventeen years after the *Brown v. Board* decision, the school system implemented a desegregation plan that affected both African American and white students.[29]

Under the HEW plan, black children in grades one through four would be bused to suburban schools and white fifth- and sixth-graders would attend formerly black, inner-city schools. Junior high school and high school attendance zones would be redrawn to produce a racially balanced student body; 25 percent of each school would be African American, and there would be no black student majorities. The plan excluded thirty-three schools on the county's outer fringes at distances deemed too far to transport students.

After reviewing the board's new rezoning plan and dismissing the *Kelley* plaintiffs' proposal to implement countywide desegregation, on June 28, 1971, Judge Morton approved HEW's plan for elementary and junior high school grades and the board's revised plan for senior high school grades. To appease the NAACP plaintiffs, Morton decided that the school system could not construct any new schools intended for a proposed black population of less than 15 percent.

Although Casey Jenkins was on the frontlines of protests, few public officials approved of busing. The *Nashville Banner*, for instance, editorialized that "Busing to Create Racial Balance in Public Schools Is Not Required by Law and Is Opposed by the Congress, by the President, and by the People." Mayor Beverly Briley, moreover, expressed outrage over the plan and refused to support increased taxes to pay the more than $2 million needed for new buses.[30]

Despite the vitriolic outbursts of angry parents, Nashville's citizens attempted to reestablish the city's progressive reputation by reelecting the more moderate Mayor Briley over Jenkins in a run-off. Although he still opposed busing, Briley promised to uphold the judge's order in an effort to distance himself from his militant opponent. The mayor even went to the city council for more money for buses, but the council refused, and the federal government denied the Metropolitan Nashville school system's requests for funding for buses from the Emergency School Assistance Act, which had granted millions of dollars to Nashville and school systems across the South since 1970. Nevertheless, President Richard Nixon disagreed with the programs' focus on busing and cut its funding. Judge Morton ordered the school system to add thirty more buses to the 193 in use. Only eighteen were acquired, and school starting times were staggered so buses could make multiple trips.[31]

After the Supreme Court refused to hear the board's appeal of Morton's decision in August, Jenkins, now leader of the Concerned Parents Association, held another antibusing rally in September and called for thousands of parents to boycott schools. He later urged them to picket on opening day.

On September 15, 1971, almost two hundred yellow school buses rolled down Nashville's highways and streets to transport more than forty-four thousand students for the first day of school. When the black students stepped off buses at forty-one of the system's schools they were greeted with shouts of "go home Niggers" from white parents and other protesters.[32] Unlike cities such as Boston, Massachusetts, and Pontiac, Michigan, where white parents pelted children with rocks and vandalized buses, there was no large-scale physical violence in Nashville, but tension ran high nonetheless.[33]

White parents objected to sending their children to dilapidated, educationally inferior, and possibly dangerous inner-city black schools with children of supposedly different cultural values. Some especially feared sending their daughters to school with black boys, whether the supposed results were violent or sexual. Others complained of inconvenience when their children could no longer attend a neighborhood school.[34] As one white mother in Nashville put it, "I moved there so that my children would be only one block from school, and then they were put on buses. Busing is horrible—especially for working mothers."[35]

Most parents did not object to integration in the abstract but did not want their children to suffer for a social experiment. Goldie Sinor, another white Nashville mother, lamented, "My daughter drives a Metro school bus and takes black children from their neighborhood into the white neighborhood. In the meantime, her own children are being picked up by buses and carried into the black neighborhoods—and her five children are going off in all directions."[36]

Avon Williams and the other lawyers for the *Kelley* case supported the plan but pointed out that it placed too much responsibility on blacks because only young African American children were being bused for the early grades and several black schools were being closed. Although most black Nashvillians were behind Williams's fight for desegregation, one mother explained, "There were so many things they did not have in their schools that the white schools had—like certain books that the white schools had and that the black schools couldn't even get. Negroes have been riding buses for a long time."[37] Some of Nashville's black parents disapproved of busing because they thought their children would bear the heaviest burdens of desegregation. The new plan enabled them to send their children to state-of-the-art schools, but some students had to catch their bus at 6:15 A.M. in order to attend a facility sometimes more than ten miles away.[38]

As picketing continued, the African American teachers who worked in white schools prepared to meet new students and colleagues. Sometimes they encountered negative feelings toward busing from white educators. Virginia Westbrook recalls that the assistant principal at Apollo led public prayer at an antibusing rally.[39] As the buses carrying young African American children drove up to Paragon Mills Elementary School, formerly all-white, one of the first black teachers at the institution, Mary Alice Goldman, ran from her class to escort the young boys and girls into the building. She did so amid a crowd of angry whites and against the wishes of her principal. Such incidents reinforced black teachers' fears. Although they labored consistently to dispel negative stereotypes about themselves, they also worried that white teachers might mistreat African American students. "We learned," Goldman says, "that children knew how to identify people. [They could] tell us just as well the white people who were genuine from those who were phony."[40]

Several "genuine" white teachers did their best to alleviate fears. Colleen Whitver, who transferred to Pearl Senior High School in 1970, maintains that she and her white colleagues wanted African American students to feel equal and special and tried to "recognize kinships rather than differences." Roberta Jackson, a former primary grade teacher, also attempted to dispel black parents' anxieties by frequently hugging her first-graders. Mary Driscoll, who taught English, remembers stories of white instructors who placed black students in the back of classrooms, but she vowed to integrate the seating in her room.[41]

After a few days many parents put down picket signs and protested by removing their children from the system. Although social science researcher James Coleman wrote a groundbreaking study in the late 1960s that civil rights lawyers used to support desegregation and busing, by 1975 he had changed his tune.[42] In the latter book he caused controversy when he contended that busing for desegregation led to white flight and resegregation. His findings proved true in Nashville. In the first ten years of full desegregation there, white flight, the increase in private schools, and low birth rates led to a 24,717 decline in white student enrollment by 1981.[43]

The carefully designed ratios and percentages in the school system's desegregation plan only worked if whites attended the schools. Over the years, however, white parents, both in Nashville and across the nation, expressed hatred of busing by relocating to the suburbs or enrolling their children in

Table 2. Total Enrollment of Metropolitan Nashville–Davidson County Public Schools, 1970–81

School Year	Whites	Blacks	Others	Total	Percent Black
1970–71	68,421	21,525	—	88,996	23.9
1971–72	70,481	22,519	—	83,000	24.2
1972–73	58,183	21,697	—	79,880	27.2
1973–74	55,729	21,326	—	77,052	27.7
1974–75	53,471	21,227	—	74,698	28.4
1975–76	51,804	21,065	—	72,869	28.9
1976–77	49,721	20,816	—	70,537	29.5
1977–78	45,942	20,634	—	68,802	30.2
1978–79	45,942	20,634	—	64,576	31.0
1979–80	43,888	20,391	—	64,279	31.7
1980–81	45,252	22,725	860	68,827	33.0

Source: Metropolitan Nashville–Davidson County Schools.

newly established private schools. In Memphis city schools, white enrollment fell from 48.2 percent in 1970 to 21.8 percent in 1987; Atlanta recorded a decline from 55 percent in 1961 to 18 percent in 1970; and Houston's white student population fell from 50 percent in 1970 to 17 percent in 1975.[44] Nashville's North High School, once predominately white, became predominately black in the early 1970s after the white students fled. Although the populations of resegregated schools remained black, their faculties did not.

A year before the busing controversy erupted, thousands of Nashville teachers received letters directing them to report to new schools. The massive transfer reflected similar efforts at faculty desegregation throughout the country as school systems attempted to comply with court-ordered desegregation plans. Both black and white teachers left their segregated surroundings to work in new schools. Some, such as Iola Taylor in Austin, Texas, transferred to schools where many students were Mexican American. The teachers had to adjust to a different environment and also had to become fluent in another language. Taylor has described how she felt when she received notice of the transfer: "I think they never ever took the vantage point of at least talking to you, encouraging you, making some type of support commitment to you. You never got that: you just got a letter. I don't know if they did that with Anglo teachers."[45]

In other cities, many black teachers lost their jobs after districts closed black schools. According to Michele Foster and an HEW study of the period, between 1968 and 1971 more than a thousand black teachers across the nation lost their jobs and five thousand more white teachers were hired.[46] In

1971 the HEW amended its 1966 guidelines for faculty desegregation to stress that demotions and dismissals of African Americans would result in federal investigation. Nashville's black high school teachers were not fired as were those in smaller cities or rural areas, but they, like hundreds of others, were moved to new positions as junior high school and elementary school instructors.[47]

Some, such as Anne Lenox, a former guidance counselor who was assigned to teach junior high school mathematics, protested the demotions or reassignments. Others left the system.[48] Most African American teachers, whether eager to escape the financial burdens of racial uplift or protective of their jobs and roles as supporters of the African American community, however, did not openly resist the mandate to transfer. Lillian Dunn Thomas recalls complying with sorrow: "We really liked one another so well that when they integrated we got sick. We didn't want to part. The children were so lovely, and I have letters saying, 'We sure hate to see Mrs. Thomas leave.'"[49]

Nashville's white citizens did not protest faculty integration with large rallies, but some black teachers received threatening telephone calls. "They got all of the names and telephone numbers [of some transferring teachers] and harassed us," recalls Sadie Madry. The voices proclaimed, "Hi nigger! Nigger you are not going to teach my boy! I am going to kill you nigger." The police, moreover, were little help. "We were told," Madry says, sadly, "there was nothing we [the police] could do about it." When she and other African Americans requested aid, they were advised, "You have fathers and brothers? Have them sit in your yard at night." During that period, Madry observes, "Black teachers worked together. We did our part. We didn't fight back with them. The only way we fought back was to do a good job. I figured if I did a good job, it was better than fighting with a knife. We were going to do a good job come hell or high water."[50] Ossie Trammel, who taught kindergarten, remembers an angry caller threatening that she "better not come over to that white school."[51] Nevertheless, most of these women resolved to spite racist callers by reporting to work. They could not expect students to integrate if teachers refused.

Most of the transfers were black, but some white teachers also received letters to move. As Nashville wrestled with race relations, white teachers in black schools had to reevaluate their attitudes about the issue. Mary Driscoll relates that some of her peers thought the board punished white teachers deemed problematic or incompetent by sending them to black schools. Middle-class white teachers also objected to laboring in what they considered potentially dangerous, run-down, inner-city schools. Some, according to Betty Tune, a white teacher who went to a black school, were racists. As she suggests, "They probably wouldn't have been good teachers anyway."[52] The change was too much for them, and they soon left the system. But thousands remained and attempted to adjust.

Many who taught in integrated schools were relatively new to the field. New or younger black teachers such as Helen Adams and LaMona McCarter began their careers in Nashville's desegregated school system. The Metropolitan Nashville Board of Education asked Adams, who came to Nashville with her husband in 1969, whether she would be willing to work in an integrated school, and she observes, "When you are looking for a job, you are not choosy. So, I said it wouldn't make me any difference. I'd give anything a try. So, I was the first black teacher at Central High School."[53] McCarter, who came of age during the civil rights movement and whose mother was a teacher, had been a student in Nashville's African American schools. She began her teaching career at the desegregated Bellevue High School.[54]

These young teachers did not have to experience the tearful goodbyes and painful separations that older educators endured. They did, however, need to develop personal teaching philosophies and styles without the supportive guidance of older African American teachers and in sometimes hostile environments. The majority of white teachers assigned to black schools were younger and had little or no teaching experience. Lynda Thompson, who had been teaching for a few years when she received notice to leave McCann Elementary School with its poor white students, looked forward to going to McKissack. She and others, such as Roberta Jackson, were happy to have jobs.[55]

The majority of Nashville's African American teachers received letters directing them to white schools, but others did not have to relocate. The board permitted school principals to keep 20 percent of their faculties in order to ease the transition and ensure that the same educational structures continued.[56] Both Ola Hudson, who taught home economics at Cameron High School, and Minerva Hawkins, a history teacher for almost thirty years at Pearl Senior High School, remained at their jobs. Mary Driscoll also stayed at her high school, a suburban institution profoundly affected by white flight. She saw the influx of black teachers and students as the school's upper-middle-class population went elsewhere.[57]

Beginning with the struggle to gain employment in the 1880s, Nashville's African American teachers combated perceptions that they were incompetent and unequal to their white counterparts. Faculty integration, however, could change the perceptions of some whites. As Betty Tune explains, "After working with black teachers, I realized that all the things that my parents had told me about black people were wrong. They [black teachers] were so wise." Although eager to prove themselves to white peers and represent the best of the African American community, some black teachers also wanted to see whether white educators deserved their reputation. Mary Alice Goldman faced her transfer with curiosity. "I wanted to see what it was like to be in school with white teachers," she remembers. "They [whites] had always said, white teachers taught better than blacks [and] that they knew more. I wanted to see if it was true."[58]

On occasion, the situations of black teachers were not as bad as might have been imagined. As Overton Senior High School's only African American teacher in 1967, for example, Helen Anne Mayes was prepared to face racism. She knew she had to represent African American educational excellence and present herself as a professional. When administrators assigned her to be a roving teacher she was outraged. She thought she was refused a classroom because she was African American, but later she discovered that it was the policy to place all new staff as roving teachers. Her apprehension ended, and she felt she belonged, when several white colleagues visited her home after her father died. Mayes's perceptions, in short, were worse than the reality.[59]

Virginia Westbrook's case, however, was quite different. Although she had grown weary of struggling against poverty and racism at segregated Washington Junior High School, she encountered even more troubling issues when transferred to Apollo Junior High. An exemplary teacher, Westbrook was accustomed to respect from colleagues and administrators. At Apollo, however, she was just the new African American woman. A person who once maintained sole control of her classroom, she now had to adapt to team-teaching methods that eliminated individual autonomy, and she worked with colleagues she did not respect. "I was stunned to see these teachers on the faculty with me," she observes. "They were more like English students to me. My intelligence and experiences were so far above theirs that I couldn't believe it. I was really aghast. Yet I was never made the team leader. Whenever something happened they would always go to me to get an idea of how it ought to go. I was never the one to receive the credit for it. I tell you, away with integration and that kind of stuff for me. I tell you honestly."[60] Surrounded by younger teachers who did not value her experience and refused to view her as an authority figure, Westbrook experienced daily incidents with colleagues and administrators.

For teachers like Westbrook, adjusting to white schools included dealing with the loss of status and respect. Many women who were leaders in their former schools suddenly became minorities who had neither voice nor power to influence policy. Ola Hudson had expressed the frustration of many other African American teachers: "Egos can get crushed when nothing you say seems to matter. Dislike me if you want. I'd rather you like me, that's your prerogative, but please don't ignore me."[61]

Other African American women teachers experienced overt hostility, and their isolation mirrored a realization that their work environments were now contingent on the actions of others. Shortly after Donzell Johnson transferred to a white school from Pearl, for example, he overheard a fellow teacher refer to African Americans as "niggers." As Johnson remembers, "When the janitor said, 'Don't you see Mr. Johnson is in the room?' he stated that he didn't give a damn."[62] After Johnson complained to the faculty, the board, and the director of schools, the white teacher was forced to apologize publicly.

Receptions were not always unfriendly, however, and some teachers were overwhelmed with kind words and gestures. Dorothy Baines, who taught with Virginia Westbrook at Apollo but in another department, had an entirely different experience than Westbrook's. The other teachers in the science unit were so close that they would cover for each other when one was absent so pay would not be lost.[63]

Some of the women helped white teachers become more aware of discrimination. Gwendolyn Vincent recalls that one of the white teachers at her new school, Rosebank Elementary, repeatedly mentioned how much she enjoyed spending time in the whirlpool at a health club that refused admittance to African Americans: "We were sitting in the cafeteria, when she was talking about how relaxing it was. I said, 'It sounds wonderful to me. It sounds like something I would really like to do.' She dropped her fork in shock at the thought that I would go sit in a hot tub. The very next day this teacher came to me almost crying. 'Gwen, it never dawned on me that you would want to do this, go to the health club and you could not go. I know what a wonderful person you are and to think that you wanted to do the same things as I do and you can't do it.'"[64]

For some, a transfer helped change their views about the disparities between black and white. "After listening to those [white] teachers, all of my stereotypes were blown out of the water," recalls Margaret Whitfield, who transferred to Antioch High School in 1971.[65] Teaching expertise gained through educating African American children applied to all children, regardless of race. Team-teaching meant that some African American teachers lost the power to design and implement curriculum, but they gained the self-knowledge and self-confidence of being able to compete on the same level with white teachers.

One positive surprise was no longer having to help finance extracurricular activities. Ossie Trammel remembers that she and other teachers had to use their own money to decorate their classrooms. Sponsoring cheerleaders or advising the student council sometimes meant contributing personal funds or selling tickets but receiving no additional pay for doing so. "At Pearl," Thelma Tears says, "I had worked with cheerleaders for many years. I had to sell tickets. I had never been paid for it until I got to Stratford [High]. It was a pleasant experience."[66]

The women also had to change the way in which they interacted with administrators. Many, such as Gwendolyn Vincent, welcomed the new freedom of having less authoritative supervisors. Her former principal had ruled with an iron hand. "His style of communication was always threatening. He said, 'School comes first. Family comes second. You either do this job or you don't need to be here.' If you rebelled you were on the bad list."[67] Still other African American administrators stressed excellence among their teaching staffs because the teachers were responsible for helping students learn in segregated schools.

The majority of Nashville's black women teachers transferred to white schools in 1970 and 1971, but most black principals did not. As in other cities, they either lost their jobs when black schools closed or were demoted to assistant principal positions. Tennessee had seventy-three African American principals in 1968 but only seventeen in 1970. By 1975, after several black schools were closed or their staffs reduced, the number of African American principals had further been lessened, but the number of assistant principals had increased from seven to sixteen.[68] The majority of the new positions were at formerly all-white schools.

White teachers responded to black principals in a variety of ways. Betty Tune enjoyed talking with the one at her school because he offered teaching advice and knew a great deal about world events. Roberta Jackson considered her principal to be very nice, but she tried to keep misbehaving students out of his office because she viewed his discipline style as overly severe. Lynda

Thompson greatly admired the firm administrative style of Ivanetta Davis, the black principal at her school, when she told the faculty that they were now integrating and she expected no problems. From giving counsel regarding teaching techniques to advising Thompson to wear more comfortable shoes, Davis helped her become a better teacher.[69]

The African American women who taught at white schools soon acclimated themselves to their new surroundings. Trained to instruct students from a variety of economic backgrounds, black teachers were able to adapt to many situations, whether they involved substandard materials or hungry children. They used the same flexibility when interacting with white children. As Thelma Tears contends, "Kids are kids."[70] Historically, African American women often worked as care-givers for white children. Those had been service positions. Now, as teachers, they occupied new roles as leaders.

White students who sought nurturing and understanding sometimes formed strong bonds with their African American teachers. Gwendolyn Vincent remembers that one white first-grader at Rosebank would rub her hand to see if the color would wear off. "In time," she points out, "those kids got so attached to me that being different really faded away. I received so many gifts at Christmas that I had to have shopping bags to take them home. They gave me Avon products, boxes of candy, and even a robe." Virginia Westbrook, who later transferred to Overton High School after teaching at Apollo for five years, also describes positive relationships with students: "One girl, tall, blond and blue-eyed said, 'I wish you were my mother.' And that to me was sort of humorous, but I could appreciate it when they would say, 'I wish my mother was more like you. I can talk to you. You are not like my mother.' They understood that I was not only a teacher but also a person, one who was interested in them and one they could share ideas with."[71]

Other African American women teachers struggled. Anne Lenox, who resented losing her guidance counselor position at Pearl Senior High School and having to teach the "new math," an unfamiliar subject, grew apathetic but then realized, "If you are going to take that attitude, you need to go and get yourself another job. You can't take this out on those kids. They didn't send you here. So the next day when they came in, I was still standing there and they started playing, and I said, 'Okay, playtime's over. We are going to work' because I felt that I was being unfair to them."[72]

African American female teachers reshaped the message of racial uplift that they promoted in segregated settings to fit integrated environments by attempting to form alliances across racial lines, constructing new identities as racial and class mediators, and protecting African American children. The teachers' goals included helping black and white students acclimate and ensuring that they learned. Some teachers refused to transfer to less hostile surroundings in order to remain available to black students. In previous years the women had struggled to prepare students to live in a discriminatory world. Now they had to help them deal with racism within their schools. As Margaret Whitfield observes, "I loved working with black kids. I felt like I was giving them some things that integration wasn't doing for them. I was the first black teacher at Antioch High School, a suburban school. I could have asked for a transfer, but there were a few black kids out there and I felt that I needed to stay to provide a role model."[73]

Some teachers had to contend with administrators and other people in order to protect African American students. After Anne Lenox left Dupont, she received another unwanted transfer to suburban Hillwood Senior High School. As one of the guidance counselors, she was responsible for discipline and mediating disputes:

> I remember a time in a faculty meeting when a man was talking about the "Nigras" and how the standards had been lowered because the "Nigras" had come. This is the kind of stuff we had to put up with. When he was approached, he was told to say "blacks." He said he couldn't say "blacks." I told the principal I would suggest that he talk with him because we had some words, too, because he was going to call the wrong student "boy" or "Nigra" and [that student] wasn't going to call him "poor white trash" or "honkey," he was going to call him "son of a bitch." And I was going to the board of education and defend [the student]. So we never heard the word "Nigra" again.[74]

Although most of the faculty demonstrated less prejudice after several years, Lenox continued to remain in the halls between classes in order to safeguard African American pupils from possible mistreatment. After years of being a thorn in the principal's side because she continued to defend students, especially those accused of crimes they did not commit, the principal suggested she transfer. "I didn't ask to come here," Lenox responded. "I was sent here. I didn't know this school existed. But since I am here and I see what you are doing to my poor little black students, I am going to stay here as long as I can."[75]

Some white teachers also endeavored to mediate between whites and blacks. Jeanne Gore, who later worked at Hillwood, attended one of the first desegregated high schools in Atlanta and began her teaching career at a desegregated school in that city. After attempting to calm and heal wounds in that Atlanta school in the aftermath of a race riot, she worked to prevent racial incidents at Hillwood by integrating classroom groups and being in a neutral setting when discussing racial issues.[76]

Novella Davis's work environment at Hillsboro, another white high school, was so unpleasant that she "would go to school praying all the way." An assistant librarian, she increased the school's collection of books on African Americans and helped black students when her superior ignored their requests. "I think I was the saving grace for them in the library," Davis remembers. "The lady wouldn't help them. It got to the place that they would never ask for anything." A former participant in the civil rights movement, Davis had learned the benefits of keeping good records. She maintained a daily ledger of discriminatory events and reported her boss to the superintendent of schools, the director of personnel, and the principal.[77]

There was even opposition from some African American teachers when efforts to protect black students stirred controversy. "The other black teachers just said 'Yessum,'" maintains Mary Alice Goldman. "They tried to make me less militant; they distanced themselves from me. It's not my style. I am a person who will speak out. I refuse to have others thinking for me."[78]

Some sought to mold black female students into traditional gender roles and considered it a responsibility to convey their thoughts about femininity, class, and sexuality to them. In an age in which young people openly questioned authority figures and challenged women's roles, students sometimes dismissed or misunderstood their teachers' advice. In the mid-1970s Virginia Westbrook disappointed a group of girls when she refused to sponsor the Half-Timers, an African American dance team at Apollo. "They wanted to get out there and do their thing," she says, "and they called me in to discuss it with me and I didn't think it was appropriate. I have taught a lot of dance, but these were not the little girls that you would choose to dance because of their physical build. I could see in these white communities how they would be laughing at our black girls doing our thing, and I didn't want them to hurt their feelings. I didn't want to put them through that. I failed them. They didn't understand what I was thinking."[79]

Westbrook's desire to "protect" students from the ridicule of whites who possibly would not appreciate the girls' dance moves and mature appearance, or even laugh at them, reflected her efforts to ensure that black students did not inadvertently embarrass themselves or disgrace the African American teachers. Westbrook came from an environment in which students represented their teachers, who were, in turn, responsible for training young black girls to act and look like ladies. Her distaste for the students' gyrating dance moves reflects a time when girls faced expulsion if they became pregnant and when adoption centers, then called "homes for unwed mothers," refused to accept African Americans. As a new youth culture called for new social attitudes, Westbrook continued to model conservative professionalism to female students even as they sought new images to emulate. Years later, she encountered some of them and received a warm greeting. They might not have agreed with her attitude toward dance, but they respected her as their teacher.[80]

In some cases, integration strained the student-teacher connection when students misconstrued their teachers' efforts to restrain them as attempts to force them to emulate whites. The same image of middle-class conservatism these women portrayed in segregated schools now aroused resentment among many black students. Social influences such as African American cultural nationalism and the youth culture provoked them to reject middle-class conventions and celebrate nontraditional forms of expression. It is ironic that while being pushed to succeed academically in order to prove they were worthy of equality some rebelled, believing that speaking "correct" English or excelling in integrated classrooms represented a loss of black identity and could cause them to be ostracized among their peers for "acting white."

Black students had to learn, however, to traverse two worlds in language and behavior. Those desperate to embrace and define African American culture in a sea of whiteness sometimes accused teachers who insisted they speak properly or were strict of not "acting black." Margaret Whitfield declares, "Some of the girls resented me. They said, 'She thinks she is white. She thinks she is sharp.' I told them, "You want to be different. You want people to think that you think that you are something because you are. You don't have to like me, but try to emulate some of my traits.'"[81]

Elene Jackson at first faced awkward stares of surprise from white faculty and students as she announced that she was one of the new French teachers at formerly all-white Hillsboro High School. "They just couldn't understand a black person speaking French," she says. A former faculty member at Pearl High School, she believed teachers and students had a responsibility to dress properly. After she overheard a white teacher laughing at a black girl who came to school with rollers in her hair, she went into the teacher's classroom, found the girl, and took her to the lavatory, where she told her, "Take those curlers out of your hair." When the girl asked, "What for?"

Jackson responded, "Ladies leave the boudoir in the boudoir!" She adds, "Black girls wore these crazy hairdos and short dresses that went up the nose. You're in a school with 90 percent whites. You have to act civilized because whites are going to look at you."[82]

Veteran teachers believed they were responsible for always portraying African Americans in a positive manner, but Jackson thought her new black students did not care how they appeared to others. In reality, however, her objections to girls having "unattractive plats" or braids reflected her own unawareness of the fashion to embrace natural hairstyles.

Students wore jeans and preferred long hair, Afros, or cornrows during the 1970s, and some young white teachers also challenged traditional conservative attire. Roberta Jackson ignored her black principal's suggestion that she wear more professional clothing. She thought that overly dressed teachers intimidated young children; moveover, such apparel hindered her ability to play with students and get messy.

Some younger African American teachers celebrated cultural nationalism by wearing Afros and calling themselves "black" instead of "Negro," but many continued to favor conservative dress. In the late 1960s and early 1970s, while faculties across Metropolitan Nashville voted to allow women to wear pantsuits instead of skirts, some black teachers, including Gwendolyn Vincent, voted no. Even black male teachers adhered to professional dress standards. No one ever directly told history teacher Donzell Johnson how to dress when he arrived at Pearl in the mid-1960s, but he only had to see how well his colleagues were decked out to know what to wear. Pearl's reputation for excellence was so strong in the black community that he would not disgrace his position and others on the faculty by not wearing the proper attire.[83]

Albert Shaw hated to pay the frequent dry-cleaning bills, but he knew that dressing well was part of his professional presentation. Even the physical education teacher at his school wore a suit to work and changed into athletic attire before class. When Shaw was transferred to John Trotwood Moore Junior High School in the 1970s, white students asked why he dressed so formally. He replied that he felt most comfortable that way. Although his peers wore casual slacks and comfortable sportswear, he continued to wear suits. Roberta Jackson, who once dressed casually to be more approachable to young students, concluded in later years that "perhaps when we stopped dressing as professionals is when we lost some of our respect as teachers."[84]

During the 1970s, integration and the possibility of having to control feuding black and white students frightened some teachers. Students in segregated schools fought, but the altercations escalated into racial conflict with integration. No large-scale riots broke out in the Metropolitan Nashville school system, but white schools such as Glencliff and Hillsboro High had several incidents of fights between black and white students. A white teacher at Hillsboro suggested that those in his classroom led him to reevaluate how he viewed racial issues. "It has made me start doing a lot of psychological work to try and get my students not to use racial slurs," the teacher says. "Using terms such as *nigger* or *redneck* may begin as a joke, but you never know when the line will be crossed and it isn't a joke anymore."[85]

When the Nashville police shot a Tennessee State University student in 1973 some blacks retaliated by starting a fistfight with three white Pearl High School students. Although school officials could not determine whether students or outsiders had initiated the attack, the school system sent police to patrol the school.[86] Donzell Johnson remembers solving one potential racial incident between two students by having the entire class diagram the offensive sentences the two parties used. The surprised students stopped focusing on the disagreement. Of course, fights still occurred within racial groups. A 1974 incident at McGavock High School between two black girls, for example, resulted in Afro hair picks being banned.[87]

Racial clashes were not the only student conflicts that faced teachers. Following the suggestions of the Coleman Report that the overall performance of poor black students would improve if they attended school along with more affluent whites, the Metropolitan Nashville School System bused to achieve that goal.[88] The new zoning plan with comprehensive high schools also enabled more whites from various levels of society to interact, so students differed by class as well as race. Sometimes conflicts occurred. Mary Driscoll complained about the tension at Hillwood between whites from various social classes. She thought that some of the wealthy looked down on less-fortunate classmates. One Hillsboro teacher maintained that some incidents or fights between blacks and whites were about class differences not racial ones. Lynda Thompson claims that small incidents occurred at her elementary school between poor whites and more affluent blacks, but the disputes were often due to personality conflicts rather than class or race. Betty Tune adds that when she transferred to Whites Creek High School, a large new comprehensive facility with a high percentage of more affluent blacks, she realized that the standards they set for being in style were ones their poorer classmates could not attain.[89]

Some older teachers of both races disliked the more permissive atmosphere in public schools and refused to abandon attitudes that equated stern discipline with proper teaching. Other African American teachers, however, thought that their white counterparts inadequately disciplined African American children. For them, punishing misbehaving students was a sign of care, and parents relied on their judgment at segregated schools. Thus, if a teacher corrected a misbehaving student, his or her parents often reinforced the discipline by punishing the child again at home. When students failed to act appropriately in a school setting, black parents and teachers worked together to punish them. Perhaps because they used corporal punishment as a deterrent, the teachers instilled fear, yet overall they generated respect. According to Myra Dixon, a strict disciplinarian, she knew how to "give just as much as I got."[90] Integration diminished the trust between parent and teacher, and teachers often had to follow formal procedures to chastise a child.

Discipline was tricky in integrated schools, especially between white teachers and black students. Anne Lenox remembers, "Many white teachers were afraid of black students. That's another reason they didn't do anything. They could see students doing things in the hall they knew were wrong and they wouldn't correct them, but they would correct the white students."[91] "When the black child asked too many questions," Thelma Tears adds, "they [white teachers] would sit him out in the hallway instead of dealing with him. All over Metro, all over the South, we have lost a lot of black children from sitting in hallways."[92]

Black teachers and students complained about that issue in other cities as well. Robert Pratt explains that some black students in Richmond, Virginia, considered white teachers to be either paternalistic or bigoted, but one explained, "Sometimes we felt as though we were walking on eggs. Some were afraid to walk up to students and ask them to put out cigarettes. I know that most teachers were well-intentioned, but they often used the wrong words like 'boy,' which triggered conflict. They made mistakes, but they learned from them."[93]

Black teachers' concerns with white teachers and their methods of discipline often stemmed from contrasting ideas about corporal punishment. Newer techniques of child-rearing downplayed the need for spanking, and some white teachers thought black parents punished their children too severely. When one disrobed her child and spanked her in the principal's office, Betty Tune was horrified and could not understand why the principal allowed it. Even after parents gave her permission to spank their children Roberta Jackson refused to use corporal punishment and employed more modern disciplinary techniques instead. When a kindergartener consistently threw temper tantrums, Jackson asked the mother, who had a reputation for violence, to meet with her. "I just beat the child" the woman commented, but Jackson nervously refused to follow that course of action. On one occasion she decided to get on the floor beside the screaming student and mimic a tantrum. When the girl stopped and asked what she was doing, Jackson replied, "Don't we look funny doing this?" The number of tantrums reduced drastically.[94] Jeanne Gore, another young white teacher, controlled high school students by becoming quiet and staring them down. The teachers considered discipline to be more a student problem than a racial one. Betty Tune gained such a reputation as a disciplinarian that misbehaving students were sent to her class. She was intimidated only once when she had to retrieve a gun from a mentally disturbed junior high student.[95]

The white teachers who failed to discipline students properly may have done so because of inexperience, having a missionary attitude, or out of fear of negative reprisals from parents and administrators rather than from prejudice or indifference. Ola Hudson, a temporary assistant principal at Cameron Senior High School in 1970, described such discipline problems: "My office was filled everyday with referrals from new teachers. The offenses probably would not have happened if the teachers knew how to manage a class. I think that by not having some of the experiences that the children have had, they either overlook or feel sorry and let kids get away with a lot they don't need to get away with. I have seen children play on the sympathy of teachers who will buy it."[96]

In response, some African American teachers took it upon themselves to correct black students. If white teachers chose not to make them behave, then African American teachers would. Margaret Whitfield decided to remedy the lack of discipline at her school by standing in the halls and becoming a "holy terror," ready and willing to make sure black pupils behaved.[97]

During the 1970s and 1980s African American teachers faced changing social customs as well as racial issues. Their ideas concerning chastity and what constituted proper womanhood were passe by the 1970s and early 1980s. During segregation, black women teachers were mandated to uplift students by helping them obtain an education. Discrimination and poverty, however, oftentimes hindered those efforts. Cynical, post–civil rights African American students now deemed participation in middle-class organizations irrelevant. Teachers recognized that black children had more educational opportunities in desegregated schools, but they faced new responsibilities for uplift as they saw some succumb to the drug culture. They nevertheless continued to apply their philosophies of discipline and community responsibility to nurture and help the students.[98]

When black teachers taught in segregated schools the message they conveyed was that African American children would need to prove their competence to white society and be "ten times better just to be treated equally." While teachers promoted that idea, the students could grow and thrive in an environment that required excellence. With desegregation, black children were often tracked into classrooms for lower-achieving students on the assumption that "culturally deprived black children" should be separated from higher-achievers. In an effort to rebel against the perception of African American inferiority, and frustrated by society's negative perceptions of them, some African American students stopped trying to prove themselves. Some underachieved on purpose.

Those who remained at formerly all-black schools entered the same buildings, but little remained recognizable; white teachers had replaced their former colleagues. The new teachers, sometimes unfamiliar with African American culture and people, relied on the remaining faculty for information and guidance. A white graduate of Vanderbilt University, Ann Carter (pseudonym) taught in two predominantly African American junior high schools in Nashville during the late 1960s. In a 1969 interview she described her experiences, "I was one of five whites there—but the faculty was the best I've ever worked on. They were on top of the situation, they knew what they were doing, helped those of us that were new. But my preparation was totally inadequate. There are high points—kids who do really well, others who go from nothing to mediocre—but the frustrations outweigh all of that. I don't want to continue." Carter added that economic poverty caused more problems for students than racial issues.[99] Other white teachers also indicated they had difficulty adjusting. Lynda Thompson, for example, recalls that nothing she learned in college prepared her to teach at an inner-city school. Betty Tune remembers a black teacher who served as her mentor during her first year at Washington Junior High School: "She taught me so much about teaching. My classroom was a wreck. I didn't know what I was doing. I always felt I should have paid Metro for my first few years I taught school."[100]

Some African American women teachers experienced new pressures in working with young and inexperienced white instructors and took on the additional duty of helping their new colleagues adjust so students would not suffer. Ola Hudson stressed her frustration: "Many of these new teachers didn't have a clue about what was going on in the community. They were pulling at you, needing so much. They were always asking questions. I didn't have time to think. They were always asking questions."[101]

The teachers also mourned the absence of former colleagues and lamented that the schools did not seem the same without their friends and peers. As Hudson explains, "I realized that I wasn't as good as I thought I was. What helped me to be the strong teacher that I thought I was, was the co-workers that I had and the rapport that I had built, and the sharing." These instructors suddenly had to abandon old circles or expand them to include the few remaining African American teachers and the new white faculty. They also had to guide the black students who had lost mentors and favorite teachers. "You talk about tired," Hudson adds. "It was the worst year I ever spent in my entire life." As Tune puts it, "Of course students were upset when white teachers arrived at Washington. They had their faculty that they loved for generations. They just worshipped those teachers and they pulled them all out."[102]

With student and faculty integration, African American teachers became minorities in their own schools. Many who remained assumed new positions of leadership and authority, but their new minority status weakened their power. Minerva Hawkins recalls her eyes filling with tears as she saw new white teachers walk into her friends' former classrooms at Pearl Senior High School.[103]

In 1973 the Metropolitan Nashville School System received a grant from the U.S. Department of Education to work with several area universities, including Fisk, Tennessee State, and Vanderbilt, to initiate the Teacher Corps Project, which offered workshops for teachers in several inner-city schools. McKissack's principal, Ivanetta Davis, sent Lynda Thompson to participate. The National Teacher Corps also operated a Learning Resource Center for students after school at Ford Greene Elementary School. By 1977 the Teacher Corps offered lesson plans and programs to help teachers incorporate multicultural education into their classrooms. One of the project's main objectives was to help elementary and junior high school students learn "that it's okay to be different and not to apply negative stereotypes to people just because they are different."[104]

In a survey of black and white Nashville teachers in 1980, African Americans were ambivalent about busing for integration. Although 38 percent of the black teachers surveyed stated that busing did not improve the educational achievement of black students, 36 percent believed it had. The numbers were similar when it came to issues of self-esteem. Of the black teachers surveyed, 39 percent thought busing did not enhance the self-esteem of black children and 33 percent were unsure. The teachers were well aware of the many problems African American children faced in integrated schools, but 79 percent of them nonetheless thought that busing for desegregation helped black and white students better understand and appreciate each other.[105] Alternatively, most white teachers polled saw little benefit in busing. Lynda Thompson maintains that busing at her school enabled poor white students to interact with blacks of a higher socioeconomic status. "They must not be that bad," the white students would say. "Look at their houses."[106]

Integration provided an opportunity for African American students to take advantage of programs ranging from Latin and computer mathematics classes to the individualized elementary reading programs and commercial art offered in the system's new schools. Although appreciative of the ability of desegregated schools to lessen racism, Pearl High student Pam Streator contended, "A lot of people wouldn't know prejudice unless they are taught it. Little kids don't have prejudice. It's sad to see them grow up and learn it." By the late 1970s the majority of Nashville's African American students attended schools that had been predominately white.[107]

Integration may have helped reduce racial prejudice by providing all students with greater opportunities to interact with each other, but desegregation sometimes had a detrimental effect on African American students. Once in schools that cherished their presence, they now encountered environments that were often unwelcoming. For Donzell Johnson, busing severed the bonds between black schools and the community; increased distance between homes and schools made it difficult for African American parents to visit their children's teachers. Moreover, although their new schools offered a variety of extracurricular activities, some African American students could not participate because their parents had limited transportation and relied on buses to pick them up. In a controversial article, legal scholar Derrick Bell maintained that civil rights lawyers placed too much emphasis on meeting desegregation goals and that well-meaning lawyers, in the quest to secure civil rights, neglected to listen to some African Americans' call to improve the educational quality of neighborhood schools and stop the wide-spread closings of black ones.[108]

Bell quotes Marian Wright Edelman, who lamented her experiences as an NAACP legal defense attorney in Mississippi before she moved to Washington, D.C.: "We are up here filing desegregation suits, but something else is going on in the black community. I sensed it before I left Mississippi. We hear more about non-desegregation, about 'our' schools, about money to build up black schools. I'm not sure we are doing the right thing in the long run. We automatically assume that what we need to do is close lousy black schools. But desegregation is taking the best black teachers out of the black schools. It has become a very complex thing."[109] By the late 1970s Williams and the city's civil rights leaders expanded the fight for desegregation to place more focus on retaining schools in predominately African American neighborhoods and balancing busing requirements to ease the burden on black children.

Pearl Senior High School had an excellent reputation as one of the most prestigious African American high schools in the South. Nevertheless, in 1971 more than 70 percent of the 908 whites zoned to attend Pearl Senior High transferred or did not enroll; by 1977 they made up only 25 percent of the student population.[110] When white parents contended that they transferred their children to suburban comprehensive high schools because Pearl did not offer the special courses that those schools did, the board added more subjects at Pearl. The white students zoned to Pearl still refused to attend. They would not attend an older school in a poor and declining black neighborhood.[111] In this case, desegregation did not erase fears and stereotypes.

A major reason that Pearl's role in the community changed was the loss of many of its African American teachers to other schools. White teachers made up more than 80 percent of its faculty despite the fact that Pearl remained a black school in student population. Among those teachers were men and women who had no prior connection to the school or its mission. Pearl's reputation as a beacon for academic excellence rested not only on the successes of its students but also on its teachers. They had resisted the idea that Pearl was inferior to white schools, arguing that it only received fewer funds and supplies. Without the presence and leadership of African American faculty to connect a school to a community, former educational and social icons such as Pearl lost their status as cultural centers; the bonds among schools, teachers, and the neighborhood loosened. Racial discrimination, the Great Depression, world wars, and changing social values could not destroy Pearl Senior High School, but desegregation and the loss of its black faculty caused the decline of a school that had educated black students for almost eighty years.

At first, desegregation primarily involved moving black children and teachers, but by the late 1970s the board of education endeavored to close several African American schools to achieve racial balance. Nashville's African American community watched as the board turned Cameron and Meigs High Schools into junior highs and closed North High School. Pearl was now the only high school still located in an African American neighborhood.[112]

Nashville was not alone in closing African American schools. In the name of integration, school boards across the nation shut down black facilities to avoid sending white children to such institutions. Some schools were sub-standard, but others, built in the effort to impede desegregation during the early 1950s, were fine structures. Some black parents and community leaders considered the push for integration necessary, but their sacrifice stopped at the closing of their schools. In a study of a North Carolina community's valiant fight to keep its new high school, David Cecelski points out that many African Americans were not willing to sacrifice their beloved institutions for the sake of token desegregation.[113]

In 1977 the board developed a new plan that called for constructing several new comprehensive high schools in the suburbs and closing several smaller white high schools and Pearl. The NAACP responded by filing suit in 1979. Williams maintained that the board's efforts would cause black students to be bused for most of their school years. The plaintiffs also claimed that the board was too lenient toward white students; transfer policies allowed them to leave a black school if it failed to offer a needed course. The NAACP added that Pearl was capable of expanding to become a comprehensive high school. Although they continued to seek redress through the courts, concerned African American citizens formed community groups and voiced their protests.[114] In response, Thomas Wiseman now the presiding judge, agreed to re-open the *Kelley* case.

The judge then mandated that the board reevaluate the plan and incorporate the entire county rather than just the city limits and also review transfer policies. Community opinion was sought, and the Nashville Urban League stated its objection to closing of Pearl and other black schools:

> Schools in the inner city have a right to exist. Schools are a living part of a community and to close a school in a Black community is to take some of

the life away from that community. Moreover, it places an unequal burden on the Black child when schools in his or her community are closed and the Black child must be bused into a White community to be educated. Equality in education and society calls for equality in busing demands. If little black children must wait on snowy street corners for the school bus, fair play calls for little white children to do the same.[115]

The Nashville NAACP, more than a hundred years after black Nashvillians first petitioned to replace southern white teachers with African Americans in segregated schools, implored the board of education to reinstate black teachers at schools that had African American populations and hire more African American teachers in white schools to serve as role models for black students there.[116]

When school systems across the nation started to transfer experienced African American teachers to white schools, students there benefited from those instructors' abilities. In the process, however, African Americans lost valuable cultural capital. The black community realized that its losses were more profound than the schools'. The heart and soul of those institutions, the people who had made prestigious urban schools like Pearl achieve amid a white supremacist society, were being lost as well.

Judge Wiseman rejected the board's plan to extend busing to the outer areas of the county and close more black schools, including Pearl. He asked for a new plan that would end busing in the early grades, limit it in the upper ones, eliminate a prescribed set racial ratios, and include new educational programs. Williams and the NAACP then looked to the appeals court, which overturned Wiseman's decision. Busing continued in Nashville. In 1983, after three years of court challenges and negative community responses, federal courts approved the Metropolitan Nashville Board of Education's new desegregation plan for extending busing to thirty-three previously exempted schools. The plan also allowed for schools to be within 15 percentage points of the local black-to-white student ratio. In addition, the board called for construction of Pearl-Cohn High School where Washington Junior High and Ford Greene Elementary once stood, the reopening of some African American schools, and creation of magnet or specialized schools designed to draw white students. Pearl became Martin Luther King Jr. Magnet High School for the Sciences. The reassignment allowed it to remain open yet attractive to white students.[117] Finally, under the new plan African American teachers no longer faced tight placement restrictions.

As middle-class whites throughout the nation flooded into suburban areas to avoid busing, and as several studies of the benefits of busing on African American and white students proved inconclusive, the conservative Reagan-era Supreme Court took on integration. In *Milliken v. Bradley* the Court limited the reach of desegregation orders by preventing students from being bused across county and city lines. After several other Supreme Court rulings during the 1980s that weakened school districts' responsibility for desegregation, school systems across the country petitioned the courts to be relieved from the court order.[118]

In Nashville during the early 1990s, the school system created a committee of community leaders and education professionals to develop a "Commitment to the Future" plan that stressed more focus on magnet and neighborhood schools. There was far less emphasis on busing for racial balance. After years of court battles for desegregation, busing, and now the protection of black schools, the plaintiffs and the schools jointly asked the District Court if the school system could be released from the court order so it could implement a five-year school improvement plan. It would build more magnet schools, provide more parental choice in school selection, and eliminate racial goals in school population. Citing progress in desegregation efforts, the U.S. District Court released the Metropolitan Nashville School System from the desegregation order in 1998. Ironically, as Williams and other civil rights lawyers staged a more than forty-year struggle to integrate local schools and faculties, African Americans sacrificed community control for better access to educational opportunities. Eventually, both African American and white students benefited from the development of comprehensive and magnet schools and increased funding for specialized programming.[119]

The second wave of the women's movement emerged from the civil rights movement, but there were African American women teachers who did not identify with some of the movement's goals. They had always balanced their work and family life, and working outside their homes was often necessary in maintaining a middle-class lifestyle. Nevertheless, in promoting professionalism and academic excellence for women they endorsed some feminist beliefs. Whether sewing missing buttons on children's coats, seeking financial aid for a female student so she could remain in school, or escorting elementary-school children to safety amid angry mobs, the women exhibited the tenets of womanist philosophy. Womanism is a concept developed by a host of scholars and writers, including Alice Walker, Clenora Hudson Weems, Delores Williams, and Jacquelyn Grant, to describe the multiple and integrated battles that black women must fight. Against a complex mixture of sexism, racism, and classism, they have had to develop new strategies that take their "multiple jeopardy" into account. Consequently, their self-concept as black female teachers involves promoting the progress of the entire African American community.[120]

As greater numbers of women teachers assumed administrative positions they relied on the independence and self-sufficiency garnered from classroom teaching to accomplish their new jobs. One of the first black teachers at Overton, Helen Anne Mayes rose to become supervisor of business education for the school system. In 1969 Ola Hudson's principal and assistant principal became too ill to work. To her surprise, the board asked if she would serve as acting assistant principal. "This was before women were in administration," she remembers. "I said no and I started naming every man on the faculty. It was the farthest thing in my imagination. But I dearly loved Cameron School, and I was a team player; and if they thought that I was the one that could do it, I would."[121] After serving as assistant principal, Hudson then sat on the Human Relations Committee, where she designed programs to help teachers adjust to desegregation. She later became supervisor of home economics for the Metropolitan Nashville schools.

Throughout the 1980s the percentage of African American women in elementary and secondary education dropped significantly. There were a variety of reasons for the decline. As the civil rights and the women's movements provided new economic opportunities for African American women, teaching was no longer their only or even best professional option. The ability to obtain more lucrative careers in business, engineering, and higher education led to a decline in numbers of black women entering education. "Now, there are more ways to progress," contends Helen Adams, who taught and was an assistant principal as well. "For example, my daughter went to Vanderbilt and is a mechanical engineer. I did not have that opportunity. I didn't know anybody that was an engineer. Everyone went the education route when I came along. That was the way to go."[122] Although such positive changes have led to fewer black women teachers, other negative factors, including discriminatory hiring practices and unfair testing as well as the lack of respect accorded to teachers, have also contributed to the numbers of them decreasing from 12.5 percent in 1974 to 8 percent in 1990.[123]

During segregation, the Nashville Teachers' Association for Negroes worked for increased funding and better material for the all-black schools. As members of the integrated Metropolitan Nashville Education Association, those teachers worked to gain a voice within the association and help facilitate desegregation. Gwendolyn Vincent, an African American teacher, rose from the ranks of the MNEA to hold top administrative office in the 1980s. She also struggled to promote the aims of all Nashville teachers, including increasing their salaries and improving their benefits, while protecting African American interests. Her knowledge of procedures and guidelines helped inform her colleagues.[124]

Under federal pressure to provide racial balance, the board of education never asked how African American women teachers, who often taught under adverse conditions and with inadequate material, managed to produce successful graduates. Once powerful forces in their schools, Nashville's African American women teachers saw their individual authority diminish. Their objections at not having input into the issues of teacher placement, instruction, and discipline did not resonate as loudly as outbursts of angry antibusing protesters or outcries from influential civil rights lawyers and activists. The former NAACP desegregation lawyer Robert Carter claimed that instead of looking at the work of social scientists to determine negative consequences of segregation, he would in hindsight have recruited teachers to create a definition and model for equal education and base his argument on that definition.[125] The failure to listen to African American concerns about desegregation has been labeled a type of "cultural ignorance," which explains why the Metropolitan Nashville School System and others across the nation saw little worth in preserving African American schools and gaining advice from those who taught there.[126]

The black women teachers from inner-city schools attended PTA meetings to explain what their schools had to offer and answer questions from incoming students.[127] Had they had more opportunities to speak with apprehensive parents or share their educational philosophies about discipline and nurturing students from impoverished backgrounds, perhaps some African American students would not have suffered isolation or lacked understanding. Lillian Thomas has commented, "I always thought they didn't integrate right. If they had the parents come to meetings we [teachers] could talk with them about teaching their children to appreciate blacks and to appreciate one another then they would know how they should integrate. How they should get along, and then they wouldn't have had all of that trouble. But they didn't do that. They [parents] would get a notice—this week that white students go here, twenty teachers go there."[128] Although most white teachers held negative views concerning busing, many now believe that desegregation should have occurred. Betty Tune cherishes her friendships with black teachers, an opportunity she realizes she would never have had if she were not transferred.[129]

When black women teachers reminisce and discuss the powerful roles they once held in the African American community they seem to portray a romanticized view of segregated schools with eager happy children and loving instructors. Their seemingly nostalgic praise for the past is a reminder of their overwhelming yet powerful roles as women who sometimes taught in overcrowded hallways and with tattered textbooks. The recollections describe beautiful new schools built to obstruct integration or illustrate memories of nurturing teachers from these women's childhoods. Nonetheless, the stories tell less about African American female teachers' affection for segregated schools and more about disillusionment with the desegregation process.[130] Once teachers of children from different socioeconomic classes, as the minister's son who went to Pearl with the janitor's daughter, those who work in newly resegregated black schools now face an economically homogeneous school population of poor and working-class students. Middle-class families, both black and white, have flocked to the suburbs.

Integration was supposed to alleviate the massive burdens of black teachers, not diminish their role or cause new obstacles to African American educational progress. As Thelma Tears puts it, "I think the black child was hurt in the process to get a better building." Despite their call for the creation of more nurturing public school environments, most of the women deny ever wanting to return to the substandard segregated schools of the past, and teachers, both black and white, denounce school resegregation because, as Roberta Jackson says, they "went through so much to make it work."[131] These teachers suggest, however, that the true and lasting benefits of desegregation are still unrealized for most African American students in Nashville.

Conclusion

In 1998 Judge Wiseman approved a $206 million desegregation plan and dismissed the forty-three-year-old *Kelley v. Maxwell* case. For the first time since 1970 the Metro Nashville–Davidson County schools were not under court supervision and the board had sole control over which school the city's students would attend. Part of the system's plan included gradually dismantling busing in the lower grades and constructing new neighborhood schools as well as instituting programs for low-achieving students. The NAACP's new attorney, Richard Dinkins, celebrated the ruling. One of the original plaintiffs, Henry Maxwell, maintained, "I think that this plan brings us closest to a neighborhood school concept without going back in time and segregating the schools once again . . . I do not see us regressing. We've come too far. Students will now have to attend only three different schools during their tenure instead of seven."[1] In 1998 only one school in the Metro system had a 90 percent black student population; by 2003 there were nine, and almost 60 percent of the system's students attended racially unbalanced schools.[2]

African American teachers now work alongside whites in every school in the Metro system, but the faculty was the only group to fully integrate. Most of Nashville's formerly all-white schools still have small percentages of African American students, and the board of education closed or reconfigured several black institutions. By the early twenty-first century, the racial makeup of the system's public schools reflected the aftermath of desegregation in southern urban areas. African Americans gained access to white schools, but to obtain greater opportunities they often had to sacrifice their own institutions. The loss was more than one of actual school structures. A foundation of Nashville's African American community had disappeared.

As integration opened new employment and housing opportunities, some African Americans relocated from segregated neighborhoods to integrated ones. Those who remained had to fight to protect their neighborhood institutions, including schools. These cultural centers had connected residents through shared experiences and goals, and many residents felt that the neighborhood's schools belonged to them. Desegregation opened the doors to a larger white world, but it severed the bonds between school and neighborhood and between black teachers and the African American community. It also changed the relationships between black teachers and African American students.

Connections first formed more than one hundred years ago when newly freed slaves struggled to secure educational opportunities for their children. Black parents and community leaders sent their children to overcrowded and substandard public schools after they re-opened in the late 1860s. They did so because they equated education with power and opportunity. Although they appreciated white northern teachers, African Americans in Nashville wanted black teachers to train their children. They also wanted to exercise control over the educational destinies of their children as much as possible. That desire propelled black teachers to elevated status in the African American community. They became not only responsible to their students but also to their race. Racial uplift became the foundation of a black teacher's pedagogical philosophy.

As African Americans during the late nineteenth and early twentieth centuries attempted to circumvent the constrictions of segregation by equating racial progress and social betterment with educational attainment, teachers helped promote that philosophy as they inspired students by word and deed to obtain an education and rise to affluence. Although the belief in the emancipating power of education influenced individuals, collectively it had little impact upon employment among African Americans during segregation. The promise of equality through education did nevertheless help instill confidence and hope in black children that they could have a better life within the confines of segregation.

African American women flocked to teaching because it offered professional status and respect. After learning the tenets of middle-class behavior at black institutions of higher learning, the women embraced being regarded as professionals. Some attempted to safeguard their middle-class status by participating in exclusive clubs and sororities in order to escape the overwhelming poverty of the Great Depression and the rampant racism of American society. These teachers were bound by the black community to behave in a matter deemed appropriate, which sometimes included social separation from impoverished or working-class African Americans. Although they mastered their classrooms and organizations they succumbed to the larger dictates of the African American community because it created their role. Their status relied on its sentiment.

As the NAACP initiated its legal effort to end segregation, teachers were on the frontlines as plaintiffs in salary-equalization cases. In Nashville they challenged the board of education to pay them the same wages that whites received and won their case in 1942. During World War II and the cold war segregation and discrimination remained despite calls for patriotism and democracy. African American teachers responded to the contradiction by teaching an inclusive interpretation of democracy and patriotism that stressed tolerance and equality. By promoting the idea that the United States supported freedom and equality, they planted seeds of discontent that would blossom into full-scale student protest by the late 1950s and 1960s. Ironically, as the NAACP pushed for desegregation it implicitly and subtly condemned segregated schools and their teachers. The studies the NAACP used, which used dolls and children's response to them, suggested that black children had low self-esteem, so black teachers fought valiantly to instill self-confidence in students. These contradictions signaled a change in the NAACP's strategy for racial progress. The South's black teachers, once in charge of uplifting the race, now had to sacrifice their status as professionals in order to support the idea that segregated schools were unequal. They also had to experience whatever negative consequences resulted from the new push for desegregation.

After the *Brown v. Board of Education* decision in 1954, public school systems across the South enacted massive measures to evade the Court's ruling. African Americans in Nashville supported the NAACP's desegregation efforts publicly and in spirit, but they nonetheless embraced African American schools and worked to obtain more funding for them. The dual approach to educational equality that black Nashvillians supported stressed integration and retaining black schools. Although some African American parents thought white schools were better than theirs, most feared sending their children to unwelcoming environments. Whether from fear of reprisal or by choice, very few offered to send their children to desegregated schools. Black Nashvillians never wanted to abandon their institutions or lose their teachers; they merely desired more options for the children. Coupled with white resistance, that reluctance ensured that most Nashville schools remained segregated until the early 1970s.

Meanwhile, African Americans took to the streets to put Jim Crow to death in businesses and restaurants. Although black teachers endured the implied suggestions of inferiority and possible job loss, they provided background support as the lawyers and activists grew more prominent. They also adapted to a more effective way to achieve racial progress by standing back and letting go.

In 1971 the federal government enacted new measures, including busing and black-and-white percentage ratios, to force whites to participate in local desegregation efforts. Desegregation had become a one-sided endeavor, and only token blacks attended white schools. Nevertheless, the new plan could not overcome white flight to suburban or private schools. The black community expressed alarm and outrage when plans were proposed to close their community institutions.

The plan caused extensive change in the work environment. Although black Nashvillians had worked to have black teachers in the community's classrooms, by the 1980s most black students in Nashville public schools had few teachers who were African American. There was no wide-scale protest to stop the transfer of black teachers to white schools; the black community underestimated the detrimental effect their removal would have on schools, communities, and students. African American teachers, along with parents and other community members, were responsible for developing positive self-concepts in African American children and often served as surrogate parents. Without them, black pupils lacked a crucial resource.

Some black teachers were lost in their new environments after desegregation because they were no longer accountable to the black community in general but only to their few remaining black students. The African American community also suffered at the hands of a board of education that insisted that eliminating black institutions was the best way to achieve desegregation. Whites bore the smallest burden during desegregation, blacks the most severe.

African American teachers are still respected, but they no longer hold positions of prestige and power in Nashville's black community. With the advent of the women's movement and the positive results of the civil rights era, black women now assume professional status in positions that range from astronaut to Web-site developer. Nevertheless, something changed when black women teachers lost their place in society. Many left the profession, and in most cases black children now have few African American educational influences to support them.

Some black teachers suggest that desegregation was detrimental to African American students, but it was problematic for them as well because they had to reevaluate their roles in the educational system and the black community. Black women teachers were compelled to provide support from the background, and doing so limited their power to speak for themselves and their schools. If the black community and the Metropolitan Nashville Board of Education had given more thought to these teachers' importance, perhaps more African American schools would have remained open and more consideration would have been given to students' emotional needs.

The story of black women teachers in Nashville's public schools is one of triumph and tragedy. During segregation they consistently managed to educate their sometimes poverty-stricken students despite substandard schools and society's racist environment. African American teachers now face new challenges resulting from desegregation, changing concepts of pedagogy, and shifting social values. Nevertheless, their mission continues: help students.

In more recent years, schools have re-segregated, the number of black teachers has decreased, and issues of parental neglect and violence have increased. African American female teachers helped shape urban education in the South, and their achievements and experiences offer insight into how to solve the mounting problems of today. These women believed that children could progress despite economic status. By establishing relationships with a student's parents, they achieved support from home in manners of discipline and academics. Now, the bond between parent and teacher is easily broken. As the number of neighborhood schools in Nashville continues to increase, the city has the opportunity to correct its mistakes. The Metropolitan Nashville School System must combine black teachers' ability to nurture and be role models, whether in the classroom or outside it, with their experience in forming bonds with parents and their abilities to connect the school to the community through technological and academic advances. Then the true goals of desegregation—educational equality for all—can be achieved.

Notes

INTRODUCTION

1. James D. Anderson, *The Education of Blacks in the South, 1860–1935* (Chapel Hill: University of North Carolina Press, 1988); Adam Fairclough, *Teaching Equality: Black Schools in the Age of Jim Crow* (Athens: University of Georgia Press, 2001); Michael Fultz, "African American Teachers in the South: Powerless and the Expectations of Protest," *History of Education Quarterly* 35 (Winter 1995): 401–22; Linda M. Perkins, "The History of Black Teaching: Growth and Decline within the Profession," in *American Teachers: Histories of a Profession at Work*, edited by Donald Warren (New York: Macmillian, 1989); Vanessa Siddle Walker, *Their Highest Potential: An African American School Community in the Segregated South* (Chapel Hill: University of North Carolina Press, 1996); Stephanie Shaw, *What a Woman Ought to Be and to Do: Black Professional Workers in the Jim Crow Era* (Chicago: University of Chicago Press, 1996).

CHAPTER 1: "BY PRECEPT AND EXAMPLE": SCHOOLS, COMMUNITY, AND PROFESSIONAL TEACHERS FROM 1867 THROUGH THE 1930S

1. Joseph H. Cartwright, *The Triumph of Jim Crow: Tennessee Race Relations in the 1880s* (Knoxville: University of Tennessee Press, 1976), 29; Herbert Leon Clark, "The Public Career of James Carroll Napier, Businessman, Politician, and Crusader for Racial Justice, 1845–1940," Ph.D. diss., Middle Tennessee State University, 1980, 26; see also James Carroll Napier Papers, Special Collections, John Hope and Aurelia E. Franklin Library, Fisk University, Nashville. Randall Brown was the first black person to win a seat on the city council in 1868.

2. Public Acts of the State of Tennessee, Tennessee General Assembly, ch. 108, Senate Bill 108, March 18, 1901. Vincent P. Franklin uses the term *cultural capital* to describe the black community's social, cultural, and/or financial efforts to support its children and African American schools. Franklin, "Cultural Capital and African American Education," *Journal of African American History* 87 (Spring 2002): 175–81. Nashville's public schools began in 1855 and reopened after the Civil War.

3. George Hubbard, *History of the Colored Schools of Nashville, Tennessee* (Nashville: Wheeler, Marshall and Bruce, 1874), 7.

4. For more information about northern teachers working in the Reconstruction-era South, see Henry Lee Swint, *Northern Teachers in the South* (New York: Octagon Books, 1967), and Jacqueline Jones, *Soldiers of Light and Love: Northern Teachers and Georgia Blacks, 1865–1873* (Athens: University of Georgia Press, 1992). For a broader discussion of the role of religious institutions in Reconstruction see Edward J. Blum,

Reforging the White Republic: Race, Religion, and American Nationalism, 1865–1898 (Baton Rouge: Louisiana State University Press, 2005).

5. Ester W. Douglass to Adam K. Spence, May 27, 1870, microfilm no. H-9509, Records of the American Missionary Association Archives, Amistad Research Center, Tulane University, New Orleans.

6. Hubbard, *History of the Colored Schools*, 7.

7. Bobby Lovett, *The African American History of Nashville, Tennessee, 1780–1930: Elites and Dilemmas* (Fayetteville: University of Arkansas Press, 1999), 136; James D. Anderson, *The Education of Blacks in the South, 1860–1935* (Chapel Hill: University of North Carolina Press, 1988), 23–25.

8. Lovett, *The African American History of Nashville*, 136. Belle View opened in a former two-story home in 1867.

9. Minutes, Nashville City Board of Education, July 6, 1868, Metropolitan Nashville Board of Education Office.

10. Annual Report, Superintendent of Schools, 1873.

11. Lovett, *The African American History of Nashville*, 138; Harold Rabinowitz, "Half a Loaf: The Shift from White to Black Teachers in the Negro Schools of the Urban South, 1865–1890," *Journal of Southern History* 40 (Nov. 1974): 579. Nashville's first black female public school teachers continued a tradition of instruction established by free black women such as Sarah Player Porter, who had opened her own institution in 1841 (Lovett, *The African American History of Nashville*, 36).

12. Ibid., 272; Rabinowitz, "Half a Loaf," 578.

13. Annual Report, Board of Education, 1871.

14. Stanley Jon Folmsbee, Robert Ewing Corlew, and Enoch Lockwood Mitchell, *History of Tennessee* (New York: Lewis Historical Publishing, 1960), 2: 244.

15. Rabinowitz, "Half a Loaf" 566.

16. Minutes, Nashville City Board of Education, Nov. 5, 1878.

17. A list of board of education information is in supporting documents for *Thomas v. Hibbits* (46 F. Supp. 368 [M.D. Tenn. 1942]), see "Negro Applicants and Employees," Minutes, Nashville City Board of Education, 1880. The Knowles Street School opened in 1879 but was closed in 1883 after the opening of Meigs and Pearl Elementary School. Knowles reopened in 1890. Although board minutes list the name of the school as Vandaville, it was named after Randall Vandavall, a prominent minister who has several spellings of his last name listed.

18. Lovett, *The African American History of Nashville*, 138–39; Rabinowitz, "Half a Loaf," 582.

19. Rabinowitz, "Half a Loaf," 586. Du Bois did not teach in the Nashville schools.

20. Annual Report, Nashville City Board of Education, 1884; Lovett, *The African American History of Nashville*, 138–39.

21. Yollette Trigg Jones, "The Black Community, Politics, and Race Relations in the Iris City," Nashville, Tennessee, 1870–1954," Ph.D. diss., Duke University, 1985, 59.

22. Rabinowitz, "Half a Loaf," 582.

23. Michele Foster, "Constancy, Connectedness, and Constraints in the Lives of African American Teachers," *National Women's Studies Journal* 3 (Spring 1991): 240.

24. Rabinowitz, "Half a Loaf," 583.

25. Annual Report, Nashville City Board of Education, 1886. McKee was reopened in the late 1870s.

26. Anderson, *The Education of Blacks in the South*, 186.

27. Table 6.2, "High School Enrollment by Age, Race, and Southern States, 1910, U.S. Census Records," cited in Anderson, *The Education of Blacks in the South*, 191.

28. The quotation is cited in D. N. Crosthwait Jr., "The First Black High School," *Negro History Bulletin* 37 (June–July 1975): 267; see also Leslie Carnes, "History of Pearl High," 1974, 1, unpublished document on file at the Pearl High School Archives, Nashville.

29. Crosthwait, "The First Black High School," 267–28.

30. Ibid.

31. Lovett, *The African American History of Nashville*, 138.

32. Ibid., 139.

33. Annual Report of the Nashville Public Schools, 1897.

34. Lovett, *The African American History of Nashville*, 139.

35. U.S. Bureau of the Census, *Thirteenth Census of the United States Taken in the Year 1910; Statistics Statistics for Tennessee, Containing Statistics of Population, Agriculture, Manufactures, and Mining for the State, Counties, Cities, and Other Divisions* (Washington: Government Printing Office, 1913).

36. *Plessy v. Ferguson* 163 U.S. 537 (1896) 163 U.S. 537.

37. Anderson, *The Education of Blacks in the South*, 25–27; Horace Mann Bond, *The Education of the Negro in the American Social Order* (New York: Prentice-Hall, 1934), 158.

38. Jones, "The Black Community," 141.

39. William McMakin, "The History of Nashville City Schools, 1930–1960," M.A. thesis, East Tennessee State University, 1973, 7–8.

40. Redding S. Suggs Jr., *Motherteacher: The Feminization of American Education* (Charlottesville: University Press of Virginia, 1978).

41. U.S. Bureau of the Census, *The Negro Population in the United States, 1790–1915* (Washington, D.C.: Government Printing Office, 1918), 526, cited in Earl Lewis, "Discourse of Class Formation: The Inner World of Black School Teachers," presented at the annual meeting of the Organization of American Historians, 1991, 15.

42. Nashville Public School Directory, 1912, box 7, folder 12, Metropolitan Nashville Archives.

43. Glenda Gilmore, *Gender and Jim Crow: Women and the Politics of White Supremacy in North Carolina, 1896–1920s* (Chapel Hill: University of North Carolina Press, 1996), 36; Andrew Ward, *Dark Midnight When I Rise: The Story of the Fisk Jubilee Singers, Who Introduced the World to the Music of Black America* (New York: Farrar, Straus, Giroux, 2000); Stephanie Shaw, *What a Woman Ought to Be and to Do: Black Professional Workers in the Jim Crow Era* (Chicago: University of Chicago Press,

1996), 83; Kevin Gaines, *Uplifting the Race: Black Leadership, Politics, and Culture in the Twentieth Century* (Chapel Hill: University of North Carolina Press, 1996), 56.

44. John Odgen, circular letter, Oct. 3, 1865, in Selected Records of the Tennessee Field Office Bureau of Refugees, Freedmen, and Abandoned Lands, 1865–1872, microfilm publication T142, roll 24, National Archives.

45. Joe M. Richardson, *A History of Fisk University, 1865–1946* (Tuscaloosa: University of Alabama Press, 1980), 2–4. Odgen, the former principal of the Minnesota State Normal School and a lieutenant in the Second Wisconsin Cavalry during the Civil War, received the appointment of superintendent of education for the Freedmen's Bureau in Tennessee in 1865. Cravath, raised in an abolitionist family in Homer, New York, was a pastor in Berlin Heights, Ohio, before resigning in 1863 to work as the chaplain of the 101st Regiment of Ohio Volunteers, an experience that led him to work with former slaves. After the war Cravath became the field secretary of the AMA. Smith also worked for the AMA as the district secretary of the newly created Middle West Department.

46. Richardson, *A History of Fisk University*, 7.

47. John Ogden, letter, June 1866, microfilm no. H9221, Records of the American Missionary Association, Amistad Research Center, Tulane University, New Orleans.

48. Emma Grisham interview in "Born in Slavery: Slave Narratives from the Federal Writers Project, 1936–1938," WPA Slave Narrative Project, Tennessee Narratives, 15:28–31, Federal Writers Project, Manuscript Division, Library of Congress.

49. Richardson, *A History of Fisk University*, 15. Nashville's first public schools for whites opened in 1855. The schools closed during the Civil War and reopened shortly thereafter.

50. Ward, *Dark Midnight When I Rise;* Cynthia Fleming, "A Survey of the Beginnings of Tennessee's Black Colleges and Universities, 1865–1920," *Tennessee Historical Quarterly* 39 (Summer 1980): 198–99; Richardson, *A History of Fisk University*, 14.

51. Lovett, *The African American History of Nashville*, 161.

52. Miss E. A. Easter to Adam Spence, Feb. 12, 1866, microfilm no. H9049A, Records of the American Missionary Society Archives, Amistad Research Center, Tulane University, New Orleans; Ward, *Dark Midnight When I Rise*, 64.

53. Ibid.; Richardson, *A History of Fisk University*, 11.

54. Booker T. Washington, "An Article in the Independent," March 24, 1910, in Washington, *The Booker T. Washington Papers*, vol. 10: *1909–11*, assistant editors Geraldine McTigue and Nan E. Woodruff (Urbana: University of Illinois Press, 1981), 613–18.

55. Richardson, *A History of Fisk University*, 64.

56. Fleming, "A Survey of the Beginnings," 198.

57. Ibid., 199.

58. Ward, *Dark Midnight When I Rise*, 65; Phillips, "Education of Blacks in Tennessee," 161.

59. William Brownlow and Western Freedmen's Aid Commission, *Second Annual*

NOTES TO PAGES 15–19 / 145

Report of the Western Freedmen's Aid Commission (Cincinnati: Methodist Book Concern, 1865), 1–48.

60. Adam Spence to Erastus M. Cravath, Oct. 4, 1870, microfilm no. H9529, Records of the American Missionary Association Archives, Amistad Research Center, Tulane University, New Orleans.

61. Jessie Carney Smith, "Minnie Lou Crosthwaite," in *Notable American Black Women*, book 2, edited by Jessie Carney Smith (New York: Gale Research, 1996), 156–57.

62. "Negro Applicants and Employees" list.

63. "Principal's Rating of Teacher Reports," June 10, 1938, Metropolitan Nashville Archives.

64. Luther Carmichael, "Stately and Grand," *Nashville Globe and Independent*, May 27, 1955, 8.

65. Author interview with Sadie Madry, July 17, 1995, Nashville, tape recording, in author's possession.

66. Patrick Connolly, "Pearls of Wisdom," *The Tennessean*, July 26, 1998, 2F.

67. Anderson, *The Education of Blacks in the South*, 104. General autobiographical information about Du Bois appears in David Levering Lewis, *W. E. B. Du Bois, Biography of a Race, 1868–1919* (New York: Henry Holt Publishers, 1993).

68. W. E. B. Du Bois, "The Talented Tenth," in *Du Bois on Education*, edited by by Eugene F. Provenzo Jr. (Walnut Creek: Rowman and Littlefield, 2002), 92.

69. Information about the concept of the "talented tenth" appears in W. E. B. Du Bois, *The Souls of Black Folk: Essays and Sketches* (Chicago: A.C. McClurg, 1903).

70. Du Bois, *The Souls of Black Folk*; Lewis, *W. E. B. Du Bois*, 68.

71. General Education Bill, Public Acts of Tennessee, House Bill 242, 1909; Fleming, "A Survey of the Beginnings," 202.

72. Clark, "The Public Career of James Carroll Napier," 116.

73. *Tennessee Agricultural and Industrial State Normal School Bulletin* 3, no. 8 (1914–15): 3, Special Collections and Archives, Tennessee State University Library, Nashville; Fleming, "A Survey of the Beginnings," 203.

74. Clark, "The Public Career of James Carroll Napier," 117.

75. Lovett, *The African American History of Nashville*, 170–71.

76. Cynthia Fleming, "The Development of Black Education in Tennessee, 1865–1920," Ph.D. diss., Duke University, 1977, 129.

77. *Nashville Globe*, June 21, 1912, 1.

78. Lester Lamon, *Black Tennesseans, 1900–1930* (Knoxville: University of Tennessee Press, 1977), 102; Lovett, *The African American History of Nashville*, 170. Washington, a former slave who rose to become the founder and president of Tuskegee Institute in Alabama, eventually promoted industrial education and was designated as spokesperson for the race. Born in 1854, he endured slavery and saw the widespread disenfranchisement of African Americans and expansion of racial violence in the South. He worked his way through Hampton Institute, an industrial school for African Americans that offered training in trades such as carpentry, printing, sewing, and cooking as well as teacher preparation.

79. Anderson, *The Education of Blacks in the South*, 102; Louis Harlan, *Booker T. Washington: The Wizard of Tuskegee, 1901–1915* (New York: Oxford University Press, 1983).

80. "Commencement at Fisk University: Booker T. Washington Delivers Address to Class," *Nashville Globe*, June 13, 1913, 1.

81. Booker T. Washington, "An Account of a Speech in Columbus, Ohio, May 24, 1900, Address at the 1900 General Conference of the A.M.E. Church, in Booker T. Washington, *Booker T. Washington Papers*, vol. 5: *1899–1900*, assistant editor Barbara S. Kraft (Urbana: University of Illinois Press, 1976), 542.

82. Anderson, *The Education of Blacks in the South*,82.

83. William H. Baldwin Jr., "The Present Problem of Negro Education, Industrial Education," 1899, in *Proceedings of the Capon Springs Conference on Christian Education in the South*, subseries C, Southern Education Board Records, Southern Historical Collection, Louis Round Wilson Library, University of North Carolina at Chapel Hill.

84. Anderson, *The Education of Blacks in the South*, 94–95; Annual Reports, Nashville City Schools, 1887–1912.

85. Harlan, *Booker T. Washington*.

86. Washington, "An Article in the Independent"; Edward L. Ayers, *The Promise of the New South: Life after Reconstruction* (New York: Oxford University Press, 1992), 324; Virginia Lantz Denton, *Booker T. Washington and the Adult Education Movement* (Gainesville: University of Florida Press, 1993), 140.

87. J. G. Merrill, "Fisk University after Thirty-nine Years," *American Missionary* (June 1904): 165.

88. Untitled and undated speech in James Carroll Napier Collection, container 1, Special Collections, John Hope and Aurelia E. Franklin Library, Fisk University, Nashville.

89. Thomas Jesse Jones, ed., *Negro Education: A Study of the Private and Higher Schools for Colored People in the United States* (1917, repr. New York: Arno Press and the New York Times, 1969), 541.

90. W. E. B. Du Bois, "Negro Education," *The Crisis* 15 (Feb. 1918): 173–78.

91. Anderson, *The Education of Blacks in the South*, 147.

92. Taylor, "The History of the Teacher Education Program at Tennessee State University," 51.

93. Anderson, *The Education of Blacks in the South*,148.

94. Samuel Henry Shannon, "Agricultural and Industrial Education at Tennessee State University during the Normal School Phase, 1912–1922: A Case Study," M.A. thesis, George Peabody College for Teachers, 1978, 174; Taylor, "The History of the Teacher Education Program at Tennessee State University," 51; Lovett, *The African American History of Nashville*, 169.

95. Du Bois, "The Talented Tenth," 85.

96. Booker T. Washington letter, March 1910.

97. Shaw, *What a Woman Ought to Be and to Do*, 90–91.

98. *Tennessee Agricultural and Industrial State Normal School Bulletin* 2, no. 7 (1912–

13), Special Collections and Archives, Tennessee State University Library, Nashville.

99. Shaw, *What a Woman Ought to Be and to Do*, 78.

100. Linda M. Perkins, "The History of Black Teaching: Growth and Decline within the Profession," in *American Teachers: Histories of a Profession at Work*, edited by Donald Warren (New York: Macmillan, 1989), 389; Lovett, *The African American History of Nashville*, 169.

101. Lovett, *The African American History of Nashville*, 169; *Tennessee Agricultural and Industrial Normal College Bulletin* 2 (1913), Special Collections and Archives, Tennessee State University Library, Nashville.

102. Shaw, *What a Woman Ought to Be and to Do*, 89–90; Shane White and Graham White, *Stylin: African American Expressive Culture from Its Beginnings to the Zoot Suit* (Ithaca: Cornell University Press, 1998), 164.

103. Ozana Vineyard, "Our Girls," *Tennessee Agricultural and Industral College Bulletin* 16 (Oct.–Nov. 1927): 2–3.

104. Shaw, *What a Woman Ought to Be and to Do*, 81; Michael Fultz, "African American Teachers in the South," *History of Education Quarterly* 35 (Winter 1995): 408.

105. Jones, "The Black Community," 140. The schools were Ashcraft, Belleview, Carter, Clifton, Hadley, Knowles, Lawrence, Meigs, Merry, Napier, Peebles, and Pearl Senior High School. Records of the Public Schools, reel 3, box 14, James Emerick Nagy Collection, Tennessee State Library and Archives, Nashville.

106. "Knowles School Alliance Wants Pure Water for the Children," *Nashville Globe*, May 18, 1913, 1.

107. McMakin, "The History of Nashville City Schools," 13.

108. Lovett, *The African American History of Nashville*, 137, 143, 141; Carnes, "History of Pearl High," 1.

109. Anderson, *The Education of Blacks in the South*, 197–98.

110. Nashville statistics given in Annual Reports of the Public Schools, 1915–16, cited in Anderson, *The Education of Blacks in the South*, 200.

111. Jones, "The Black Community," 140.

112. Minutes, Nashville City Board of Education, Dec. 9, 1919, Jan. 9, 1920, July 31, 1922; McMakin, "The History of Nashville City Schools," 19. Pensions for retired teachers also began during the 1920s.

113. Shaw, *What a Woman Ought to Be and to Do*, 135.

114. "School Teachers," *Nashville Globe*, March 28, 1913, 4.

115. Sharon Harley, "Beyond the Classroom: The Organizational Lives of Black Female Educators in the District of Columbia, 1880–1930," *Journal of Negro Education* 51 (Summer 1982): 3.

116. Joanna P. Moore, *In Christ's Stead: Autobiographical Sketches* (Chicago: Women's Baptist Home Mission Society, 1902), 204–5, in the "Documenting the American South," Louis Round Wilson Library, University of North Carolina at Chapel Hill, http://docsouth.unc.edu/church/moore/moore/htm/ (accessed May 8, 2007).

117. Stephanie J. Shaw, "Black Club Women and the Creation of the National Association of Club Women," *Journal of Women's History* 3 (Fall 1991): 19; Deborah Gray White, *Too Heavy a Load: Black Women in Defense of Themselves, 1894–1935* (New York: W. W. Norton, 1999); *Minutes of National Convention of the National Association of Colored Women Clubs, Nashville, Tennessee, September 15–18, 1897* (Washington: Smith Brothers, 1901), in *Records of the National Association of Colored Women, 1895–1992*, part 1, reel 2: *Convention Minutes and Reports, 1897* (Bethesda, Md.: University Publications of America, 1993).

118. The revolutionary-era poet spelled her name *Phillis*.

119. Lamon, *Black Tennesseans*, 213.

120. Jones, "The Black Community," 153; Fleming, "The Development of Black Education in Tennessee," 29.

121. Sharlon Harley, "For the Good of Family and Race," *Signs* 15 (Winter 1990), 348–49.

122. "Mrs. Washington to Women's Clubs," *Nashville Globe*, June 20, 1913, 1.

123. Gilmore, *Gender and Jim Crow*, 25; Shaw, "Black Club Women," 114; see also Dorothy Salem, *To Better Our World: Black Women in Organized Reform* (Brooklyn: Carlson Publishing, 1990), and Evelyn Brooks Higginbotham, *Righteous Discontent: The Women's Movement in the Black Baptist Church, 1880–1920* (Cambridge: Harvard University Press, 1993), 152.

124. White, *Too Heavy a Load*, 70; Gaines, *Uplifting the Race*; E. Franklin Frazier, *The Black Bourgeoisie: The Rise of a New Middle Class in the United States* (1957, repr. New York: Collier Books, 1975).

125. White, *Too Heavy a Load*, 71, 77.

126. Ibid., 55.

127. Mary E. Frederickson, "'Each One is Dependent on the Other': Southern Churchwomen, Racial Reform, and the Process of Transformation, 1880–1940," in *Visible Women: New Essays on American Activism*, edited by by Nancy Hewitt and Suzanne Lebsock (Urbana: University of Illinois Press, 1993), 297.

128. For more information about white clubwomen's work in Nashville see, Tennessee State Federation of Women's Clubs, *Woman's Work in Tennessee* (Memphis: Jones-Briggs Publishers, 1916).

129. "Report of the Director from September 22 to October 20, 1913 to the National League on Urban Conditions Among Negroes" and Haynes to Mr. L. Hollingsworth Wood, Oct. 23, 1915, George Edmund Haynes Papers, Special Collections, John Hope Franklin and Aurelia E. Franklin Library, Fisk University, Nashville; Richardson, *A History of Fisk University*, 64; Lynda Wynn, "Bethlehem Centers of Nashville," http:/www/tnstate.edu/library/digital//beth.htm (accessed May 9, 2007); Yolette Trigg Jones,"The Black Community, Politics, and Race Relations in the 'Iris City,'" 164–66.

130. Gilmore, *Gender and Jim Crow*, 174.

131. Editorial, May 17, 1918, quoted in Jones, "The Black Community," 183.

132. Elizabeth Lindsay Davis, *Lifting as they Climb* (1933, repr. New York: G.

K. Hall, 1996), 396; Lovett, *The African American History of Nashville*, 100; Wynn, "Bethlehem Centers of Nashville," 1

133. Shelia Wisner, "Whites Found Ways to Silence Black Vote for Nearly Forty Years," *The Tennessean*, Feb. 9, 1992, 1B, Board of Education News and Views press clippings, box 4, folder 27, Metropolitan Nashville Archives.

134. Elsa Barkley Brown, "Negotiating and Transforming the Public Sphere: African American Political Life in the Transition from Slavery to Freedom," *Public Culture* 7 (Fall 1994): 134; Rosalyn Terborg-Penn, *African American Women in the Struggle for the Vote, 1850–1920* (Bloomington: Indiana University Press, 1998).

135. "Negro Women Prepare to Vote," *Nashville Banner*, Aug. 5, 1919, reel 10, Tuskegee Institute Newspaper Clipping Files, Special Collections, Hollis Burke Frissell Library, Tuskegee University, Tuskegee, Ala.; Anita Shafer Goodstein, "A Rare Alliance: African American and White Women in the Tennessee Elections of 1919 and 1920," *Journal of Southern History* 2 (May 1998): 227, 228; Adele Logan Alexander, "Adella Hunt Logan, the Tuskegee Woman's Club and African Americans in the Suffrage Movement," in *Votes for Women: The Woman Suffrage Movement in Tennessee, the South, and the Nation*, edited by Marjorie Spruill Wheeler (Knoxville: University of Tennessee Press, 1995).

136. Minnie L. Crosthwaite to Charlotte Hawkins Brown, July 15, 1921, Brown Collection, July–Dec. 1921 file, reel 3, no. 41, Arthur and Elizabeth Schlesinger Library on the History of Women in America, Radcliffe College, Cambridge, Mass., quoted in Gilmore, *Gender and Jim Crow*, 157.

137. A. W. Hunton, *Young Women Christian Association: Beginnings among Colored Women* (New York: Young Women's Christian Association, 1913).

138. Jane Olcott, *The Work of Colored Women* (New York: Colored Work Committee War Work Council, 1919), 77; Louis Kyriakoudes, *The Social Origins of the Urban South: Race, Gender, and Migration in Nashville and Middle Tennessee, 1890–1930* (Chapel Hill: University of North Carolina Press, 2003), 148.

139. U.S. Census, *Statistics of Population Composition*.

140. Paul Mowbray to George Haynes, Aug. 31, 1917, George Haynes Papers, Special Collections, John Hope and Aurelia E. Franklin Library, Fisk University, Nashville.

141. Lovett, *The African American History of Nashville*, 252. For more on the history of the NAACP see Gilbert Jonas, *Freedom's Sword: The NAACP and the Struggle against Racism in America 1909–1969* (New York: Routledge, 2004).

142. Goodstein, "A Rare Alliance," 227–28; Lovett, *The African American History of Nashville*, 140.

143. Lamon, *Black Tennesseans*, 213.

144. Marcus Garvey's United Negro Improvement Association (UNIA) argued that the New Negro celebrated the manhood of African American men. It contended that the race would progress through the efforts of its men to assume their rightful place in society. That contradicted the philosophies of the National Association of Colored Women's Clubs, which argued that the future of the race depended on the condition of its women. Organizations that promoted interracial interaction, such

as the National Association for the Advancement of Colored People, embraced the tenets of the New Negro philosophy that promoted equality and positive imagery while discarding some of its nationalistic proponents. For more information about women in the UNIA see Ula Yvette Taylor, *The Veiled Garvey: The Life and Times of Amy Jacques Garvey* (Chapel Hill: University of North Carolina Press, 2002).

145. Raymond Wolters, *The New Negro on Campus: Black College Rebellions of the 1920s* (Princeton: Princeton University Press, 1975).

146. W. E. B. Du Bois, "Diuturni Silenti," in *The Education of Black People: Ten Critiques, 1906–1960*, edited by Herbert Aptheker (New York: New York Monthly Review Press, 2002), 57.

147. Wolters, *The New Negro on Campus*, 29–69.

148. Richardson, *A History of Fisk University*, 100, 102–3 author interview with Minerva Johnson Hawkins, July 21, 1995, Nashville, tape recording in author's possession.

149. Author interview with Minerva Johnson Hawkins.

150. Du Bois, "Diuturni Silenti," 55.

151. Lawrence C. Ross Jr., *The Divine Nine: The History of African American Fraternities and Sororities* (New York: Kensington Books, 2002). Both sororities already had alumnae chapters in the city.

152. Paula Giddings, *In Search of Sisterhood: Delta Sigma Theta and the Challenge of the Black Sorority Movement* (New York: William Morrow, 1998), 143.

153. Author interviews with Lillian Dunn Thomas, Dec. 18, 1994, and July 16, 2003, Nashville, tape recordings in author's possession.

154. Author interview with Virginia Westbrook, July 11, 1995, Nashville, tape recording in author's possession.

155. Author interview with Thelma Baker Baxter, July 27, 1995, Nashville, tape recording in author's possession.

156. Author interview with Lillie Bowman, July 25, 1995, Nashville, tape recording in author's possession.

157. Deborah Gray White, *Too Heavy a Load: Black Women in Defense of Themselves, 1894–1994* (New York: Norton, 1998), 158,159.

158. Author interview with Sadie Madry; author interview with Minerva Hawkins.

159. Kyriakoudes, *The Social Origins of the Urban South*, 149.

160. Robbins, "From Winter to Winter," 20.

161. Don H. Doyle, *Nashville since the 1920s* (Knoxville: University of Tennessee Press, 1985), 86. The Great Depression did not affect the majority of Nashville's businesses and residents until 1930, when a major bank, Caldwell and Company, declared insolvency and subsequently closed. In November of that same year the black-owned People's Savings and Loan closed its doors after twenty years of providing mortgages to black religious and fraternal institutions and loans to Nashville's black community. Depositors eventually received settlements of 35 percent of their deposits. A loan from the Reconstruction Finance Corporation (RFC) saved the only remaining black bank in Nashville, Citizens' Bank, which had survived an earlier

run on its reserves by temporarily merging with a local white bank. Although local businesspeople and politicians attempted to remedy growing unemployment, their efforts fell short.

Consequently, African American women teachers had the enormous responsibility of helping students succeed despite adverse economic conditions and substandard public schools. The jobless rate in Nashville rose to almost 25 percent by the end of 1930. During the next few years, hundreds of displaced people traveled to the city to seek jobs, but often they ended up begging for food and money. The transients set up housekeeping in Nashville's poorest slums, and the local media reported incidents of infant starvation and food shortages. The number of relief applicants at local charities such as the Salvation Army and the Community Chest rose from about 2,600 in 1929 to nearly ten thousand in 1936. Banks began offering script for currency, and businesses cut prices to attract customers. After local authorities failed to alleviate the seemingly insurmountable crisis, the city and the state welcomed President Franklin Delano Roosevelt's New Deal measures. By 1934 the population benefited from such programs as the Public Works Administration (PWA), the Works Progress Administration (WPA), and the Tennessee Valley Authority (TVA). Nashville government officials used PWA funds and other government programs to build an airport, a new capitol building, and the Steeplechase Park. See also Lamon, *Black Tennesseans*.

162. Nashville City Public Schools, *Information Concerning Nashville City Public Schools* (Nashville: Nashville City Public Schools, 1927), 5. Davidson County opened Haynes High School for African American students in 1941.

163. Frank P. Bauchman, *A Survey Report for the Division of Surveys and Field Studies* (Nashville: George Peabody College for Teachers, 1931), 198, 218, 298.

164. Bauchman, *A Survey Report*, 103. According to Bauchman, 74 percent of African American students failed one quarter or more of the school year, 22 percent made satisfactory progress, and 3 percent gained a quarter; 4 percent of the students in grades one through six were behind three years or more. The report cited late entrance to school, which caused children to fall behind, and academic deficiency as the causes for failure to pass to the next level. Grade retention eventually led to students dropping out before entering the upper grades.

165. Author interview with Novella Bass, July 18, 2003, Nashville, tape recording in author's possession.

166. Giddings, *In Search of Sisterhood*, 147, 233.

167. Robin Kelly, "We Are Not What We Seem: Rethinking Black Working-Class Opposition in the Jim Crow South," *Journal of American History* 80 (June 1993): 75–112; Tera Hunter, *To 'Joy My Freedom: Southern Black Women's Lives and Labors after the Civil War* (Cambridge: Harvard University Press, 1997).

168. Robert D. Phillips. "A Survey of Racial Conflict and Racial Adjustment in Nashville, Tennessee," senior project, Tennessee Agricultural and Industrial State College, 1939, 10, 14.

169. Whether church-sponsored or based on activities such as playing cards or needlepoint, these groups offered ways for African Americans to interact among

themselves, offering charitable services, and cultural and social outlets. Unable to attend white restaurants, forced to sit in the balconies of movie theaters, and denied admission to white dance clubs, African American men and women created their own ways to entertain.

170. Earl Lewis, "Connecting Memory, Self, and the Power of Place in African American Urban History," in *The New African American Urban History* (Thousand Oaks, Cal.: Sage Publications, 1996), 128.

171. Tommie Morton-Young, *Sable Scenes: Real Life Stories of Black Family Life and Living in a Southern Town, 1935–1965* (Nashville: AfrAgen Associates, 1996), 42–43.

172. Earl Lewis argues that scholars of African American history should discuss the social construction of class as well as race. Lewis, "Discourse on Class Formation," 4, 12.

173. Author interview with Gwendolyn Vincent, July 31, 1995, Nashville, tape recording in author's possession; author interview with Ruth Young, Aug. 2, 1995, Nashville, tape recording in author's possession.

174. Shaw, *What a Woman Ought to Be*, 6.

175. Carter G. Woodson, *The Miseducation of the Negro* (Washington, D.C.: Associated Publishers, 1933), 52–61.

176. "Alpha Beta History," written historical information donated to author by Rose Howell; author interview with Rose Howell, Aug. 1, 2003, Nashville, tape recording in author's possession; author interview with Sadie Madry.

177. "Alpha Beta History"; author interview with Sadie Madry.

178. Edmonia Grant, 1937, manuscript notes for *Patterns of Negro Segregation* by Charles S. Johnson, 232, Special Collections, John Hope and Aurelia E. Franklin Library, Fisk University, Nashville. Born in Nashville in 1903, Grant came from a family that stressed educational excellence. Her mother, Hortense Stone White, completed the tenth grade. Her father, George White, studied at Fisk, and all of her five brothers and sisters earned college degrees. During the summer months and on Saturdays she and her siblings worked their mother's family business, the McIntyre Beauty Parlor. The shop, which her mother and aunts bought from their employer, catered to elite whites. Emma Bragg, *Scrapbook: Some Family Reminiscences of a Native Nashville Septuagenarian* (Nashville: E. W. Bragg, 1985).

179. African American teachers resented the discriminatory practices of some white sales clerks. Some, for example, refused to wait on black women, instead directing the store's maids to help them. This practice placed shoppers in the predicament of possibly offending the domestic worker if they refused her service or protested. It was even more stinging for professionals such as Edmonia Grant to encounter disrespect from women they perceived as being of a lower educational and cultural class.

180. Edmonia Grant manuscript notes. Another custom that infuriated teachers and other black women involved the failure of whites to address them formally by title and last name. Most preferred that only family and friends address them by given name. The practice of doing so had originated in slavery, and white southern-

ers continued that convention or else used titles such as *gal* or *auntie*. Although they often used *professor* when adressing male educators, women teachers did not receive that courtesy. Black women countered these insults by using only their initials or their husbands' names.

181. Edmonia Grant to the Rosenwald Fellowship Committee, 1942, box 415, folder 13, Julius Rosenwald Fund Archives, Special Collections, John Hope and Aurelia E. Franklin Library, Fisk University, Nashville.

182. Author interview with Novella Bass.

183. The Nashville Board of Education permitted married women to teach in the 1920s.

184. Lewis, "Discourse on Class Formation."

CHAPTER 2: "THE LIVING SYMBOLS OF DEMOCRACY": WORLD WAR II AND THE COLD WAR

1. Author interview with Sadie Madry, July 17, 1995, Nashville, tape recording in author's possession.

2. *Mills v. Board of Education of Anne Arundel County*, 30 F. Sup. 245; Mark V. Tushnet, *The NAACP's Legal Strategy against Segregated Education, 1925–1950* (Chapel Hill: University of North Carolina, 1987), 68. The NAACP first began its fight by successfully suing for blacks to enter the University of Maryland's Law School in 1935.

3. *Alston et al. v. School Board of the City of Norfolk et al.*, 112 F. 2d. 992 (1940)

4. Tushnet, *The NAACP's Legal Strategy*, 88.

5. National Association for the Advancement of Colored People, "Report of the National Education Program 28th Conference NAACP 24 June 1937: The National Education Program and What Has Been Accomplished," Papers of the National Association for the Advancement of Colored People, part 3: Campaign for Educational Equality, ser. A, Legal Department and Central Department Records, reel 19, box 1–C-281, University of Texas at Austin Libraries; Richard Kluger, *Simple Justice* (New York: Vintage Books, 1975), 216.

6. Leander L. Boykin, "The Status and Trends of Differentials between White and Negro Teachers' Salaries in the Southern States, 1900–1946," *Journal of Negro Education* 18 (Winter 1949): 41–42, 44. The seventeen southern states are Alabama, Arkansas, Delaware, Florida, Georgia, Kentucky, Louisiana, Maryland, Mississippi, Missouri, North Carolina, Oklahoma, South Carolina, Tennessee, Texas, Virginia, and West Virginia.

7. Charles Houston to Walter S. Walker, Jan. 4, 1935, and Z. Alexander Looby to Charles H. Houston, Jan. 7, 1936, both in Papers of the National Association for the Advancement of Colored People, Teacher's Salaries, Nashville, Tennessee, part 3: Campaign for Educational Equality, ser. B, reel 10, box B-181, University of Texas at Austin Libraries.

8. Minutes, Nashville City Board of Education, Feb. 27, March 24, 1939, Metropolitan Nashville Board of Education Office.

9. Harry Walker interview with Z. Alexander Looby, June 19, 1939, manuscript

notes for *Patterns of Negro Segregation* by Charles S. Johnson, Special Collections, John Hope and Aurelia E. Franklin Library, Fisk University, Nashville.

10. Don H. Doyle, *Nashville since the 1920s* (Knoxville: University of Tennessee Press, 1985), 181.

11. Doyle, *Nashville since the 1920s;* Charles Houston to Walter S. Walker.

12. *Alston v. School Board of Norfolk*, 1123 F. 2d992, 4th Cir., cert. denied; Tushnet, *The NAACP's Legal Strategy*, 89; National Association for the Advancement of Colored People, "Memorandum of Procedure to Equalize Salaries, 28 January 1939," Papers of the National Association for the Advancement of Colored People, Teacher's Salaries, Tennessee, Nashville, part 3: Campaign for Educational Equality, ser. B, reel 10, box B-181, University of Texas at Austin Libraries.

13. Tushnet, *The NAACP's Legal Strategy*, 89.

14. National Association for the Advancement of Colored People, "Memorandum of Procedure to Equalize Salaries."

15. *Thomas v. Hibbits*, 46 F. Supp. 368, M.D. Tenn. 1942, Harold Thomas Collection, Special Collections, John Hope and Aurelia E. Franklin Library, Fisk University, Nashville.

16. Minutes, Nashville City Board of Education, 1891–1940, reel 27, James Emerick Nagy Collection, Tennessee State Library and Archives, Nashville.

17. Mildred Freeman, 1939, manuscript notes for *Patterns of Negro Segregation* by Charles S. Johnson (New York: Harper and Brothers, 1943), 232, Special Collections, John Hope and Aurelia E. Franklin Library, Fisk University, Nashville.

18. Annual Report, Nashville City Public Schools, 1940.

19. U.S. Office of Education and the Tennessee Department of Education, *A Graphic Analysis of Tennessee's Public Elementary and High Schools: An Analysis of Significant Phases of Public Elementary and High Schools Graphically Presented, Including a Ranking of County Educational Systems* (Nashville: Cullom and Ghertner, 1937), fig. 42, 43.

20. "US Judge Studies School Salaries," *Pittsburgh Courier*, March 7, 1942; *Thomas v. Hibbits*.

21. Press release, Salary Equalization, Tenn.—Nashville file, Papers of the National Association for the Advancement of Colored People, Teacher's Salaries, Tennessee, Nashville, part 3: Campaign for Educational Equality, ser. B, reel 10, box B-181, University of Texas at Austin Libraries.

22. Press release, Salary Equalization, Tenn.; "Davies Bans Discrimination in White, Negro Teachers' Pay," *Nashville Banner*, July 28, 1942, 1B. Harold Thomas resigned from teaching in 1943, shortly after winning the suit, to go into sales. His new job, selling class rings and graduation materials, enabled him to travel throughout Tennessee and Alabama.

23. Author interview with Sadie Madry.

24. *Turner v. Keefe*, 50 F. Supp 647, S.D. Fla. 1943; *Thompson v. Gibbs* 60 F. Supp 872, E.D. S.C. 1945; Tushnet, *The NAACP's Legal Strategy*, 88–104; Bruce Beezer, "Black Teachers' Salaries and the Federal Courts before *Brown v. Board of Education:* One Beginning for Equity," *Journal of Negro Education* 55 (Spring 1986): 200–213;

see also Scott Baker, "Testing Equality: The National Teacher Examination and the NAACP's Legal Campaign to Equalize Teacher's Salaries in the South 1936–1963," *History of Education Quarterly* 35 (Spring 1995): 49–64.

25. Author interviews with Lillian Dunn Thomas, Dec. 18, 1994, and July 16, 2003, Nashville, tape recordings in author's possession.

26. Arnold George Love "An Evaluative Study of the Nashville Teachers' Association, Formerly Teachers' Benefit Association," M.S. thesis, Tennessee State University, 1956, 34; Harry William McMackin III, "Nashville City Schools, 1930–1960," M.A. thesis, East Tennessee State University, 1973, 56.

27. Harold Thomas obituary, *780 Countdown*, July 30, 1968, 1; author interview with Novella Bass, July 18, 2003, Nashville, tape recording in author's possession.

28. Mildred Freeman manuscript notes for *Patterns of Negro Segregation;* author interview with Novella Bass.

29. In addition to this victory, the NAACP had expanded the fight against educational inequities in other cases across the state. In 1936 it filed a writ of mandamus to force the University of Tennessee to admit William Redmond to its pharmacy school; meanwhile, however, Redmond entered Fisk University and performed poorly there. The judge dismissed the writ, ruling that it was filed before the University of Tennessee could take proper action, and the NAACP decided not to pursue the case. In 1939 the NAACP filed another writ of mandamus on behalf of several blacks who wanted to go to graduate school at the University of Tennessee at Knoxville, but that writ was dismissed on technical grounds in 1940. In response, the Tennessee state legislature allocated funds to Tennessee A&I State College to create and strengthen its graduate programs. Papers of the National Association for the Advancement of Colored People, part 3, Campaign for Educational Equality, ser. A, Legal Department and Cultural Office Records, 1913–40, reel 17, box 1-D-98, University of Texas at Austin Libraries; Tushnet, *The NAACP's Legal Strategy*, 55–56.

30. Tennessee Department of Education, *A Graphic Analysis of Tennessee Public Elementary and High Schools* (Nashville: Tennessee Department of Education, 1934), 34–35, 3.

31. Sharon Harley, "For the Good of the Family and Race: Gender, Work, and Domestic Roles in the Black Community, 1880–1930," *Signs* 15 (1990): 336–49.

32. Jacqueline Jones, *Labor of Love, Labor of Sorrow: Black Women, Work, and the Family from Slavery to Present* (New York: Basic Books, 1985), 134.

33. Nashville City Schools, "Comparative Study of the Administrative Supervisor and Instructional Staff," report by the Department of Education, Metropolitan Nashville Board of Education Office, June 30, 1947, 2.

34. William McMakin, "The History of Nashville City Schools, 1930–1960," M.A. thesis, East Tennessee State University, 1973, 59.

35. Baker, "Testing Equality," 63; Robert A. Margo, *Race and Schooling in the South, 1880–1950: An Economic History* (Chicago: University of Chicago Press, 1990), 65; L. D. Williams, "Capital Is Paying Largest Salaries Says 1954 Report," *Nashville Globe and Independent*, Nov. 4, 1955, 1.

36. For more information about the FEPC see Herbert Garfinkel, *When Negroes*

March: The March of Washington Movement in Organizational Politics of the FEPC (New York: Macmillian, 1969).

37. Robert Spinney, *World War II in Nashville: Transformation of the Homefront* (Knoxville: University of Tennessee Press, 1998), 33; Don Doyle, *Nashville since the 1920s* (Knoxville: University of Tennessee Press, 1985), 85–89.

38. Spinney, *World War II in Nashville*, 57.

39. Ibid.; Minutes, Nashville City Board of Education, Aug. 1942.

40. Ibid.; Spinney, *World War II in Nashville*, 59.

41. Spinney, *World War II in Nashville*, 59; Yollette Trigg Jones, "The Black Community, Politics, and Race Relations in the Iris City: Nashville, Tennessee, 1870–1954," Ph.D. diss., Duke University, 1985, 279.

42. Doris Weatherford, *American Women and World War II* (New York: Oxford University Press, 1990), 191; Nashville–Davidson County Metropolitan Planning Commission, *Economy of Metropolitan Nashville: The Employment of Women in the Metropolitan Nashville Area*, staff memorandum 2, April 1964, quoted in Spinney, *World War II in Nashville*, 33.

43. Minutes, Nashville City Board of Education, Nov. 30, 1942.

44. For more information about the experiences of African American nurses see Darlene Clark Hine, *Black Women in White: Racial Conflict and Cooperation in the Nursing Profession, 1890–1950* (Bloomington: University of Indiana Press, 1989); see also Weatherford, *American Women and World War II*, 193.

45. "Eighteen New Teachers Chosen: All-Day School for Youngsters Is Now Assured," *Nashville Globe and Independent*, June 30, 1944, 1.

46. "Mrs Phynetta Nellis Is Given Surprise Party by Local USO," *Nashville Globe and Independent*, May 11, 1945, 4; Jones, "The Black Community," 280.

47. Spinney, *World War II in Nashville*, 55; Jones, "The Black Community," 279. Labor relations also changed during the war years as African American workers protested unfair treatment. In 1944 black city employees walked away from their jobs to protest discriminatory job assignments, and local black physicians sued to gain admittance to practice at General Hospital. Tired of their bosses' use of racial slurs, fourteen workers at a downtown cafe walked out in 1945. These small acts of resistance resulted in few tangible results, but they did reflect growing impatience with discrimination.

48. Spinney, *World War II in Nashville*, 56.

49. Minutes, Nashville City Board of Education, Sept. 21, 1942. The twelve black schools were Pearl Senior High School, Belleview, Cameron Junior High, Carter-Lawrence, Clifton, Ford Greene, Head, Meigs, Napier, Pearl Elementary, Peebles, and Washington Junior High School.

50. "Attached Supplemental Reports to Superintendent's Report to Board of Education," Minutes, Nashville City Board of Education, Jan. 1944–June 1944.

51. Mary L. Williams, "Unity-Action-Victory," *The Broadcaster*, June 1942.

52. "Graduates Will Get Diploma at Closing Tonight: Several Seniors Will Go from War Memorial Building Direct to Train Bound for Army Camp," *Nashville Globe and Independent*, June 9, 1944, 1; Eunice Matthew, "Teaching—A Perplexing

Job These Days," *The Broadcaster,* June 1943. The Tennessee Negro Education Association was a professional group for black teachers.

53. Author interview with Ella Thompson, July 22, 2003, Nashville, tape recording in author's possession.

54. Minutes, Nashville City Board of Education, Dec. 17, 1941.

55. Lucy Campbelle, "Unity—Action—Victory," *The Broadcaster,* June 1942; "Bond Sales of City Schools Reach $24,610 as Drive Ends," *Nashville Globe and Independent,* Feb. 18, 1944, 1.

56. "Attached Supplemental Reports to Superintendent's Report to Board of Education," Minutes, Nashville City Board of Education, Jan. 1944–June 1944; author interview with Frances McHaney Reeds, July 20, 1995, Nashville, tape recording in author's possession; Lucy Campbelle, "Unity—Action—Victory," *Broadcaster* June 1942.

57. Author interview with Lillian Dunn Thomas, Dec. 18, 1994; author interview with Lillie Bowman, July 25, 1995, Nashville, tape recording in author's possession.

58. "Mrs. Edmonia Grant Chosen to Education Post in Washington," *Nashville Globe and Independent,* Nov. 11, 1946, 1, 4.

59. "Programs Emphasize Health, Attendance, Arts, Reading Improvement, War Drives, Professional Meetings, Character," *Nashville Teacher,* March 14, 1945, 3.

60. "Subject: Use Marion Jack Letters," Marion Jack Letters, box 415, folder 13, Julius Rosenwald Fund Archives, Special Collections, John Hope and Aurelia E. Franklin Library, Fisk University, Nashville. Grant's letters also discussed human rights issues in India and China.

61. For more information about the Race Relations Institute see Patrick J. Gilpin and Marybeth Gasman, *Charles S. Johnson: Leadership beyond the Veil in the Age of Jim Crow* (Albany: State University of New York Press, 2003).

62. Spinney, *World War II in Nashville,* 62.

63. "A&I State College Expanding to Become $6,500,000 Institution," *Nashville Globe and Independent,* Oct. 31, 1947, 1, 4. Davis is the husband of Ivanetta Davis.

64. *Gray v. Board of Trustees,* 342 U.S. 517 (1952); see also *Gray et al. v. Board of Trustees of the University of Tennessee et al.,* appeal from the U.S. District Court for the Eastern District of Tennessee no. 120.

65. Frances A. Saunders, "A Summary of Activities of the Department of Elementary Education," ser. 1, 1946, Division of Education, Tennessee A&I State College Education Department, Special Collections and Archives, Tennessee State University Library, 4, 11.

66. Spinney, *World War II in Nashville,* 60.

67. *The Block Bulletin* (Oct. 1949), in Mingo Scott, *The Negro in Tennessee Politics and Governmental Affairs, 1865–1965: The Hundred Years Story* (Nashville: Rich Print, 1965), 202.

68. Spinney, *World War II in Nashville,* 67

69. Arnold George Love, "An Evaluative Study of the Nashville Teachers' Association, Formerly Teachers' Benefit Association," M.S. thesis, Tennessee State University, 1956, 35.

70. Love, "An Evaluative Study"; *Nashville Globe and Independent*, Aug. 3, 1945, 1.

71. Charles S. Johnson, "Present Status of Race Relations in the South," *Social Forces* 23 (Oct. 1944): 27–32.

72. Ronald Lora, "Education: Schools as Crucible in Cold War America," in *Reshaping America: Society and Institutions 1945–1960*, edited by Robert H. Bremner and Gary W. Reichard (Columbus: Ohio State University Press, 1982), 223, 230–31.

73. William A. Bass, "Education for American Democracy," address to Nashville City Board of Education, March 2, 1948. Located in Minutes, Nashville City Board of Education.

74. Bass, "Education for American Democracy."

75. "Supt. W. A. Bass Addresses A&I Students for Education Week Celebration," *Nashville Globe and Independent*, Nov. 25, 1949, 7. The *Nashville Globe* merged with the *Nashville Independent* in 1931.

76. Elsie M. Lewis, "Speakers and Discussion Groups Consider Many Phases of Democratic Living," *Nashville Teacher*, March 31, 1949, reel 11, box 25, 805–12, James Emerick Nagy Collection.

77. Lewis, "Speakers and Discussion Groups."

78. Eunice Matthew, "Organizing the Curriculum for Education in Democratic Living," *Nashville Teacher*, March 31, 1949, reel 11, box 25, 805–12, James Emerick Nagy Collection.

79. William Faulkner, "Organizing the Curriculum for Education in Democratic Living," *Nashville Teacher*, March 31, 1949, reel 11, box 25, 805–12, James Emerick Nagy Collection.

80. Faulkner, "Organizing the Curriculum for Education."

81. Lewis, "Speakers and Discussion Groups," 5.

82. Spinney, *World War II in Nashville*, 22.

83. Teachers' Benefit Association, *How to Belong* (pamphlet), reel 27, James Emerick Nagy Collection.

84. Idabelle Yeiser, "Are We Training Our Youth for a World Community?" *Broadcaster* (June 1948): 49.

85. The Tennessee Negro Education Association became the Tennessee Education Congress in 1953.

86. For information on U.S. government reactions to civil rights activities during the cold war see Mary L. Dudziak, *Cold War Civil Rights: Race and the Image of American Democracy* (Princeton, N.J.: Princeton University Press, 2000), 47–113.

87. Author interview with Novella Bass; "City Closes Belleview School," *Nashville Globe and Independent*, July 11, 1947, 1, 4. The spelling of the school's name later changed from Belle View to Belleview.

88. "Drastic Change Is Made in State Rule By '47 Legislature," *Nashville Globe and Independent*, Sept. 21, 1947, 1, 4.

89. Juan Williams, *Thurgood Marshall: An American Revolutionary* (New York: Random House, 1998), 131–42; Gale Williams O'Brien, *The Color of the Law: Race, Violence, and Justice in the Post-World War II South* (Chapel Hill: University of North Carolina, 1999), 48–55. In 1946 the African American business community, located

at Fourth and Cedar Streets in Nashville, was threatened when city planners decided to construct a park and demolish several businesses and community organizations such as the Colored YMCA. The city postponed the project because the National Housing Authority, in an effort to provide more homes for veterans, restricted building materials and labor for home building use only. While Nashville's black business community breathed a sigh of relief, some forty miles away, in Columbia, Tennessee, a fight between a black veteran and a white storeowner escalated into a race riot that resulted in the deaths of two black men while in police custody, threats of lynching, and the vandalism of Mink Slide, the black business center of Columbia. Twenty-five black men were arrested after black residents responded to the invading mobs with gunfire. The governor of Tennessee called in the National Guard to quell the disturbance. Surprised by the militance of their neighbors, white Columbians argued that black Nashvillians had instigated the incident by telling the small town's black population to retaliate against the white rioters. That was not the case. The black Columbians, including veterans and other citizens, were returning gunfire because they refused to stand by and let their neighborhood be destroyed. Nashville residents later offered financial support to the families of the men on trial.

In a surprise victory the NAACP lawyers, including Thurgood Marshall and Z. Alexander Looby, won acquittals for twenty-three of the twenty-five men accused. The prosecution then dropped the two remaining guilty cases because of a lack of evidence. When Marshall attempted to leave the city he narrowly escaped a lynch mob. Looby, seeing Marshall's abduction, followed the group, which led them to turn around. The officers then falsely arrested Marshall for drunken driving and took him to the courthouse. Charges were dismissed after Marshall passed a breath test. A friend who volunteered to act as a decoy and drive Looby's car out of Columbia was severely attacked; Marshall and Looby returned to Nashville safely in another car. Sadie Madry, proudly remembered, "Thurgood Marshall came to help Mr. Looby. You know, Thurgood Marshall, he was somebody in Washington. They took him to jail and Mr. Looby helped him get out!" Author interview with Sadie Madry.

Black Americans across the nation celebrated this victory. Although the judge relocated the case to the neighboring city of Lawrenceburg to ensure a fair trial, finding an impartial all-white southern jury was rare. Marshall gained popularity, and Looby also became a hero to black Tennesseans. More than three hundred attended a testimonial dinner in Nashville to celebrate the victory and congratulate him. The local attorney thanked everyone for their touching tributes by humorously stating that "it made him feel that Nashvillians really were 'behind him,' but that when the battle was in progress at Columbia and Lawrenceburg, he was suspicious that Nashvillians were so far 'behind him' that it would have been difficult to see them had he turned around to look for them." He later added that "he rather preferred to give the highest tribute to those patriots at Columbia who stood when all were against them." Williams, *Thurgood Marshall*; "Defense Attorney in Columbia Case Lauded as Hero," *Nashville Globe and Independent*, Dec. 28, 1946, 1.

90. "Big Bond Issue for City Schools, Big Money Required to Meet Need of Growing School Population," *Nashville Globe and Independent*, Oct. 10, 1947, 1, 4.

91. Margold Report, Papers of the National Association for the Advancement of Colored People, part 3: Campaign for Educational Equality, ser. A, Legal Department and Central Office Records, 1913–1940, reel 1, box 1–C-96, University of Texas at Austin Libraries; Tushnet, *The NAACP's Legal Strategy*, 28.

92. W. E. B. Du Bois, *Dusk of Dawn: An Essay toward an Autobiography of a Race Concept* (1940, repr. New Brunswick: Transaction Books, 1984); W. E. B. Du Bois, "Does the Negro Need Separate Schools?" *Journal of Negro Education* 4 (July): 328–35, in *Du Bois on Education*, edited by Eugene Provenzo Jr. (Walnut Creek, Cal.: Rowman and Littlefield, 2002), 143.

93. Tushnet, *The NAACP's Legal Strategy*, 103.

94. Amilcar Shabazz, "The Opening of the Southern Mind: The Desegregation of Higher Education in Texas 1865–1965," Ph.D. diss., University of Houston, 1996.

95. Baker, "Testing Equality"; Richard Kluger, *Simple Justice: The History of* Brown v. Board of Education (New York: Vintage Books, 1977), 291; Tushnet, *The NAACP's Legal Strategy*, 103; *Sweat v. Painter* 210 S.W. 2d 442 (1947); *McLaurin v. Oklahoma Regents for Higher Education*, 339 U.S. 637 (1950).

96. Thelma D. Perry, *History of the American Teachers' Association* (Washington: National Education Association, 1975), 175; "Organization Was Formed in City of Nashville in 1903," *Nashville Globe and Independent*, Aug. 25, 1944, 1.

97. "Organization Was Formed"; Tushnet, *The NAACP's Legal Strategy*.

98. "Organization Was Formed"; "Big Bond Issue for City Schools," 1.

99. "Happy School Days for All," *Nashville Globe and Independent*, Oct. 30, 1953, 4.

100. Anna Holden et al., *A Tentative Description and Analysis of the School Desegregation Crisis in Clinton, Tennessee* (Nashville: Anti-Defamation League of B'nai B'rith in Cooperation with the Society for the Study of Social Problems, 1956), 1–21.

101. The case remained in the circuit court until the *Brown v. Board of Education of Topeka, Kansas* decision of 1954 when Federal Judge Robert L. Taylor ruled for action consistent with *Brown*. In 1955 the plaintiffs asked for the complete and immediate desegregation of all Anderson County schools.

102. Minutes, Nashville City Board of Education, 1954; McMakin, "The History of Nashville City Schools."

103. Minutes, Nashville City Board of Education, April 1953; McMakin, "The History of Nashville City Schools."

104. Williams, *Thurgood Marshall*, 199; *Brown v. Board of Education of Topeka, Kansas*, 347 U.S. 483, 74 Sup. Ct. 686, 98 L. Ed. 873, 881 (1954).

105. Derrick Bell, *Silent Covenants:* Brown v. Board of Education *and the Unfulfilled Hopes for Racial Reform* (New York: Oxford University Press, 2004), 124, 125; Michael Fultz, "African American Teachers in the South: Powerless and the Expectations of Protest," *History of Education Quarterly* 35 (Winter 1995): 22.

106. Derrick Bell, "Time for the Teachers: Putting Educators Back into the Brown Remedy," *Journal of Negro Education* 52 (Summer 1983): 292.

107. James Patterson, Brown v. Board of Education: *A Civil Rights Milestone and Its Troubled Legacy* (New York: Oxford University Press, 2001), 44, 45.

108. Author interview with Ola Hudson, July 27, 2003, Nashville, tape recording in author's possession.

109. Author interview with Lillian Dunn Thomas, July 16, 2003, Nashville, tape recording in author's possession.

CHAPTER 3: "WE ARE READY WHENEVER THEY ARE":
BROWN AND THE CIVIL RIGHTS MOVEMENT

1. Minutes, Nashville City Board of Education, June 10, 1954, Metropolitan Nashville Board of Education Office; Atlanta NAACP, *Declaration on NAACP Policy in Public School Segregation Cases*, 1954, reprinted in Artie Thomas Pate, "An Investigation of the Desegregation Process in the Metropolitan Nashville–Davidson County Public School System, 1954–1969," Ed.D thesis, 1981, George Peabody School for Teachers of Vanderbilt University, 88.

2. William Gandy, "Implications of Education for the Southern Teacher," *Journal of Negro Education* 2 (Spring 1962): 193.

3. Author interview with Lillian Dunn Thomas, Dec. 18, 1994, July 16, 2003, Nashville, tape recordings in author's possession.

4. George N. Redd, "Education in Tennessee—One Year Afterward," *Journal of Negro Education* 24 (Winter 1955): 339.

5. Saundra Ivey, "Desegregation: Twenty-four Years Later," *The Tennessean*, May 13, 1979, 7B.

6. Glen Linden, *Desegregating Schools in Dallas* (Dallas: Three Forks Press, 1995), 38.

7. *Annual Report of the State Superintendent of Public Instruction for Tennessee of the Scholastic Year Ending June 30, 1901* (Chattanooga: Press of Times Printing, 1901), 35.

8. Minutes, Nashville City Board of Education, June 10, 1954; "Negro School Rejects Three White Students," *New York Times*, Sept. 12, 1954, collected in microfilm collection of Schomberg Center for Research in Black Culture clipping file, section 1, 1924–74: Desegregation Tennessee, Nashville Room, Metropolitan Nashville Public Library.

9. Patrick J. Gilpin and Marybeth Gasman, *Charles S. Johnson: Leadership beyond the Veil in the Age of Jim Crow* (Albany: State University of New York Press, 2003), 242.

10. Z. Alexander Looby, quoted in Minutes, Nashville City Board of Education, Sept. 9, 1954.

11. *Brown v. Board of Education*, 349 U.S. 294, 75 Sup. Ct. 753, 99 L. Ed. 1083 (1955).

12. Numan Bartley, *The Rise of Massive Resistance: Race and Politics in the South during the 1950s* (Baton Rouge: Louisiana State University Press, 1969); James T. Patterson, Brown v. Board of Education: *A Civil Rights Milestone and its Troubled Legacy* (New York: Oxford University Press, 2000).

13. Minutes, Nashville City Board of Education, June 9, July 14, Aug. 11, 1955.

14. General Education Bill, Public Acts of Tennessee, House Bill 242, 1909, 190; Minutes, Nashville City Board of Education, Aug. 11, 1955.

15. William McMakin, "The History of Nashville City Schools, 1930–1960," M.A. thesis, East Tennessee State University, 1973, 32.

16. Hugh Davis Graham, "Desegregation in Nashville: The Dynamics of Compliance," *Tennessee Historical Quarterly* 25 (Summer 1966): 135–54; John Egerton, *Nashville: The Faces of Two Centuries: 1780–1980* (Nashville: Plus Media, 1979), 251.

17. Saundra Ivey, "Desegregation: Thirty-six Years and Still Trying," *The Tennessean*, June 14, 1993, 2B.

18. Author interview with Albert A. Shaw, July 22, 2003, Nashville, tape recording in author's possession.

19. *Kelley v. Board of Education of the City of Nashville*, 139 F. Supp. 578 (1956).

20. Graham, "Desegregation in Nashville," 136. Lorch was no longer a party in the suit. A cold war casualty, he refused to state whether he currently was or had been a member of the Communist Party and provide other names of possible communist sympathizers. As a result, he was labeled a communist. In addition, the local white community pressured Fisk for harboring a professor who advocated interracial ideals and desegregation. Consequently, the university did not renew his contract and released Lorch from the faculty in 1955. After a campaign by other faculty members to have him reinstated failed, he relocated to Arkansas, taught at a small college, and eventually moved to Canada. He was acquitted of all charges in November 1957. Gilpin and Gasman, *Charles S. Johnson*, 237–38.

21. "Wharton Pupils Assured: Long-Neglected Area of City to Get Big Building," *Nashville Globe and Independent*, Oct. 14, 1955, 1.

22. Minutes, Nashville City Board of Education, Oct. 12, 1955.

23. Author interview with Charleene Spencer, July 11, 1995, Nashville, tape recording in author's possession.

24. Author interview with Lillie Bowman, July 25, 1995, Nashville, tape recording in author's possession.

25. Author interview with Helen Young, July 15, 1995, Nashville, tape recording in author's possession.

26. Minutes, Nashville City Board Of Education, June 12, 1956.

27. Robert Pratt, *The Color of Their Skin: Education and Race in Richmond Virginia, 1954–1989* (Charlottesville: University Press of Virginia, 1992), 16.

28. "Unrest Seemed to Have Left Along with John Kasper," *Nashville Globe and Independent*, Nov. 8, 1957, 4. The *Nashville Globe and Independent* published from 1907 to 1960. The newspaper appeared sporadically and ceased publishing from April to December 1954. From reading later editorials and articles, however, the *Globe and Independent* supported school integration but wanted to prevent any negative impact upon the city's black schools and teachers. M. W. Day, the NAACP's president during the 1950s, was also the publication's advertising manager.

29. V. P. Franklin, "Cultural Capital and African American Education," *Journal of African American History* 87 (Spring 2002): 176.

30. "Integration Is Near in Tennessee Schools," *Nashville Globe and Independent*, Aug. 24, 1956, 1, 4.

31. For more information concerning the southern reaction to the Brown decision

see Bartley, *The Rise of Massive Resistance*, and Patterson, Brown v. Board of Education.

32. Patterson, Brown v. Board of Education, 99.

33. "Much Dissatisfaction Expressed on Ruling of U.S. Judge Miller" (editorial), *Nashville Globe and Independent*, Aug. 15, 1958, 4.

34. Nashville Board of Education, "A Resolution Adopted by the Nashville Board of Education on 29 October 1956, 'Initiating a Plan of Desegregation in the Nashville City Schools,'" box 68, file 1, Kelly Miller Smith Papers, Special Collections, Jane and Alexander Heard Library, Vanderbilt University, Nashville.

35. "Kasper and Company Did Not Interfere in School Board Matter," *Nashville Globe and Independent*, Sept. 6, 1957, 1.

36. Pate, "An Investigation of the Desegregation Process," 59.

37. Minutes Nashville City Board of Education, 17 April 1957.

38. "Memphis State University Gives Study to Years Delay of Integration Plan," *Southern School News*, Sept. 1958, 10.

39. Pate, "An Investigation of the Desegregation Process," 64–65; Don Doyle, *Nashville since the 1920s*, (Knoxville: University of Tennessee Press, 1985), 237. The six elementary schools were Bailey, Buena Vista, Fehr, Glenn, Hattie Cotton, and Jones.

40. Anna Holden, *A First Step toward School Integration* (pamphlet), edited by Jim Peck and Alexander L. Crosby (New York: Congress of Racial Equality, 1958), 5. Nashville's chapter of the Congress for Racial Equality (CORE) was founded in 1956.

41. Holden, *A First Step*; Ivey, "Desegregation: Thirty-six Years." Hayes was president of the Nashville NAACP branch from 1960 to 1962.

42. Shelia Wissner, "Eyewitnesses to the Struggle Tell Their Stories," *The Tennessean*, June 14, 1993, 3B.

43. Background information appears in chapter 2 of this volume. After a federal court order called for the desegregation of the schools in Clinton, Tennessee, that small East Tennessee town admitted twelve black students to its high school. Two days after school began, New Jersey resident John Kasper came to the city and led violent anti-integration demonstrations. One black student was assaulted, and black parents were threatened. After being arrested and let out on bail, Kasper resumed his demonstrations. Riots ensued. The governor then called the National Guard to restore order, and Kasper was jailed again. Patterson, Brown v. Board of Education, 101–3; Anna Holden et al., *A Tentative Description and Analysis of the School Desegregation Crisis in Clinton, Tennessee* (Nashville: Anti-Defamation League of B'nai B'rith in Cooperation with the Society for the Study of Social Problems, 1957), 1–21.

44. "Nashville School Bombed, Clinton Opening Peaceful," *Southern School News*, Oct. 1957; McMakin, "The History of Nashville City Schools," 124.

45. David Halberstam, *The Children* (New York: Random House, 1998), 57.

46. Pate, "An Investigation of the Desegregation Process," 126–27.

47. Ibid.; *Southern School News*, Oct. 1957; McMakin, "The History of Nashville City Schools," 122.

48. Holden, *A First Step*, 6, 7.

49. "Redbook Article Runs Feature Story on Nashville Integration Crisis," *Nashville Globe and Independent*, Feb. 7, 1958, 1.

50. Holden, *A First Step*, 7, 8.

51. Graham, "Desegregation in Nashville," 145.

52. Minutes, Nashville City Board of Education, March 13, 1958.

53. Metropolitan Public Schools Division of Pupil Accounting, Transfers, and Records, "Number of Black Children in Formerly All-White Nashville City Schools Broken Down by School," cited in Pate, "An Investigation of the Desegregation Process," 74; Hugh Davis Graham, *Crisis in Print Desegregation and the Press in Tennessee* (Nashville: Vanderbilt University Press, 1967), 174, 177.

54. Roy Wilkins to Z. Alexander Looby, June 26, 1958, Papers of the National Association for the Advancement of Colored People, 1956–65, General Office File, Board of Directors, Z. Alexander Looby, 1956–62, supplement to part 16, Board of Directors File, 1956–65, reel 5, box 25, University of Texas at Austin Libraries.

55. Roy Wilkins to Z. Alexander Looby, June 26, 1958, Papers of the National Association for the Advancement of Colored People, 1956–65.

56. "The 1958 Convention Dr. James M. Nabrit Challenges Tennessee Teachers to Dedicate Themselves to Three Major Tasks," *Broadcaster* 30 (May 1958): 115.

57. Jacqueline Jordan Irvine, "African American Teachers' Culturally Specific Pedagogy," in *In Search of Wholeness: African American Teachers and Their Culturally Specific Classroom Practices*, edited by Jacqueline Jordan Irvine (New York: Palgrave, 2002), 142. Excellent interviews of a wide range of African American teachers who taught during segregation and also in today's schools appear in Michele Foster, *Black Teachers on Teaching* (New York: New Press, 1997). On the experiences of African American teachers who work in contemporary schools see also Gloria Ladson-Billings, *The Dream Keepers: Successful Teachers of African American Children* (San Francisco: Jossey-Bass, 1994).

58. Vanessa Siddle Walker, *Their Highest Potential: An African American School Community in the Segregated South* (Chapel Hill: University of North Carolina Press, 1996), 201.

59. Alice Epperson, "Pearl High School Memories," interview cited at http://www.pbs.org/wgbh/amex/partners/ index.html (accessed April 18, 2007).

60. Epperson, "Pearl High School Memories"; Walker, *Their Highest Potential*, 201.

61. Author interview with Thelma Tears, July 10, 1995, Nashville, tape recording in author's possession.

62. "East Nashville Pays Loving Tribute to Mrs. M. W. Thompson," *Nashville Globe and Independent*, May 11, 1956, 1, 5.

63. Author interview with Charleene Spencer.

64. Author interview with Minerva Johnson Hawkins, July 21, 1995, Nashville, tape recording in author's possession.

65. Author interview with Sadie Madry, July 17, 1995, Nashville, tape recording in author's possession.

66. Johnetta K. Williams, "The Problem of De-Segregation: The Competent Teacher Has an Important Role in Preparing Children to Meet This Crisis," *The Broadcaster*, no. 26 (April 1955): 104.

67. James E. Haney, "The Effects of the *Brown* Decision on Black Educators," *Journal of Negro Higher Education* 47 (Winter 1978): 89–90.

68. Fultz, "Displacement of Black Educators," 14.

69. "Only Three Nashville Men for 'Bad Bills' Backed by Governor," *Nashville Globe and Independent*, Jan. 18, 1957, 4.

70. Mabel Bell Crooks, "The ATA Plans a Course of Action," *The Broadcaster*, no. 13 (Oct. 1954): 12.

71. L. D. Williams, "Capitol Is Paying Largest Salaries Says 1954 Report," *Nashville Globe and Independent*, Nov. 4, 1955, 1, 4.

72. "Rough Outsiders Cause All Trouble over Segregation," *Nashville Globe and Independent*, Sept. 14, 1956, 1, 4.

73. "Interview with Dr. Omer Carmichael: Is 'Voluntary Integration the Answer?'" *U.S. News and World Report*, Oct. 5, 1956, quoted in Fultz, "Displacement of Black Educators," 41.

74. Statistical information appears in Robert W. Hooker, *Displacement of Black Teachers in the Eleven Southern States* (Nashville: Race Relations Information Center, 1970).

75. L. D. Williams, "State Teachers Hold Big Meeting," *Nashville Globe and Independent*, April 18, 1958, 1, 4.

76. "Heart Warming Are Experiences of Groups Desegregated," *Nashville Globe and Independent*, Feb. 1, 1957, 1, 4.

77. J. H. Parrish, G. W. Brooks, and M. D. Senter to Dr. Quill E. Cope, Commissioner of Education, State Board of Education, "Open Letter to the Tennessee State Board of Education," *The Broadcaster*, no. 28 (Feb. 1956): 66.

78. "Reporting Service to Tell School Story: South Carolina," *Southern School News*, Sept. 3, 1954, 124; Jonas Rosenthal, "Negro Teachers and Desegregation," *Journal of Negro Education* 26 (Winter 1957): 68, 69.

79. "John Kasper and Company Cause Unexpected Trouble in City," *Nashville Globe and Independent*, Sept. 27, 1957, 8 (part of this quotation was used in the title of this chapter).

80. Pate, "An Investigation of the Desegregation Process," 70.

81. Author interview with Albert Shaw.

82. Linda Wynn, "Nashville Sit-Ins," in *Profiles in African American History*, edited by Bobby Lovett (Nashville: Tennessee State University, 1995), 1.

83. Wynn, "Nashville Sit-Ins"; author interview with Albert Shaw.

84. Leo Lilliard, interview excerpt from "Student Sit-ins in Nashville, 1960," in *Voices of Freedom: Oral History of the Civil Rights Movement from the 1950s through the 1980s*, edited by Henry Hampton and Steve Fayer with Sarah Flynn (New York:

Bantam Books, 1990), 60–61; Ray Waddle, "Divinity School Student Helped Show Protestors They Had Strength to Win," *The Tennessean*, Feb. 19, 1990, 1A, 6A.

85. Author interviews with Virginia Westbrook, July 11, 1995 (quotation), and July 17, 2004, Nashville, tape recordings in author's possession.

86. Will Sarvis, "Leaders in the Court and Community: Z. Alexander Looby, Avon N. Williams, Jr., and the Legal Fight for Civil Rights in Tennessee, 1940–1970," *Journal of African American History* 88 (Winter 2003): 47.

87. Paul Saprod, "Nashville, Tennessee: The Rebellion of African American Students," in *A Documentary History of the Negro People in the United States: 1960–1968*, edited by Herbert Aptheker (New York: Citadel Press, 1994), 22–23.

88. Author interview with Ruth Young, Aug. 2 1995, Nashville, tape recording in author's possession.

89. Author interview with Thelma Tears.

90. Author interview with Charleene Spencer; author interview with Donzell Johnson, Aug. 8, 2004, Nashville, tape recording in author's possession.

91. Halberstam, *The Children*, 73.

92. "Fisk Faculty Approves School's 'Sit-In' Stand," *Nashville Globe and Independent*, May 6, 1960, 1. Thirteen Tennessee A&I students were expelled in 1961 because they participated in freedom rides. Attorneys Looby and Williams successfully argued their case in federal district court, where Judge William E. Miller presided. The state attorney general ordered the freedom riders reinstated, but only seven returned.

93. Diane Nash quoted in "Inside the Sit-Ins and Freedom Rides: Testimony of a Southern Student," in *We Shall Overcome: The Civil Rights Movement in the United States in the 1950s and 1960s*, edited by David J. Garrow (New York: Carlson Publishing), 989.

94. Author interview with Myra Dixon, July 22, 2003, Nashville, tape recording in author's possession; author interview with Novella Davis, July 28, 1995, Nashville, tape recording in author's possession; author interview with Albert A. Shaw.

95. "Citywide 'Freedom Sunday' Set by Women's Unity League, April 4: This and 'Talent Extravaganza' to Benefit Legal Defense of Sit-In Students," *Nashville Globe and Independent*, March 25, 1960, 1.

96. Author interview with LaMona McCarter, March 12, 1994, Nashville, tape recording in author's possession.

97. Author interview with Ruth Young.

98. Author interview with Virginia Westbrook.

99. Author interview with Dorothy Baines, July 18, 1995, Nashville, tape recording in author's possession.

100. Adam Fairclough, "Being in the Field of Education and Being a Negro Almost Seems Tragic: Black Teachers in the Jim Crow South," *Journal of American History* 87 (June 2000): 90.

101. *Henry C. Maxwell v. County Board of Education of Davidson County, Tennessee et al.* 203 F. Supp. 768 (1960).

102. McMakin, "The History of Nashville City Schools," 136.

103. Ibid., 137.

104. John H. Harris, "School Reorganization in a Metropolitan Area: The Nashville Experience," in *Metropolitanism: Its Challenge to Education: The Sixty-seventh Yearbook of the National Society for the Study of Education (Part 1)*, edited by Herman G. Richey and Robert J. Havighurst (Chicago: National Society for the Study of Education, 1968), 377.

105. Harris, "School Reorganization"; McMakin, "The History of Nashville City Schools," 137; "Teachers' Groups Vote to Merge," *Southern School News*, Jan. 1964, 15.

106. Author interview with Virginia Westbrook.

107. Fultz, "Displacement of Black Educators," 24; author interviews with Ola Hudson, Aug. 7, 1995, and July 27, 2003 (quotation), Nashville, tape recordings in author's possession.

108. Doyle, *Nashville since the 1920s*, 189.

109. Bulletin in Papers of the Student Non-Violent Coordinating Committee, 1959–72, reel 40, 245, Nashville Public Library, Nashville, Tenn.

110. "Black Power Sparks Divergent Ideals," *Nashville Tennessean*, Feb. 14, 1969, 1, 12.

111. Doyle, *Nashville since the 1920s*, 257.

112. Ibid.; Minutes, Metropolitan Nashville–Davidson County Board of Education, Dec. 10, 1964.

113. Herbert Aptheker, "Youth March for Integration" (1959), in *A Documentary History of the Negro People in the United States: 1960–1968*, edited by Herbert Aptheker (New York: Citadel Press, 1994), 466. Adam Fairclough discusses the impact of integration on black teachers and schools in "The Costs of *Brown*: Black Teachers and School Integration," *Journal of American History* 19 (Spring 2004): 53. Further information on desegregation after 1966 appears in Richard Pride and David Woodard, *The Burden of Busing: The Politics of Desegregation in Nashville, Tennessee* (Knoxville: University of Tennessee Press, 1985).

CHAPTER 4: "THE ONLY WAY WE FOUGHT BACK WAS TO DO A GOOD JOB": PUBLIC SCHOOL INTEGRATION

1. Author interview with Gwendolyn Vincent, July 24, 1995, July 25, 2003, Nashville, tape recording in author's possession.

2. Further information about the Nashville activists who participated in the Student Non-Violent Coordinating Committee is in David Halberstam, *The Children* (New York: Random House, 1998).

3. *Brown v. Board of Education*, 349 U.S. 294, 75 Sup. Ct. 753, 99 L. Ed. 1083 (1955); *Kelley v. Board of Education of the City of Nashville*, 139 F. Supp. 578 (1956); "A Resolution Adopted by the Nashville Board of Education on October 29, 1956, Initiating a Plan of Desegregation in the Nashville City Schools" (Nashville Board of Education, 1956,), box 68, file 1, Kelly Miller Smith Jr. Papers, Special Collections, Jane and Alexander Heard Library, Vanderbilt University, Nashville.

4. Metropolitan Nashville–Davidson County Public Schools, "First Year under Metropolitan Nashville 1 July 1964–1 July 1965 Annual Report of the Director of

Public Schools of Metropolitan Nashville Davidson County," in Minutes, Metropolitan Nashville Board of Education, July 1, 1965, Metropolitan Nashville Board of Education Office.

5. M. D. Neeley, March 22, 1981, cited in Artie Thomas Pate, "An Investigation of the Desegregation Process in the Metropolitan-Nashville Davidson County Public School System, 1954–1969," Ed.D. thesis, 1981, Vanderbilt University, 88.

6. Author interview with Helen Anne Mayes, July 18, 2003, Nashville, tape recording in author's possession; interview with M. D. Neeley, cited in Pate, "An Investigation of the Segregation Process," 88.

7. Author interview with Virginia Westbrook, July 11, 1995, July 17, 2003, Nashville, tape recordings in author's possession.

8. Minutes, Metropolitan Nashville Board of Education, 10 December 1965.

9. Author interview with Roberta Jackson, July 31, 2004, Nashville, tape recording in author's possession.

10. Author interview with Albert Shaw, July 22, 2003, Nashville, tape recording in author's possession.

11. Saundra Ivey, "Faculty Desegregation a Time of Adjustment," *The Tennessean*, May 23, 1979, 13; author interview with Helen Anne Mayes, July 18, 2003, Nashville, tape recording in author's possession.

12. Pate, "An Investigation of the Segregation Process," 85.

13. *Green v. County School Board of New Kent County, Virginia*, 391 U.S. 430 (1968); Gary Orfield and Susan E. Eaton, *Dismantling Desegregation: The Quiet Reversal of Brown v. Board of Education* (New York: New Press, 1996), xxi–xxii.

14. *Alexander v. Holmes County [Mississippi] Board of Education*, 396 U.S. 19 (1969); Orfield and Eaton, *Dismantling Desegregation*, xxii.

15. *Singleton v. Jackson Municipal Separate School District* 419 F. 2d. 1211 (5th Circuit 1969); Orfield and Eaton, *Dismantling Desegregation*, xxii; *U.S. v. Montgomery Board of Education*, 395 U.S. 225 (1969).

16. Richard Pride and David Woodard, *The Burden of Busing: The Politics of Desegregation in Nashville, Tennessee* (Knoxville: University of Tennessee Press, 1985), 61; *Kelley v. Metropolitan County Board of Education of Nashville and Davidson County, Tennessee*, 396 U.S. 19, 90 St. Ct. 29, 24 L. Ed. 2d. 19 (1969); Saundra Ivy, "Desegregation through the Years," *The Tennessean*, June 14, 1993, 3B. Although Nashville's civil rights lawyers continued to seek desegregation they also fought to protect the rights of students at predominantly black schools in this partially desegregated school system. In 1967 Williams re-filed the *Kelley* case in the U.S. District Court against the Metropolitan Nashville–Davidson County Board of Education. The NAACP sued the Metropolitan Nashville–Davidson County Board of Education in U.S. District Court in response to the decision by the Metropolitan Nashville schools to suspend all-black Cameron High School from participating in athletic competitions for a year after a disturbance at a basketball game. Stratford, an all-white high school, won the game, and the students began to fight. The Nashville police had to dispel the crowd.

In April 1968 the board decided to place Stratford High School on probation. The NAACP argued that racism motivated the board to impose such harsh treatment on Cameron. The judge, William Miller, ruled that the board had to discard its decision because students were denied due process. Nevertheless, the Tennessee Secondary School Association also suspended Cameron for a year. The case merited NAACP attention because it wanted to ensure that black students and schools in the new system received equal treatment in extracurricular activities. *Kelley v. Metropolitan County Board of Education of Nashville and Davidson County,* Tennessee 293 F. Supp. 485: (M.D. Tenn. 1968); Pate, "In Investigation of the Segregation Process," 88; Ada Willoughby, "The Impact of Desegregation on the Curricula of the Secondary Schools of Nashville, Tennessee," Ed.D. diss., Loyola University, 70.

17. *Swann v. Charlotte-Mecklenburg Board of Education,* 402 U.S. (1971).

18. Pride and Woodard, *The Burden of Busing,* 62; U.S. District Court Memorandum Opinion, *Kelley v. Metropolitan Nashville Davidson County Board of Education,* 317 F. Supp. 980 at 992 (M.D. Tenn. 1970), box 68, file 4, Kelly Miller Smith Papers.

19. Willoughby, "The Impact of Desegregation," 71.

20. Ivey, "Faculty Desegregation," 13; James Coleman and Ernest Campbell, "Suggestions for Desegregation of Metropolitan Nashville Faculty," Educational Statistics Division of the U.S. Department of Health, Education and Welfare, 1967, 1–9, box 10, file 2, Kelly Miller Smith Jr. Papers.

21. Ivey, "Faculty Desegregation," 1B; Joseph Garrett, "Integration Report for Metropolitan Nashville–Davidson County Public Schools Nashville, Tennessee," Oct. 1970, John Egerton Papers, Special Collections, box 6, Jane and Alexander Heard Library, Vanderbilt University.

22. U.S. Commission on Civil Rights, *School Desegregation in Nashville–Davidson County, Tennessee: A Staff Report of the United States Commission on Civil Rights* (Washington, D.C.: Government Printing Office, June, 1977), 10; Minutes, Metropolitan Nashville Board of Education, Aug. 14, 1970, Metropolitan Nashville Board of Education Office.

23. Author interviews with Lillian Dunn Thomas, Dec. 18, 1994, and July 16, 2003, Nashville, tape recordings in author's possession.

24. *Kelley* (Dec. 1970); Hugh Scott, "Desegregation in Nashville: Conflicts and Contradictions in Preserving Schools in Black Communities," *Education and Urban Society* 15 (Feb. 1983): 238.

25. Frank Sutherland, "Two Groups Protest School Busing Plans," *Nashville Tennessean,* March 16, 1971, 1A.

26. Frank Sutherland and Pat Welch, "School Suit Recessed by Morton," *Nashville Tennessean,* March 17, 1971, 1A.

27. Sutherland and Welch, "School Suite Recessed"; Sutherland "Two Groups Protest School Busing Plans," 6A.

28. *Swann v. Charlotte Mecklenburg Board of Education,* 402 U.S. 1 (1971). Information about school desegregation in Charlotte appears in Frye Gaillard, *The Dream Long Deferred* (Chapel Hill: University of North Carolina Press, 1988), and Peter Irons, *Jim Crow's Children: The Broken Promise of the Brown Decision* (New York: Viking Press, 2002), 210–33.

29. Pride and Woodard, *The Burden of Busing,* 125; Don Doyle, *Nashville since the 1920s* (Knoxville: University of Tennessee Press, 1985), 257.

30. The *Nashville Banner*, March 11, 1971, quoted in Pride and Woodard, *The Burden of Busing*, 71.

31. Frank Sutherland, "Has the U.S. Impeded School Integration?" *The Tennessean*, July 15, 1973, 1A.

32. Pride and Woodard, *The Burden of Busing*, 73.

33. Information about busing in other cities appears in Peter Irons, *Jim Crow's Children: The Broken Promise of the Brown Decision* (New York: Viking), and Orfield, *Dismantling Desegregation*.

34. Orfield, *Dismantling Desegregation*; Irons, *Jim Crow's Children*, 222; Pride and Woodard, *The Burden of Busing*, 83.

35. Frances Meeker, "Twenty Years Later . . . ," *Nashville Banner*, May 17, 1974 1A.

36. Meeker, "Twenty Years Later," 1A.

37. Ibid.

38. Scott, "Desegregation in Nashville," 239.

39. Author interviews with Virginia Westbrook, July 11, 1995 (quotation), and July 17, 2004, Nashville, tape recordings in author's possession.

40. Author interview with Mary Alice Goldman, July 13, 1995, Nashville, tape recording in author's possession.

41. Ivey, "Faculty Desegregation," 1B; author interview with Roberta Jackson; author interview with Mary Driscoll, July 26, 2004, Nashville, tape recording in author's possession.

42. James S. Coleman, *Equality of Educational Opportunity* (Washington: U.S. Dept. of Health, Education, and Welfare, Office of Education, 1966).

43. James S. Coleman, Sara D. Kelley, and John Moore, *Trends in School Segregation, 1968–1973* (Washington, D.C.: Urban Institute, 1975); Willoughby, "The Impact of Desegregation," 90; Pride and Woodard, *The Burden of Busing*, 126. The board kept no records of the enrollment of children of other races and ethnicities until 1980–81.

44. Memphis City School District, Pupil Research Division, "Enrollment in the Memphis City School System by Race, 1970–1987," Department of Research, Evaluation, and Assessment, Memphis City Schools, 1987; Adam Fairclough, *Better Day Coming: Blacks and Equality, 1890–2000* (New York: Viking Press), 329.

45. Anna Victoria Wilson and William E. Segall, *Oh Do I Remember! Experiences of Teachers during the Desegregation of Austin's Schools, 1964–1971* (Albany: State University of New York Press, 2001), 61.

46. Michele Foster, *Black Teachers on Teaching* (New York: New Press, 1997), 87.

47. Michael Fultz, "Displacement of Black Educators Post-Brown: An Overview and Analysis," *History of Education Quarterly* 44 (Spring 2004): 24, 39.

48. Author interview with Anne Lenox, July 17, 1995, Nashville, tape recording in author's possession; author interview with Donzell Johnson, Aug. 8, 2004, Nashville, tape recording in author's possession.

49. Author interview with Lillian Dunn Thomas, Dec. 18, 1994.

50. Author interview with Sadie Madry, July 17, 1995, Nashville, tape recording, in author's possession.

51. Author interview with Ossie Trammel, Aug. 4, 2003, Nashville, tape recording in author's possession.

52. Author interview with Mary Driscoll; author interview with Betty Tune, Aug. 5 2004, Nashville, tape recording in author's possession.

53. Author interview with Helen Adams, July 13, 1995, Nashville, tape recording in author's possession.

54. Author interview with LaMona McCarter, March 12, 1994, Nashville, tape recording in author's possession.

55. Author interview with Lynda Thompson, Aug. 3 2004, Nashville, tape recording in author's possession; author interview with Roberta Jackson.

56. Pate, "An Investigation of the Segregation Process," 127.

57. Author interviews with Ola Hudson, Aug. 7, 1995, and July 27, 2003, Nashville, tape recordings in author's possession; author interview with Minerva Hawkins, July 21, 1995, Nashville, tape recording in author's possession; author interview with Mary Driscoll.

58. Author interview with Betty Tune; author interview with Mary Alice Goldman.

59. Pate, "An Investigation of the Segregation Process"; Ivey, "Faculty Desegregation," 13.

60. Author interview with Virginia Westbrook.

61. Author interview with Ola Hudson, Aug. 7, 1995.

62. Author interview with Donzell Johnson.

63. Author interview with Dorothy Baines, July 18, 1995, Nashville, tape recording in author's possession.

64. Author interview with Gwendolyn Vincent.

65. Author interview with Margaret Whitfield, July 12, 1995, Nashville, tape recording in author's possession.

66. Author interview with Ossie Trammel; author interview with Thelma Tears, July 10, 1995, Nashville, tape recording in author's possession.

67. Author interview with Gwendolyn Vincent.

68. Fultz, "Displacement of Black Educators," 28; U.S. Commission on Civil Rights, *School Desegregation in Nashville–Davidson County, Tennessee,* 1B.

69. Author interview with Lynda Thompson.

70. Author interview with Thelma Tears.

71. Author interview with Gwendolyn Vincent; author interview with Virginia Westbrook.

72. Author interview with Anne Lenox.

73. Author interview with Margaret Whitfield.

74. Author interview with Anne Lenox.

75. Ibid.

76. Author interview with Jeanne Gore, Aug. 3, 2004, Nashville, tape recording in author's possession.

77. Author interview with Novella Davis, July 28, 1995, Nashville, tape recording in author's possession.

78. Author interview with Mary Alice Goldman.

79. Author interview with Virginia Westbrook.

80. Ibid.

81. Author interview with Margaret Whitfield.

82. Author interview with Elene Jackson, July 15, 2003, Nashville, notes in author's possession.

83. Author interview with Roberta Jackson; author interview with Gwendolyn Vincent; author interview with Donzell Johnson.

84. Author interview with Roberta Jackson; author interview with Albert Shaw.

85. Saundra Ivey, "Racial Slurs Can Trigger Misunderstanding, Violence," *The Tennessean*, May 24, 1979, 21B, 30B.

86. "Metropolitan Nashville Officers to Patrol Pearl High," *The Tennessean*, Nov. 29, 1973, Board of Education News and Views press clippings, box 4, folder 14, Metropolitan Nashville Archives.

87. Author interview with Donzell Johnson; Bruce Honick, "Currey Seeks School Afro Comb Ban," *Nashville Banner*, Dec. 3, 1974, Board of Education News and Views Clippings, box 4, folder 15, Metropolitan Nashville Archives.

88. Coleman, *Equality of Educational Opportunity*.

89. Author interview with Mary Driscoll; author interview with Lynda Thompson; author interview with Betty Tune.

90. Author interview with Myra Dixon, July 22, 2003, Nashville, tape recording in author's possession.

91. Author interview with Anne Lenox.

92. Author interview with Thelma Tears.

93. Robert Pratt, *The Color of Their Skin: Education and Race in Richmond Virginia 1954–1989* (Charlottesville: University of Virginia Press, 1992), 86.

94. Author interview with Roberta Jackson.

95. Ibid.; author interview with Jeanne Gore; author interview with Betty Tune.

96. Author interview with Ola Hudson, Aug. 7, 1995.

97. Author interview with Margaret Whitfield.

98. Further information on the culturally specific practices of black teachers appears in Jacqueline Jordan Irvine, "African American Teachers' Culturally Specific Pedagogy," in Irvine, *In Search of Wholeness: African American Teachers and Their Culturally Specific Classroom Practices* (New York: Palgrave, 2002).

99. John Egerton interview with Ann Carter in "Learning to Cope: A Then and Now Look at Four Teachers, 1969," box 5, John Egerton Papers, Special Collections, Jane and Alexander Heard Library, Vanderbilt University, Nashville. Egerton mentions that Carter refused to use her real name.

100. Author interview with Betty Tune.

101. Author interview with Ola Hudson, Aug. 7, 1995.

102. Ibid.; author interview with Betty Tune.

103. Author interview with Minerva Johnson Hawkins, July 21, 1995, Nashville, tape recording in author's possession.

104. "Teacher Corps Touches Five Hundred in Three Years," *Nashville Banner*,

March 17, 1976; Michael Pasternak, *What's the Difference Being Different?* videotape, Nashville Teacher's Corps, 1977.

105. Pride and Woodard, *The Burden of Busing*, 155–56. The 1980 survey was mailed to a thousand randomly selected teachers; 40 percent responded in total. African American teachers composed 14 percent of those surveyed. The survey was sponsored by the authors.

106. Author interview with Lynda Thompson.

107. Pride and Woodard, *The Burden of Busing*, 64; U.S. Commission on Civil Rights, *School Desegregation in Nashville–Davidson County, Tennessee*, 12; Saundra Ivey, "Integration 'Learning' Process Still Going on Here," *The Tennessean*, May 25, 1979, 17.

108. Author interview with Donzell Johnson; Derrick Bell, "Serving Two Masters: Integration Ideals and Client Interests in School Desegregation Litigation," *Yale Law Journal* 85 (1976): 470–516.

109. Marian Wright Edelman quoted in Bell, "Serving Two Masters," 513.

110. Pride and Woodard, *The Burden of Busing*, 180.

111. Saundra Ivey, "Resegregation: A Matter of Definition," *The Tennessean*, May 27, 1979, 1B; Pride and Woodard, *The Burden of Busing*, 187.

112. Frank Sutherland, "Comprehensive School Plan Proposes Twelve High Schools," *The Tennessean*, Aug. 11, 1974, "Schools for the 1980s" (special section), 1.

113. David Cecelski, *Along Freedom Road: Hyde County, North Carolina, and the Fate of Black Schools in the South* (Chapel Hill: University of North Carolina Press, 1994).

114. Cecelski, *Along Freedom Road*, 187.

115. James W. Davis, president, Nashville Urban League, to Metropolitan Nashville Board of Education, Nov. 28, 1979, box 69, folder 10, Kelly Miller Smith Jr. Papers.

116. Howard Rabinowitz, "Half a Loaf: The Shift from White to Black Teachers in the Negro Schools of the Urban South, 1865–1890," *Journal of Southern History* 40 (Nov. 1974): 565–94; Pride and Woodard, *The Burden of Busing*, 194.

117. Derrick Bell, *Silent Covenants:* Brown v. Board of Education *and the Unfulfilled Hopes for Racial Reform* (New York: Oxford University Press, 2004), 124, 125, 276.

118. *Milliken v. Bradley*, 345 F. Supp 918 (Ed. Mich. 1972); Orfield, *Dismantling Desegregation*.

119. Bell, *Silent Covenants*, 24.

120. Information on black women, feminism, and the definition of womanist ideology appears in Hazel Carby, *Reconstructing Black Womanhood* (New York: Oxford University Press, 1987); Patricia Hill Collins, *Black Feminist Thought, Knowledge, Consciousness, and the Politics of Empowerment* (New York: Routledge), 1990; and Alice Walker, *In Search of Our Mother's Gardens: Womanist Prose* (San Diego: Harcourt Brace Jovanovich, 1983).

121. Author interview with Ola Hudson, Aug. 7, 1995.

122. Author interview with Helen Adams, July 13, 1995, Nashville, tape recording in author's possession.

123. Fultz, "Displacement of Black Teachers," 32, 33. For information on the impact of the National Teachers' Examination on black educators see R. Scott Baker, "The Paradoxes of Desegregation: Race, Class, and Education, 1935–1975," *American Journal of Education* 109 (May 2001): 320–43. Additional statistics on African American teachers are found in Michael B. Webb, "Increasing Minority Participation in the Teaching Profession" at http://www.ericdigests.org/pre-924/minority.htm.

124. Author interview with Gwendolyn Vincent.

125. Robert L. Carter, "A Reassessment of *Brown v. Board*," in *Shades of Brown: New Perspectives on School Desegregation*, edited by Derrick A. Bell (New York: Teachers College Press, 1980), 21–27.

126. Van Dempsey and George W. Noblitt, "Cultural Ignorance and School Desegregation: Reconstruction a Silenced Narrative," in George W. Noblit, *Particularities: Collected Essays on Ethnography and Education* (New York: Peter Lang, 1999), 181–204.

127. Flora McKinnon Gutterman, "A Descriptive Study of the School Demographic Changes in Tennessee Public Schools Between 1968 and 1978 Resulting from Federal, Judicial, Legislative, and Executive School Desegregation Decisions," Ed.D. diss., University of Tennessee at Knoxville, 1983, 88.

128. Author interview with Lillian Dunn Thomas, Dec. 18, 1994.

129. Author interview with Betty Tune; author interview with Lynda Thompson.

130. Barbara Shircliffe, "'We Got the Best of that World': A Case for the Study of Nostalgia in the Oral History of School Segregation," *Oral History Review* 28 (Summer–Fall 2001): 59–84.

131. Author interview with Thelma Tears; author interview with Roberta Jackson.

CONCLUSION

1. Paul Donsky, "Schools Enter New Era as Desegregation Lawsuit Ends," *The Tennessean*, Sept. 29, 1998, 1B; "Q. and A. on Judge Wiseman's Ruling," *The Tennessean*, Sept. 29, 1998, 1B; Minutes, Metropolitan Nashville–Davidson County Board of Education, Feb. 9, 1999; Paul Donsky, "Desegregation Changes to Begin This Fall," *The Tennessean*, Feb. 10, 1999, 1B.

2. Jay Hamburg, "Racial Imbalance Returns to Schools," *The Tennessean*, July 13, 2003, 1A.

Index

SONYA RAMSEY is an associate professor of history at the University of North Carolina at Charlotte, where she specializes in African American gender studies, oral history, and the history of education. Her primary areas of research include the study of African American women, issues of African American education, and black interpretations of social class. She received a Ph.D. in U.S. history from the University of North Carolina at Chapel Hill.

Women in American History

The University of Illinois Press
is a founding member of the
Association of American University Presses.

Composed in 10/13.5 Janson Text
with Electra display
by Jim Proefrock
at the University of Illinois Press
Manufactured by Thomson-Shore, Inc.

University of Illinois Press
1325 South Oak Street
Champaign, IL 61820-6903
www.press.uillinois.edu